Leaders

The PricewaterhouseCoopers Endowment for
The Business of Government

THE PRICEWATERHOUSECOOPERS ENDOWMENT SERIES ON THE BUSINESS OF GOVERNMENT

Series Editors: Mark A. Abramson and Paul R. Lawrence

The PricewaterhouseCoopers Endowment Series on The Business of Government explores new approaches to improving the effectiveness of government at the federal, state, and local levels. The Series is aimed at providing cutting-edge knowledge to government leaders, academics, and students about the management of government in the 21st century.

Publications in the series include:

2001
Transforming Organizations, *edited by Mark A. Abramson and Paul R. Lawrence*
E-Government 2001, *edited by Mark A. Abramson and Grady E. Means*
Managing for Results 2002, *edited by Mark A. Abramson and John M. Kamensky*
Memos to the President: Management Advice from the Nation's Top Public Administrators, *edited by Mark A. Abramson*

2002
Innovation, *edited by Mark A. Abramson and Ian D. Littman*
E-Government 2002, *edited by Mark A. Abramson and Grady E. Means*
Human Capital 2002, *edited by Mark A. Abramson and Nicole Willenz Gardner*

Leaders

EDITED BY

MARK A. ABRAMSON
THE PRICEWATERHOUSECOOPERS ENDOWMENT
FOR THE BUSINESS OF GOVERNMENT
and
KEVIN M. BACON
PRICEWATERHOUSECOOPERS

ROWMAN & LITTLEFIELD PUBLISHERS, INC.
Lanham • Boulder • New York • Oxford

ROWMAN & LITTLEFIELD PUBLISHERS, INC.

Published in the United States of America
by Rowman & Littlefield Publishers, Inc.
4720 Boston Way, Lanham, Maryland 20706
www.rowmanlittlefield.com

12 Hid's Copse Road
Cumnor Hill, Oxford OX2 9JJ, England

British Library Cataloguing in Publication Information Available

Library of Congress Cataloging-in-Publication Data Available

0-7425-2333-0 (alk. paper)
0-7425-2334-9 (pbk./alk. paper)

Printed in the United States of America

™
⊖ The paper used in this publication meets the minimum requirements of American National Standard for Information Sciences—Permanence of Paper for Printed Library Materials, ANSI/NISO Z39.48-1992.

To

Jessica and Andrew Abramson
future leaders

Kim Peoples Bacon
a great example of leadership

TABLE OF CONTENTS

Chapter One: 21st Century Leaders   1
by Mark A. Abramson and Kevin M. Bacon
   Introduction
   How 21st Century Leaders Are Different
   How 21st Century Leaders Can Be Developed
   Conclusion

**Chapter Two: Managing "Big Science": A Case Study of
the Human Genome Project**   11
by W. Henry Lambright
   The Human Genome Project Today
   The Human Genome Project: A Management Case History
   Conclusions
   Implications for the Future
   Endnotes

**Chapter Three: Managing Across Boundaries: A Case Study
of Dr. Helene Gayle and the AIDS Epidemic**   55
by Norma M. Riccucci
   Introduction
   The Setting
   The Case Study
   Lessons Learned about Effective Managerial Leadership
   Conclusions
   Bibliography

**Chapter Four: Leading a Cabinet Department: Donna Shalala
at the Department of Health and Human Services**   85
by Beryl A. Radin
   Part I: Managing Decentralized Departments
   Part II: Managing Across Boundaries
   Appendix: Leading the Department of Health and Human
     Services: A Conversation with Secretary Donna Shalala
     and Deputy Secretary Kevin Thurm
   Endnotes
   Bibliography

**Chapter Five: Leadership for Change: Case Studies
in American Local Government**   143
by Robert B. Denhardt and Janet Vinzant Denhardt
   Introduction
   The Case Studies
   Steps in Leading Change
   Leadership and Learning

Conclusion
Appendix: Methodology
Endnotes

**Chapter Six: The Importance of Leadership: The Role
of School Principals**   173
by Paul E. Teske and Mark Schneider
Introduction
Principals as School Leaders: A Review of the Literature
The Role of Principals in Creating Effective Schools:
    The Case of New York City
Profiles of Successful School Principals
Principals as Leaders of Successful Schools
Conclusion
Recommendation
Appendix: Methodology
Endnotes
Bibliography

**Chapter Seven: Profiles in Excellence: Conversations
with the Best of America's Career Executive Service**   201
by Mark W. Huddleston
Introduction
The Conversations
Recommendations
Appendix: 1997 Presidential Distinguished Rank Award
    Recipients by Agency
Endnotes
Bibliography

About the Contributors   233

**About The PricewaterhouseCoopers Endowment
for The Business of Government**   238

CHAPTER ONE

21st Century Leaders

Mark A. Abramson
Executive Director, The PricewaterhouseCoopers
Endowment for The Business of Government

Kevin M. Bacon
Partner
PwC Consulting

Introduction

This book is about leaders. It is about individuals running public sector organizations at the start of the 21st century. It is premised on the belief that leaders of 21st century organizations will be required to lead and manage differently than their predecessors who led 20th century organizations. A second premise is that the way to learn about leadership is to study leaders. Leadership is not an abstract art described in textbooks; leadership is about the behavior of real people at the top of organizations. Leadership is about leaders who are now being asked to lead organizations in a more complex, interdependent world.

How 21st Century Leaders Are Different

The leaders described in this book do not fit the traditional model of the charismatic "command and control" hierarchical leader of the 20th century. While some say that that approach to leading continues to be appropriate and useful in some situations, such as the military, the complexity of the 21st century world now requires a dramatically different set of approaches and skills—the ability to forge consensus and work across organizations, sectors, and national boundaries.

In chapter two, W. Henry Lambright describes how Francis Collins is leading the Human Genome Project at the National Institutes of Health at the start of the 21st century. Lambright offers a fascinating contrast between the first two leaders of the Human Genome Project (HGP)—James Watson, the famous Noble Prize-winning biologist and co-discoverer of the double helical structure of DNA, and Francis Collins. Lambright writes:

> HGP had two very different leaders. Watson was a charismatic leader.... He was the best possible person to launch HGP at a time when it was highly controversial among scientists. Few others could, by sheer personal force, have made HGP not only legitimate, but also "where the action was" in bioscience.... Watson was also an exceptional "scientific sales-man" for HGP before Congress.

> But it is not all clear that the volatile, often abrasive Watson was the right man to implement HGP over the long haul.... Less flashy, much more con-sensual in style, Collins was able to strike an alliance with [Harold] Varmus, his superior at NIH, nurture congressional relations, and develop a team approach to management that became increasingly critical as time went on.

Dr. Francis Collins   *Dr. Helene Gayle*   *Dr. Donna Shalala*

The complex challenge facing Collins was to work closely with other government organizations (such as the Department of Energy), the private sector (Celera), and other nations (most notably the United Kingdom). Lambright concludes that such interagency, intersectoral, and transnational partnerships are likely to be dominant organizational challenges in the future. Given this new world, he speculates that a new type of leader will be necessary who is equipped and trained to grapple with "increasing complexity and greater bureaucratic, political, and cultural diversity."

The need for cross-boundary leadership is also explored in chapter three by Norma Riccucci in her examination of Dr. Helene Gayle. Riccucci describes how Dr. Gayle forged partnerships with both international organizations and nations to combat the spread of HIV/AIDS and other sexually transmitted diseases, since infectious disease does not honor national boundaries. She worked closely with private, nonprofit, and government organizations to increase the amount of resources being devoted to combating these diseases. In describing the role of government, Dr. Gayle reflects, "We are not the sole players, nor will we ever have all the resources to fix all these problems on our own. Developing collaborations is key." Riccucci also describes the creation of community-based prevention activities by Dr. Gayle.

While the need for 21st century leaders to act differently when forging consensus and creating cross-boundary partnerships is clear, Beryl Radin describes in chapter four how Donna Shalala, former Secretary of Health and Human Services (HHS), attempted to manage a single, although highly diverse, federal department in much the same way as Dr. Gayle and Dr. Collins managed their programs. Instead of using the "command and control" approach of previous HHS secretaries, Professor Radin explains, Shalala attempted to manage by "shared values, personal relationships, and professional respect." Radin observes:

While the Shalala HHS approach may not be the only way to manage a
large and diverse organization, it does provide an alternative example of
the traditional command and control strategy often suggested for such
agencies.... The experience of flexibly managing HHS as a largely decentralized department does attest to the possibility of adopting a management strategy that is an alternative to the traditional centralized mode.

Like Lambright, Radin speculates that the increased complexity of managing large organizations will require more leaders at the top to act like Shalala
in managing large organizations. She concludes that the trend toward flatten-
ing organizations, reducing hierarchies, and devolving federal responsibilities
for implementation of programs to other organizations have all contributed to
more complex federal organizations. As a result, writes Radin, "the techniques and approaches that have been used in the past to manage large public organizations require rethinking." She describes a variety of techniques
and approaches Secretary Shalala used in defining new roles for "top management in the context of decentralized, flat, and devolved organizations."

While Collins, Gayle, and Shalala were all located in the federal government, it is incorrect to assume that 21st century leaders show up only at the
federal level. In chapter five, Professors Robert Denhardt and Janet Vinzant
Denhardt describe how three local government leaders engaged in a much
more "open, free-flowing, engaging, and collaborative" style of leading than
the traditional top-down approach. Unlike 20th century top-down leaders,
these 21st century local leaders redefined their role as one in which they:

- help the community and their organization understand their needs and
  potential;
- integrate and articulate the community's vision and that of the organization; and
- act as a trigger or stimulus for group action.

In their study of school principals in chapter six, Professors Paul Teske
and Mark Schneider describe how New York City school principals also
exhibit many of the qualities of 21st century leaders. Teske and Schneider
observe that nearly all the principals they profiled attempted to actively
engage their school's network of parents, teachers, and staff. In several of
the schools examined, panels of teachers, parents, staff, and the principal
jointly select new teachers. All strove to develop a shared culture among
their staff. In describing, Eric Nadelstern, principal of International High
School, Teske and Schneider write:

Nadelstern's leadership style is to let teachers have as much control and
autonomy as they prove themselves capable. Teachers, instead of only the
principal, help to evaluate each other. Decision making is shared collectively by parents, teachers, and students.

Chapter seven presents the results of a series of conversations conducted by Dean Mark Huddleston with members of the federal government's Senior Executive Service (SES). In wide-ranging discussions, Huddleston asked members of the SES about the qualities of an effective leader. Teamwork and the ability to "animate" others were deemed crucial, both components of 21st century leadership.

How 21st Century Leaders Can Be Developed

A major theme of Huddleston's interviews with members of the Senior Executive Service was the importance of developing future leaders and concern that the current development process in government is largely serendipitous. Huddleston writes, "Like farmers harvesting bumper crops without ever seeding, watering, or fertilizing, Americans and their elected officials have consistently received the fruits of outstanding administrative leadership without investing any time or effort."

Concern was expressed by several of the Senior Executive Service members that the federal government is not developing future leaders by broadening the experiences of those currently in government. One SES member observed that you can be a "desk officer for 20 years without being disturbed or developed. Consequently, people become so narrow that they are rightly not looked upon as material for higher positions in the SES, much less for deputy or assistant secretary slots."

Many of those interviewed discussed their own commitment to mentoring future leaders as a way of compensating for inadequate executive development programs in many agencies. One senior executive was cited for being "the consummate mentor, tutor, trainer, and developer of professional staff and talent." But Huddleston concludes that this is not enough. He writes:

> But personal mentoring and internship programs alone ... obviously cannot fill the career development vacuum. What is needed is a more fully articulated structure that directs career development from recruitment to retirement, a structure in which the needs of the government for executive talent are treated as a question of design, not a matter of chance. The changing character of the workforce makes this even more essential.

If government sincerely aspires to create 21st century leaders, there is clearly much that can be done. Over the past decade, many organizations in both the public and private sectors have learned much about effective ways to develop future leaders, including the skills necessary to lead and

manage in the complex world of the 21st century. Effective leadership development approaches include:
- Building leadership skills through a broad range of assignments.
- Building self-awareness of leadership skills through better feedback and skill-building experiences.
- Encouraging and monitoring the use of "job enlargement" to develop staff.
- Building on the ethos of public service.
- Conducting "leadership audits" within organizations.

Building Leadership Skills through a Broad Range of Assignments

The leadership attributes needed by 21st century leaders cannot be learned in a classroom. They must be cultivated through a range of practical experiences gained in the process of solving real problems encountered by real organizations. To provide such experiences, leadership development in the public sector must rely heavily on the conscious cultivation of career mobility. Such mobility can help individuals broaden their understanding of the mission, processes, issues, and stakeholders of important public sector agencies. This breadth of experience will build flexibility and adaptability. It can also give opportunities to understand strategic issues, the range of possible visions that can be achieved in public agencies, and the value of building networks and alliances to accomplish agency missions.

Such mobility and broad experience can be promoted with a number of tools already available to senior government leaders. By making conscious use of these tools as a mechanism for leadership development, senior executives can take positive steps to improve the future supply of leadership within their organization. Examples of these tools include:
- Using lateral transfers, within large departments or between departments, designed to expose individuals to a variety of new problems, work settings, and managerial issues.
- Consciously choosing staff to participate on special projects and task forces to give them opportunities to "stretch" their skills and capabilities by helping solve real problems facing their organizations.
- Rotating key managerial assignments among "up and coming" managers and executives as a conscious way to broaden their career experience and test their ability to adapt to new circumstances, manage diverse groups, and respond to new customer groups.

If the cross-boundary challenges faced by the leaders profiled in this book do represent the future, a strong case can be made for rotating future government leaders to nonprofit organizations, state and local governments, international organizations, and even the private sector. If the future of government is tied to forging new partnerships and close working relationships with such organizations, it would appear to be highly worthwhile to give future leaders firsthand experience in those organizations.

Organizations such as the various branches of the United States military, the Department of State, and various state government departments routinely use mobility tools such as those described above. These organizations typically have much larger pools of managers and executives with well-developed leadership capabilities than do agencies with more passive approaches to leadership development and mobility.

Building Self-Awareness of Leadership Skills through Better Feedback and Skill-Building Experiences

Research by Professor Warner Burke of Columbia University has shown that successful leaders in business tend to be more self-aware than their less successful peers. Self-awareness can be cultivated by providing feedback about an individual's managerial and leadership skills through the performance appraisal process. A very valuable tool in this regard is 360-degree feedback. Such feedback involves structured collection of input from subordinates, peers, and superiors. This range of feedback can help individuals gain a better perspective on their skills in working within and leading teams, the clarity of their communication, and their particular management style.

The questions covered in such feedback instruments can be tailored to the leadership competencies and values that each public sector organization requires. Organizations that are truly committed to developing more and better leaders have embraced the use of 360-degree feedback. Since initially such systems are likely to be perceived as threatening to traditional notions of the relationships between superiors and subordinates, it is essential that senior executives in a public agency support such a system and participate in it themselves. (Another benefit of such systems is that they provide hard data on the extent to which an organization and its managers really practice the values and principles espoused in many vision and strategy statements.)

Such feedback will highlight areas where developing leaders will need help in mastering a variety of interpersonal skills. Such skills include giving and receiving constructive feedback on performance, conflict resolution, forming and working in teams, and utilizing different management styles to match the needs of different staff. Such skills must be developed through on-the-job experience. However, formal training can be helpful in giving developing leaders the tools and insights they need to develop their capabilities in these areas. Top agency leaders should ensure that these training resources are available to support the development of future leaders.

Encouraging and Monitoring the Use of "Job Enlargement" to Develop Staff

Regular and effective use of "job enlargement" by managers and executives is a tool that can be used to enhance leadership development within an organization. Staff members grow when given the opportunity to "stretch" beyond their area of current competence. All too often, managers and executives turn to the same group of proven performers to tackle a crisis, staff a task force, or lead an interdepartmental work group. While this might make the executive rest easier, it misses a golden opportunity to test and develop leadership skills in other staff. Government organizations must operate on the twin assumptions that leadership is in short supply within their organization and that it is unlikely that leadership skills can be bought on the external labor market. Consequently, every opportunity to provide practical leadership development opportunities to existing staff must be used to expand the supply of skilled leaders within organizations.

Reluctance to provide such "job enlargement" challenges to younger staff is usually based on concern about whether they are capable of meeting the challenge. This reluctance is ironic in light of much experience in the public sector. It is routine for the armed forces of many nations to assign major organizational responsibilities in time of war to men and women in their mid-20s. Another illustration of calling on younger staff to solve a complex problem under crisis conditions involved the Apollo 13 mission to the moon. In the spring of 1970, the lives of the three astronauts on the mission were in jeopardy due to an explosion in their space vehicle while it was over 100,000 miles from Earth. The solution that brought the men home safely was developed over a period of 72 hours by a team that averaged slightly less than 27 years of age.

Building on the Ethos of Public Service

High-performing career public sector executives can usually obtain higher salaries by pursuing private sector employment. By an overwhelming margin, they indicate that the principal reason they chose to join and stay with the public service (despite the lower pay) is the social significance and challenging nature of the work performed by government. Since it is unlikely that the public sector will ever be able to fully compete with the private sector on compensation alone, it is essential that it make full use of its major competitive advantage in this area—the very work it performs. In recruiting, developing, and nurturing future leaders, the public sector should consciously attempt to give promising staff opportunities to test and develop leadership skills by working on the most complex and important public sector problems. At the same time leadership skills are developed and problems solved, staff commitment to public service will be reinforced, making it less likely that they will be enticed to join the private sector.

Conducting "Leadership Audits" within Their Organization

If leadership development is to be a priority of top management, then it is necessary to monitor performance and make adjustments in response to such information. A simple set of performance measures in this area would include:

- Monitoring the number and location of staff currently on rotational or other developmental assignments.
- Requiring all senior executives and managers to develop succession plans naming individuals who could assume their post should they retire or move to another post. (While civil service systems may prevent formal designation of successors through this process, the act of developing such succession plans forces discussions about specific individuals and the overall state of leadership development in an organization.)
- Reviewing the aggregate results of 360-degree feedback surveys to identify the specific leadership competencies that are lacking within the organization. This information can be used in career counseling, training, and assignment decisions to help build the missing competencies.
- Monitoring the amount of time top agency leaders devote to developing future leaders and their impact in terms of assisting younger staff in gaining exposure to "job enlargement" opportunities.

Conclusion

As Radin observes in chapter four, there is increasing agreement that organizations in the future will likely be "flatter" or less layered than they are now. This "de-layering" of public sector organizations will create the need for more leadership skills (flexibility, business acumen, customer focus, etc.) throughout the organization. The rapid advance of the Internet and electronic commerce will only accelerate this trend, breaking down the barriers to information flow between and within government agencies. Consequently, leadership development will have to become a priority of public sector senior executives; it can no longer be an optional activity.

The very de-layering of government that makes leadership development a pressing need also creates a great opportunity for developing new leaders at all levels within career government service. Whole new approaches need to be developed for managing core business processes, interacting with customers and other stakeholders, and demonstrating how government functions create value for the public. In all of these challenges, there are great opportunities for current government staff to develop and exercise the very leadership skills that the future will require. Senior political leaders and senior career executives should seize these opportunities to increase the breadth and depth of leadership skills in the public sector to meet 21st century challenges.

CHAPTER TWO

Managing "Big Science": A Case Study of the Human Genome Project

W. Henry Lambright
Professor of Political Science and Public Administration and
Director, Center for Environmental Policy and Administration
The Maxwell School
Syracuse University

This report was originally published in March 2002.

The Human Genome Project Today

On June 26, 2000, President Bill Clinton, joined via teleconference by British Prime Minister Tony Blair, proclaimed a momentous event in history: "the completion of the first survey of the entire human genome."[1] The human genome represents a blueprint of a person, and has been likened to an instruction manual. It has also been called the Holy Grail of biology. Nicholas Wade wrote: "It provides the basis on which to understand the human body almost as fully and precisely as an engineer understands a machine. From that understanding, physicians can hope to develop new ways to fix the human machine and in time to correct most—perhaps almost all—of its defects."[2]

However, on June 26, 2000, at the White House ceremony, politicians, scientists, administrators, media, and others were not contemplating the future, good or ill. They were celebrating the moment. It had taken a decade and a half to get there, huge amounts of money, and an army of researchers and technicians spread over six countries. Responsible for reaching this epochal event was a large-scale federally funded project of international scale—and a private company, Celera, which inspired a race between public and private sectors to sequence (order the chemical letters of) the genome. The public-private contest was intended to end at this White House fete, where it was officially called a tie. In February 2001, the federal Human Genome Project (HGP) and Celera separately published their findings, at virtually the same time, thus gaining an equal share in scientific credit. The quest to decode the human genome was regarded universally a success.

The focus of this study is the governmental project, although the story of the private activity is interwoven, as it well deserves to be. Our principal interest is in what makes government programs work—critical factors in success, as well as failure. The aim is to look at the HGP as a result not only of science, but also of public management. It is to look at the forces—technical and political—that impact on management decisions. HGP has been likened to other great technical projects, such as the Manhattan Project and Project Apollo. While far smaller in scale than these, HGP is still huge. The figure $3 billion is generally used as its cost, measured over project lifetime. This figure includes about $2 billion from the National Institutes of Health and $1 billion from the Department of Energy.[3] The full reality is several hundred million more, since the Wellcome Trust, a huge philanthropy in England, became joint sponsor after the U.S. genome project was under way. In addition, other governments have contributed. However, at $3 billion for the U.S. portion, HGP is easily the biggest science project ever in the biological field.

What is really the reason to compare HGP with other major monumental efforts in science and technology, like the Manhattan Project and

J. Craig Ventor, President Bill Clinton, and Francis Collins at the White House, June 26, 2000.

Project Apollo, is that it represents "Big Science" in pursuit of a major breakthrough in technical capability. The Manhattan Project opened up the atom for use. Apollo made human space travel possible. And HGP will enable man to develop new methods of prevention and cure for a host of illnesses. Such breakthroughs do not come every day, year, decade, or century. They do not come easily. Hence, the projects that bring them about stand out from most large-scale science and technology efforts that abound in the United States and abroad. They are worthy of serious study and an effort to derive lessons for government administration and policy.

That is the purpose of the present analysis, for HGP is a remarkable instance of successful public enterprise. The role of private enterprise was also extremely interesting and important. It shared the platform when success was proclaimed. However, this study concentrates on the public venture and the role of the private activity in affecting what public managers did. HGP, whatever its bumps along the way, wound up achieving its objectives and was speeded in doing so by private competition.

Before looking at the administrative history of HGP, it is important to see where the project stands today. Some call this the post-Genome Project Era. They are not correct. The reality is that HGP is not quite finished, and the world is just entering the genome era. The climax to the project that helped introduce the era came in February 2001 with the publication in *Nature* and *Science* of the respective findings of HGP and Celera.[4] At the time, 90 percent of the human genome was completed in terms of sequencing. What happened was that the original HGP scientific goal of a complete genome was retained, but an interim goal added—the 90 percent "rough draft"—which was set forth as the symbolic finish line. The last 10 percent was targeted subsequently, and it is expected that a complete, "polished" draft of the human genome will be ready in 2003. This is the 50th anniversary year of the discovery of the double helix structure of DNA.

Since 2001, HGP (as well as Celera) has moved forward with post-Genome Project activity, even as they finished what they had started. Their projects are in a transition phase. For HGP, the transition marks a sixth phase.[5] The first phase, extending from approximately 1980 to 1986, was one of conceptualization. Phase two, from 1986 to 1990, was the period when a national program to sequence the human genome was adopted by the U.S. government. By "national" is meant a program that involved two agencies in coordination, the Department of Energy (DOE) and the National Institutes of Health (NIH).

In the third phase, 1990–1993, the initial implementation took place, and NIH established itself as lead agency. The program was expanded to an international venture and initial scientific and organizational strategies activated. The fourth phase, from 1993 to 1998, was a time of maintaining momentum and of project growth. It included actions to find ways to accelerate the pace of research via pilot projects. It began with an internal crisis in terms of HGP leadership and ended with another crisis due to external threat.

The fifth phase ran from 1998 to 2001. It marked a reorientation of HGP to a crash program style of operation. The period ended with the achievement of the reorientation goal—the draft genome—and acclamations of triumph. As noted, the present sixth period—2001–2003—is one of transition, completing work on the genome sequence, while simultaneously moving to the next research frontier of applications.

That frontier seems limitless. HGP is charting new goals aimed at understanding how the human blueprint functions. In particular, HGP will ask how the genome makes people different, with some more vulnerable to genetically based disorders than others. Answering such a question is a first step to what may be eventual HGP applications: "individualized medicine" and "regenerative medicine."[6] People will be diagnosed from their genetic makeup to determine what diseases they are likely to get. In some cases, those malfunctions may be headed off through new drugs and other genetic therapy. That future, while not yet here, is arriving fast, and its implications are vast for government and the biotechnology industry.

HGP continues, as does its budget and organizational structure. The budget is rising and the organization is growing. The present organization of HGP is that of an international consortium. There is a de facto "lead" organization. This is the U.S. National Institutes of Health. NIH has two principal partners in funding: the U.S. Department of Energy and the Wellcome Trust. The Wellcome Trust, reputed to be the wealthiest health-oriented foundation in the world, has made HGP a priority.

While HGP has a significant intramural research program, the great bulk of its funds are spent externally, mainly by universities. Early on, HGP adopted, as a principal management strategy, the establishment of research centers as the way to accomplish its goals. In 2001 there were 16 major centers in the United States and abroad involved in human genome sequencing. Several other centers are concerned with different aspects of genome research and technology. Five of these formed the core of the human sequencing component of HGP: the Whitehead Institute for Biomedical Research; Washington University in St. Louis; Baylor College of Medicine; the Joint Genome Institute (a cluster of three national laboratories under DOE); and the Sanger Centre (now Sanger Institute) in England. Known as the G-5, these centers will have performed 85 percent of the genome sequencing by the time the project ends in 2003.

The remaining centers will have undertaken 15 percent of the sequencing. NIH has only nominal control over its university centers, and none directly over those of DOE or the Wellcome Trust. What ties the consortium together is the informal leadership of NIH and the mutually agreed upon requirement that all performers must place their findings into a common repository—the GenBank—maintained by NIH. They are required to do so within 24 hours of discovery, and what is in GenBank is open to all. It was this particular HGP requirement of total openness that made it difficult for Celera, concerned about its proprietary rights, to cooperate with HGP.[7]

As noted, the present period is one of transition for HGP. The public management challenge today is to hold the consortium together to finish the human genome blueprint, while moving forward to new objectives. The HGP has undertaken projects to sequence the genomes of the mouse, rat, and other living creatures. It is also probing relations between genes and proteins. Three new research centers beyond the major 16 have been established to work on particular research initiatives relating to human variation.[8]

Comprehending the genetic bases of such differences is critical before taking steps to apply this knowledge. In doing so, HGP is developing novel relationships with pharmaceutical companies and others. It has even found ways it and Celera can work in partnership, although Celera is still a rival, having already produced a draft sequence of the mouse. The likelihood is that rivalry will diminish in the future. A decision by Celera's parent company to move Celera in a different direction caused J. Craig Venter, HGP's competitor, to resign from Celera in early 2002.

HGP has pioneered a frontier not only in science, but also in organization. The Manhattan Project and Project Apollo were concentrated national projects, and industrial relations were those of sponsor-performer.

HGP has been a pluralistic transnational project, involving management by two U.S. agencies and a major partner that is a private foundation in a foreign country. It has utilized universities and national labs as performers. While having cordial relationships with a number of companies,[9] its best known relation with industry, Celera, has been adversarial. Whether this is a model for the future remains to be seen, but it is certainly different from earlier Big Science ventures.

At the same time, like Manhattan and Apollo, there will be long-lasting impacts on policy, for genome knowledge can be used not only to help people, but also for negative purposes. Like every powerful technology, what happens depends on human judgment. HGP has supported research in legal, ethical, and social impacts in recognition that it was creating a dual-edged sword. Finally, HGP may have a transformative impact on NIH. The project's "large-scale approach" is seen by some other institute directors as a potential way to accelerate advances in other spheres of NIH research.[10] Those who have managed HGP have presided over the first steps in what will be a multifaceted revolution.

The Human Genome Project:
A Management Case History

On May 10, 1998, J. Craig Venter, a former NIH scientist turned biotech entrepreneur, announced he was setting up a new company, Celera, that would sequence the human genome within three years for $300 million. This was four years ahead of the target date for the publicly funded, $3 billion Human Genome Project. The announcement was taken by virtually everyone as a direct challenge to the government effort and the bioscience establishment.[11]

The media called it a race for the Holy Grail of biology, the complete description of the human genome. James Watson, Nobel Prize-winning biologist, co-discoverer of the double helical structure of DNA, and first director of the Human Genome Project, saw the struggle as one of good versus evil, public versus private interests. He likened Venter's assault on the genome project to Hitler's annexation of Poland. He asked his successor as project director, Francis Collins, whether he was up to the challenge. Would he be a Churchill or a Chamberlain?[12]

Two years later, in 2000, at a White House ceremony led by President Clinton, in which British Prime Minister Tony Blair participated by teleconference, a draw was declared. Although the public and private projects were still not finished, they had reached a climactic point where the human

Francis S. Collins, M.D., Ph.D., Director, National Human Genome Research Institute, National Institutes of Health, Bethesda, Maryland

Francis S. Collins, M.D., Ph.D., is a physician-geneticist and the director of the National Human Genome Research Institute, NIH. In that role he oversees a complex multidisciplinary project aimed at mapping and sequencing all of the human DNA, and determining aspects of its function. Many consider this the most important scientific undertaking of our time. A working draft of the human genome sequence was announced in June of 2000, an initial analysis was published in February of 2001, and the completed sequence is anticipated in the spring of 2003. From the outset, the project has run ahead of schedule and under budget, and all data has been made immediately available to the scientific community, without restrictions on access or use.

Collins was raised on a small farm in Virginia and home-schooled until the sixth grade. He obtained his undergraduate degree in chemistry at the University of Virginia and went on to obtain a Ph.D. in physical chemistry at Yale University. Recognizing that a revolution was beginning in molecular biology and genetics, he changed fields and enrolled in medical school at the University of North Carolina. After a residency and chief residency in internal medicine in Chapel Hill, he returned to Yale for a fellowship in human genetics, where he worked on methods of crossing large stretches of DNA to identify disease genes. He continued to develop these ideas after joining the faculty at the University of Michigan in 1984. This approach, for which he later coined the term "positional cloning," has developed into a powerful component of modern molecular genetics, as it allows the identification of disease genes for almost any condition, without knowing ahead of time what the functional abnormality might be. Collins' team, together with collaborators, was successful in applying this approach to genes for cystic fibrosis, neurofibromatosis, Huntington's disease, multiple endocrine neoplasia type 1, and a particular type of adult acute leukemia.

In 1993, Collins accepted an invitation to become the director of the National Center for Human Genome Research, which became an Institute in 1997. In addition to overseeing the International Human Genome Sequencing Consortium and many other aspects of the Human Genome Project, Collins founded a new NIH intramural research program in genome research, which has now grown to become one of the premier research units in human genetics in the country. His own research laboratory continues to be vigorously active, exploring the molecular genetics of breast cancer, prostate cancer, adult-onset diabetes, and other disorders. His accomplishments have been recognized by election to the Institute of Medicine and the National Academy of Sciences.

genome could be almost fully sequenced in a preliminary way. In 2001, scientific papers were published by HGP and Celera, and biology's own "Project Apollo" was heralded a resounding success.[13]

How did this huge project—involving thousands of researchers, costing billions, and extending well over a decade—get started? How did it get organized? What was its scientific strategy and how was it implemented? What were the factors that affected its pace and direction? What lessons can be learned about leadership and management of large-scale technical ventures from this particular experience?

To answer these questions, it is necessary to review HGP's history. The present period is one of transition, as the HGP finishes and polishes the human genome draft and initiates new research paths. A number of these activities involve partnerships with the private industrial sector, in contrast to earlier experience. HGP is moving from development of a tool to its uses.

In getting to this transition period, HGP has gone through five previous phases. The following study of the project tracks events through these eras, which include:

1. Conceptualization—when HGP was developed, 1980–86.
2. Adoption—when HGP began, first as a DOE project, then as a national effort, involving NIH and DOE, 1986–90.
3. Initial implementation—when James Watson gave shape to the effort, 1990–93.
4. Maintaining momentum and growing—when Francis Collins succeeded Watson and sought to speed the venture, 1993–98.
5. Reorientation—when HGP shifted dramatically to a crash project, 1998–2001—and achieved its reorientation goal.
6. The present transitional phase, 2001–2003, when HGP is being fully completed as the post-genome sequencing projects are begun.

HGP is often called the most significant federal science and technology undertaking since Project Apollo. It certainly has been a historic milestone for biomedical research, not just technically, but managerially. It has been controversial throughout its history.[14]

Conceptualization, 1980–86

In 1953, James Watson and Francis Crick discovered the double helical structure of DNA, later winning Nobel prizes for their achievement. In succeeding years, biologists all over the world continued advances, probing deeper and deeper into the mysteries of life, particularly the basic building blocks of heredity, genes.

By the beginning of the 1980s, biologists were deciphering the human genetic code, one gene at a time. Some individuals speculated that it might some day be possible to sequence the entire human genome (i.e., the full complement of DNA in human cells). This was a technological vision that leapfrogged existing knowledge and technical capabilities. It entailed unraveling 3.1 billion base molecules making up DNA, a project whose scale was far beyond the mainstream of human genetics research.[15]

The first major meeting to discuss the feasibility of sequencing the human genome took place in 1985. Robert Sinsheimer, president of the University of California, Santa Cruz, invited a group of leading life scientists to his campus to discuss such a project's feasibility. Sinsheimer was looking for a large initiative he could promote to build his institution into a major center for genomic research. The meeting stimulated discussion, with plenty of views, most of which opposed the HGP idea. Big Science—research costing billions and organized as a project with milestones, expensive equipment, and a managerial hierarchy—was not in the tradition of biology. It had been pioneered in physics, sparked by the Manhattan Project, and in space with the Apollo experience, but had not penetrated biology to a significant extent. Sinsheimer also ran into bureaucratic obstacles within the University of California system and abandoned the idea.[16]

However, the notion of a human genome project continued to percolate within the scientific community. In early 1986, Sydney Brenner of the Medical Research Council (MRC) laboratory in Cambridge, England, urged the European Union to undertake a concerted program to map and sequence the human genome. What enhanced the technical feasibility of the project was the rapid advance of a range of relevant technologies. What might otherwise require thousands of scientists doing extremely difficult and dull tasks over decades could be expedited by the first automated sequencing machines, invented in 1986 by Leroy Hood and Lloyd Smith of the California Institute of Technology.[17]

There was another issue that made for conflict. Even if feasible, was deciphering the human genome really the best way to spend limited research money? The work was more like developing a technology, or (worse) data gathering, than conducting basic research experiments driven by theory. It was more industrial than academic in style—not what a good academic scientist was supposed to do. The money and talent would detract from smaller, less expensive, "better" science in the view of many researchers. Also, it would take money from many scientists and give it to a relative few willing to prostitute themselves, said critics. The principal agency supporting biomedical research, the National Institutes of Health, was responsive to the scientific community in setting its agenda. While scientists debated, NIH waited.[18]

Human Genome Project Milestones

1953	Watson and Crick discover the helical structure of DNA.
September 1986	DOE reallocates $5.3 million to initiate a human genome initiative.
1987	DOE establishes three genome research centers among its national labs.
1988	National Research Council of the National Academy of Sciences panel of prominent genetics researchers publishes report endorsing the HGP. Recommends incremental approach: first mapping and then sequencing.
1988	NIH Director Wyngaarden establishes new Office of Human Genome Research and appoints James Watson as its director. NIH and DOE sign memorandum of understanding to collaborate on HGP.
1990	Watson develops strategic plan for the project of 15 years, endorsing phased approach of mapping and then sequencing. Six centers established in the U.S. to do the HGP work.
April 1992	Watson resigns over conflict with Bernadine Healy, NIH's director.
July 1992	Venter resigns from NIH to accept offer to proceed with gene sequencing at a new non-profit, The Institute for Genomic Research (TIGR).
January 1, 1993	Healy appoints Francis Collins of the University of Michigan to direct HGP, effective in April.
1993	The Wellcome Trust opens new sequencing lab, the Sanger Centre, headed by John Sulston, near Cambridge, England.
August 1993	Clinton appoints Harold Varmus to be NIH director.
October 1993	NIH and DOE agree on revised plan for 1993-98. GenBank shifts to NIH.
1994	NIH rejects proposal from Venter's nonprofit, TIGR, to speed up gene sequencing with "shotgun" method.

(continued on next page)

Human Genome Project Milestones (continued)

May 1995	Venter announces TIGR has sequenced first entire genome of a living organism, *H. Influenzae*. Collins makes new grants to pilot projects at HGP centers to test new strategies and techniques aimed at speeding pace of HGP.
February 1996	Wellcome Trust organizes first International Strategy Meeting on Human Genome Sequencing in Bermuda. Forty leaders in genome research agree to make available all results within 24 hours.
January 1998	Applied Biosystems produces "next generation" sequencing technology, greatly accelerating the process of sequencing. Partners with Venter to form new profit-making company, Celera. Venter leaves TIGR to become president of Celera.
May 9, 1998	Venter announces Celera will sequence entire human genome in three years.
May 12, 1998	Collins meets with senior HGP staff, center directors, and key advisors and discusses response to Venter's challenge.
1998	Collins shifts to crash program with a 2000 interim goal deadline.
Summer 1999	Celera announces successful sequencing of Drosophila in just four months.
December 21, 1999	Meeting between HGP team and Venter's group.
March 14, 2000	Clinton and Blair issue joint statement on human genome issues.
June 26, 2000	Clinton and Blair proclaim a "tie" in completion of the first survey of the entire human genome.
February 15 & 16, 2001	HGP and Celera publish separately their genomic findings.
January 2002	Tony White, head of parent company, reorients Celera to develop new drugs rather than to pursue Venter's interest in research and sales of genetic information. Venter resigns.
2003	Projected completion of HGP.

Adoption, 1986–90

The trigger for moving beyond talk to action for NIH was the decision by the Department of Energy in September 1986 to reallocate $5.3 million from its budget to initiate a human genome initiative. The principal decision maker was Charles DeLisi, a cancer biologist who headed DOE's Office of Health and Environmental Research.

To DeLisi, a human genome project was a logical outgrowth of DOE's long-term research mission to study the effects of radiation on human health. Also, it was Big Science, the staple of DOE's national laboratories, which faced a diminishing demand for nuclear work. To the extent Big Science had established any foothold in biology, it had been at DOE in connection with radiation experiments. The DOE move caused great chagrin among many academic bioscientists, one of whom denounced the effort as "a scheme for unemployed bomb makers."[19] It was clearly seen as a threat. Many non-DOE observers held that if there was to be a Human Genome Project, NIH and the academic scientists who performed research under its purview had to be in charge.

Formulating a Plan

In 1987, as DOE established three genome research centers among its national labs, the National Research Council (NRC) of the National Academy of Sciences convened a panel that included many of the most prominent genetics researchers of the day, including both advocates and skeptics of a human genome project.

The NRC report came out in 1988. It endorsed the HGP. The skeptics and optimists united, but in doing so emphasized the need for a comprehensive, scientifically sound effort to generate maximum knowledge and create as perfect a picture as possible of the genetic makeup of any individual. If the Human Genome Project could be likened, metaphorically, to producing a "book of life," there was a first stage called mapping, which was the stage of defining the chapters. This meant identifying milestones or markers along the enormous length of a DNA molecule.[20] Once these chapters were delineated, the second stage of sequencing could commence. Sequencing meant going deeper, decoding the material in chapters and giving order to the letters within chapters, between the markers. This steady, incremental approach was geared to a total understanding, irrespective of whether some chapters might be more potentially valuable in terms of health or economic benefit than others. It aimed at as complete and accurate a product as was possible. Because the human genome was seen as a giant puzzle, decoding and arranging more than 3 billion chemical letters, it was viewed as a task that would necessarily have to be divided among many investigators.

U.S. Human Genome Project Funding* ($Millions)

The Human Genome Project is sometimes reported to have a cost of $3 billion. However, this figure refers to the total projected funding over a 15-year period (1990-2005) for a wide range of scientific activities related to genomics. These include studies of human diseases, experimental organisms (such as bacteria, yeast, worms, flies, and mice); development of new technologies for biological and medical research; computational methods to analyze genomes; and ethical, legal, and social issues related to genetics. Human genome sequencing represents only a small fraction of the overall 15-year budget.

The DOE and NIH genome programs set aside 3% to 5% of their respective total annual budgets for the study of the project's ethical, legal, and social issues (ELSI). For an in-depth look at the ELSI surrounding the project, see the ELSI website.**

For explanation of the NIH budget, contact the Office of Human Genome Communications, National Human Genome Research Institute, National Institutes of Health.***

FY	Wellcome Trust	DOE	NIH	Total
1992-2000	306			306
1988		10.7	17.2	27.9
1989		18.5	28.2	46.7
1990		27.2	59.5	86.7
1991		47.4	87.4	134.8
1992		59.4	104.8	164.2
1993		63.0	106.1	169.1
1994		63.3	127.0	190.3
1995		68.7	153.8	222.5
1996		73.9	169.3	243.2
1997		77.9	188.9	266.8
1998		85.5	218.3	303.8
1999		89.9	225.7	315.6
2000		88.9	271.7	360.6
2001		86.4	308.4	394.8
2002		87.8	346.7	434.3
Total	306	948.5	2066.3	3320.8

* *These numbers do not include construction funds, which are a very small part of the budget.*
** *www.ornl.gov/hgmis/elsi/elsi.html*
*** *This information is from: www.ornl.gov/hgmis/project/budget.html*

NRC recommended spending $200 million a year in new money (meaning the funds would not be taken away from other NIH research). It estimated that HGP would take between 10 and 15 years to complete, and cost as much as $3 billion. This figure included expenses for infrastructure, as well as the sequencing of simpler organisms for purposes of comparison with the much more complex human genome. NRC recognized there could be more than one agency involved in the HGP, but called for a "lead" agency. It did not specifically name which agency should play that role, but its view in favor of NIH was obvious. This was a project with a goal, but a relatively uncertain timetable. It was not a top-down, managed "crash project" like Manhattan or Apollo. The NRC declared:

> A large-scale, massive effort to ascertain the sequence of the entire genome cannot be adequately justified at the present time.... the Council wants to state in the clearest possible terms our opposition to any current proposal that envisions the establishment of one or a few large centers that are designed to map and/or sequence the human genome.... it is of the utmost importance that traditions of peer-reviewed research, of the sort currently funded by the National Institutes of Health, not be adversely affected by efforts to map or sequence the human genome.[21]

Not everyone on the NRC went along with the recommended incremental approach. Significantly, one of the members of the panel, Walter Gilbert, a Harvard University Nobel Prize-winning biologist, resigned from the NRC committee before it issued its report. He announced plans to start a private company, the Genome Corporation, that would move much more quickly than NRC recommended, employing a different scientific strategy than the one NRC favored. His new company could potentially gain a proprietary advantage and sell genome data for profit.[22]

Gilbert's venture never got off the ground because he could not raise venture capital. However, his action raised many alarms among bioscientists who wanted knowledge to flow freely so they could have access to it for research. Also, some scientists saw the human genome in symbolic terms. It was a gift of God. To make a profit from something so intrinsic to humanity was immoral. If many academic scientists and their allies in NIH looked askance at DOE and its national labs, they were even more wary of business.

Getting a Director

Armed with the NRC report, James Wyngaarden, NIH director, now made his move. Obtaining a small appropriation from Congress, he established a new Office of Human Genome Research, which reported to him. As director of the office, he appointed, in September 1988, James Watson, who had been one of HGP's strongest proponents in advising him.[23] The appointment of Watson was extraordinarily important. He was the most famous biologist in the world. His appointment brought immediate scientific legitimacy to HGP. Scientific carping diminished quickly. In addition, the Watson appointment to NIH immediately put DOE's program in the shadows. Watson said he had no choice in accepting the appointment: "I would only once have the opportunity to let my scientific life encompass a path from double helix to these billion steps of the human genome."[24]

NIH and DOE signed a memorandum of understanding and agreed to collaborate on HGP. HGP thus became a national program. In form, the two agencies might be equal. In reality, NIH was dominant. Watson was not only a great scientist, he was a flamboyant showman. DeLisi soon left DOE, replaced by leaders unknown in comparison to Watson. Also, Congress proved far more generous in funding NIH than DOE. DOE had little choice but to be the junior partner. For better or worse, HGP became associated primarily with NIH, an agency that had little experience in managing large-scale science and technology projects. Big Science and NIH had to adapt to one another.

In 1989, NIH elevated HGP from an office to the National Center for Human Genome Research (NCHGR). Congress appropriated funds directly to this new entity and gave Watson authority to award grants through an extramural program. He was now in a position to put some of his ideas into action.

Initial Implementation, 1990–93

Keeping his position as director of the Cold Spring Harbor Laboratory on Long Island, New York, Watson commuted regularly to Washington, D.C., and NIH's Bethesda campus. He started with just two employees, with staff gradually expanding. In a move unusual for NIH, Watson developed a strategic plan stretching 15 years. He began with an initial five-year plan. In a move that made it abundantly clear who was in charge of this national program, he declared that the HGP would start "officially" in 1990—thus peremptorily dismissing the four years of effort DOE had expended, as well as NIH's own previous work. Watson said the project would run until 2005, by which time the entire human genome would be sequenced as accurately as possible. He endorsed the phased approach espoused by NRC—mapping, then sequencing. In an unprecedented and bold action, Watson also announced that 3 percent of his budget (later raised to 5 percent) would go to social, legal, and ethical studies of the impacts of the research. He said that there would be societal impacts from HGP, and he wanted them studied so that the technology—and he regarded HGP as developing a new technology or capability—could be used wisely.

Watson was extremely effective with Congress. "My name was good," he recalled. Leslie Roberts wrote in *Science*:

> ... members of Congress were spellbound when the eccentric Nobel Laureate swept in to testify. Watson was eloquent in touting the project's goal: "to find out what being human is." He also had the refreshing quality of saying what he thought, no matter how politically incorrect—an unusual quality in Washington, D.C.[25]

There were debates within Watson's advisory panel about scientific strategy. Instead of the steady, phased, comprehensive approach of Watson, some advisers favored targeting and understanding disease genes. This was the real payoff, they said. It was what Congress cared about. Watson, however, held his ground. He likened the human genome to a particle accelerator. There was a proper way to build such a machine if it was to work effectively.

Watson pushed the first stage of the project, which was to chart maps of human chromosomes. With chromosome maps in hand, he believed the genes within could be better found and sequenced, and the disease genes would be a byproduct.[26]

Administrative Strategy

To achieve his purposes, however, Watson could not go along with NIH's traditional single investigator approach. This approach mainly involved grants to individual academic investigators who submitted ideas through peer-reviewed proposals to NIH. It was a basic research model that had served NIH well. However, Watson adopted a "center" strategy, which had been previously used primarily for clinical research, relying on universities. He did not build up an intramural laboratory within NIH. While he allowed university and other research institutions creative freedom to compete for center awards and go through peer review, it was clear that they had to gear their pursuits to HGP goals and fit into a pattern of his design. This was mission-oriented research in a basic science NIH setting. There were six initial centers established to do the work of HGP in the United States, all six at universities. These were the Whitehead Institute for Biomedical Research, affiliated with MIT; the University of Michigan; Baylor College of Medicine; University of Utah; University of California, San Francisco; and Washington University in St. Louis.

In addition to the initial centers, Watson expanded the project to other research institutions in the United States and other countries. He wanted broad involvement, as he insisted the human genome belonged to the world, not just the United States. Soon researchers from England, France, Israel, Germany, Canada, and Japan were involved, usually supported by their own governments. The linkages of U.S. centers with partners abroad placed NIH at the hub of a consortium of institutions. Watson imposed certain rules through force of his personality. In particular, he was emphatic that researchers in the United States and other countries share information toward a common goal.

While Watson saw HGP in technological terms, he was not really building a machine but aggregating information into a blueprint. The work of HGP was distributed widely, among individuals, institutions, and countries that were in some respects competitors. But, ultimately, information had to be brought together so the blueprint would make sense. What made this "large-scale approach" to science different from other life-science research at NIH was that there was less emphasis on theory and hypothesis as in the traditional model of science. This was a project focused on technical capacity to gather huge data sets of a particular type and assemble them in a meaningful pattern.

This Big Science approach was new to NIH and biology, but had some precursors at DOE. However, the model of organization Watson adopted was one of "distributed" or decentralized Big Science. He built up to perhaps a dozen major academic centers as HGP evolved. Each had its own procedures and quality controls. They coordinated with one another and through Watson's office to divide the labor of HGP. Watson was "directive" and sometimes abrasive, but, as one former center head recalled, he was so able and such a towering figure in biology, "you forgave him."[27] Nevertheless, the consortium model was an unwieldy structure for HGP.

Whatever its scientific merit (or limits), this spreading of the project had political dividends in that it meant many institutions (and, in the United States, congressional districts) had stakes in the project. Such support was especially important in the early days of HGP, when it was getting off the ground. This was a period of budget deficit and cost-cutting in government. Other Big Science projects at the time—the Superconducting Supercollider and the Space Station—were under heavy fire. The Space Station barely survived, and the Collider project was terminated by Congress in 1993.

One of the key technical decisions Watson made was to support Robert Waterston of Washington University in St. Louis, and John Sulston, then with the Medical Research Council laboratory in England, on a pilot project, the sequencing of the roundworm. This partnership ultimately became a backbone of HGP in some ways—a "transatlantic alliance."[28]

Conflict at NIH

While Watson coordinated various elements of the international consortium of organizations he had established, he ran into increasing problems with his own NIH organization. Watson did not have an intramural research program, but there was genome work under way at NIH. J. Craig Venter was a scientist who ran a large lab at NIH's National Institute for Neurological Disorders and Stroke, an entity over which Watson had no control. Venter not only had biomedical ability, but also was attracted to the applications to his science of information technology. He had been among the first scientists at NIH to acquire sequencing machines. Initially, Watson and Venter saw common purpose, but after a while began to contend.[29] Venter had developed with a colleague, Mark Adams, "a new technique, called expressed sequence tags, which enabled them to find genes at unprecedented speed." Venter was an outspoken individual, and he said his approach "was a bargain in comparison to the genome project." He boasted that his approach would allow him to find 80 percent to 90 percent of the genes within a few years, for a fraction of the HGP cost. Watkins dismissed Venter's "cream-skimming approach."[30]

Venter, however, had the backing of NIH's new director, Bernadine Healy, an M.D. who had been appointed in 1991 by President George H. W. Bush following her stint at the White House Office of Science and Technology Policy (OSTP). She and Watson had crossed swords earlier when she was at OSTP. Watson had disparaged her ability and suggested she had her job only because she was a woman. Now she was his boss. Moreover, she was actively promoting NIH's patenting inventions from its employees as part of a technology transfer strategy she espoused.[31] Venter was her poster child. Watson argued that if NIH patented genes, it would undermine the policy of openness and information sharing he had established for HGP participants.

The dispute became public in the summer of 1991, when both Venter and Watson appeared before a congressional hearing. Venter noted that NIH liked what he was doing, so much so that it was filing patent applications on the partial genes he was identifying—at the rate of 1,000 a month. Venter's bravado caused Watson to blow up. He called Venter's patenting "sheer lunacy," and declared "virtually any monkey" could do what Venter was doing. Aside from his concern about communication within the project, Watson's approach was to identify whole genes and determine what they did. He explained that if the patents on sequencing tags held, then anyone could lay claim to a gene without knowing its function. "I am horrified," Watson told Congress.[32]

The Watson-Healy feud worsened. In April 1992, Healy backed an examination by NIH of Watson's personal shareholdings in biotechnology companies for possible conflict of interest. Outraged, Watson resigned—via a fax from his Cold Spring Harbor lab. He declared that no one could work with that woman.[33] Ironically, Venter, who apparently could work with Healy, resigned in July from NIH to accept an offer of $70 million from a venture capital company. He intended to demonstrate his gene identification strategy at a new nonprofit, The Institute for Genomic Research (TIGR).[34] Venter was utterly determined to proceed with gene sequencing with the approach he chose, and felt the need for an organizational setting that gave him more freedom than NIH. A nonprofit model seemed to make sense, although he felt at the time he was taking a huge personal risk.[35]

Maintaining Momentum and Growing, 1993–98

A New Leader

The Human Genome Project was in trouble. Unless a new leader of great ability could be found soon, the project would founder. The centrifugal forces operating in the consortium Watson had established were immense. Healy knew she had to find a replacement, fast. While she may not have wanted Watson, she did want NIH to lead HGP. On January 1, 1993, NIH announced that Francis Collins of the University of Michigan had agreed to direct the NIH genome program, effective in April. Collins had achieved renown for co-discovering the genes associated with several dreaded maladies—cystic fibrosis, neurofibromatosis, and Huntington's disease. He was a medical doctor/scientist and headed a laboratory that had a secure base of funding from several sources. His laboratory was one of the original genome centers Watson had established. He had to take a cut in pay to become director of HGP. If Watson was a superstar in bioscience, Collins was a very bright star on the rise.

Why did he take the job? One reason was that many other scientists in the program believed he had the right blend of technical and administrative skills, and they pressed him hard. Another was that he wanted it, he said, "because there is only one human genome program. It will happen only once, and this is that moment in history. The chance to stand at the helm of that project and put my own personal stamp on it is more than I could imagine." He also stated, "My whole career has been spent training for this job— this is more important than putting a man on the moon or splitting the atom."[36] He recounted that it was Healy who made him realize this was his calling. She asked him to imagine a time in the future when they met as old people in a nursing home. He would say to her: "Damn it, Bernie, you should have made me take the job."[37]

The Collins appointment was regarded as a major coup for Healy and allowed her to show her own commitment to HGP. With Clinton taking office January 20, she was on the way out, and hiring Collins to bolster HGP might well be seen as her principal NIH legacy. If Watson was universally regarded as the ideal man to get HGP off the ground, Collins was seen by many as the right choice to bring it to fruition.

Collins had a very different leadership style from Watson. Watson was a scientific celebrity and loved the limelight. Collins was relatively unknown, quiet, and did not particularly enjoy the goldfish bowl aspect of heading HGP. Watson was a "big picture" leader, a scientific visionary who would delegate a lot of work. Collins was much more into the nitty-gritty and hands-on details of management. Watson worked hard, but maintained his Cold Spring Harbor lab. Collins was totally absorbed in HGP and left the University of Michigan.[38] Watson was a biologist and Collins a doctor and researcher. As a scientist, Watson always spoke of HGP as creating a technology that would advance the scientific frontier. Collins spoke about the health impacts of the technology. Watson assumed he was always "number one," an attitude that brought his ego into conflict with that of Healy. Collins was more consensual, more comfortable in a team concept of leadership.

In coming to NIH, Collins extracted two promises from Healy. First, he wanted laboratory space at NIH, so he could continue his research even while serving as an administrator and also build an intramural research program staffed by NIH researchers reporting to him. Second, he wanted the organization he headed to have institute status, the major designation at NIH. The Watson office had been established administratively, with minimal congressional authority. With Watson in charge, it had a high status in spite of its bureaucratic base. But without a stronger mandate and position, it was extremely vulnerable to NIH directors and their whims. NIH legislation was thus approved at the beginning of the Clinton administration, and this gave Collins' operation "permanent" status—meaning an NIH director or HHS secretary could not arbitrarily reorganize it out of existence. This action also meant the HGP ultimately would have the same bureaucratic status as the institutes with a research focus on the heart, cancer, and other diseases.[39] Eventually, HGP's organizational home was renamed the National Human Genome Research Institute (NHGRI).

Healy set in motion the machinery to provide Collins what he wanted and she left June 30. Ruth Kirschstein, a long-time NIH career administrator, served as interim director. President Clinton announced in August that his appointee as NIH director would be Harold Varmus, a Nobel Laureate cancer researcher from the University of California, San Francisco. As it turned out, Varmus and Collins got along well and formed a cohesive team. Varmus removed an issue by ending his predecessor's drive to patent partial genes.[40] Moreover, Varmus, unlike Healy, worked easily with Congress, and before too long the NIH budget, HGP included, rose substantially. This internal top-level support aided Collins enormously in managing HGP.

Taking Stock

When Collins took command, he found HGP making progress, but not quickly enough. Most positive was the discovery of disease genes. As Watson had predicted, they were coming as "spinoffs" from the mapping work.

These gave Collins ammunition in testifying before Congress. Every week, it seemed, the discovery of another deadly disease gene could be announced. "The reason the public pays and is excited—well, disease genes are at the top of the list," said Collins.[41] Also, the consortium was growing. Particularly important was an infusion of new funds from Great Britain's Wellcome Trust, possibly the world's largest medical philanthropy, which in 1993 opened a major new sequencing lab, the Sanger Centre, near Cambridge, England. The lab was headed by John Sulston. This meant that the Waterston-Sulston transatlantic connection Watson had funded became potentially more significant in the Collins era.

On the negative side, the mapping was not phasing into sequencing as fast as Collins believed was necessary if the 2005 deadline was to be met. With President Clinton anxious to hold the line on federal expenditures and much of HGP's money still concentrated on mapping, Collins was worried that "we have mortgaged part of our future."[42]

Nevertheless, he maintained the general approach he inherited. It was an approach he was sure would work, but it was slow, and the various academic laboratories made for a cumbersome structure. Collins' initial change was not in Watson's scientific strategy or organizational approach, but in trying to speed the execution of the project. In October, NIH and DOE agreed on a revised plan for 1993–1998. The plan was to accelerate work toward the goal of completing the human genome by 2005. The database for HGP information, called GenBank, which had been under DOE during the tenure of former Secretary James D. Watkins, now was shifted to NIH, a move that further underlined the NIH leadership role in the project. Moreover, to bolster that role even more and help in project acceleration, Collins continued to add staff and start the building of HGP's intramural research. He achieved a major coup when he enticed a former colleague at Michigan to leave the university to head the intramural laboratory, which Collins wanted to look ahead to applications.[43]

The Shotgun Alternative

In 1994, NIH received a proposal from Craig Venter's nonprofit institute, TIGR. It involved a dramatic bacterial gene sequencing method called "shotgun." It had been devised by Hamilton Smith, a Johns Hopkins biochemist, Nobel Prize winner, and member of TIGR's advisory board. Instead of spending months, possibly years, mapping, Smith proposed to Venter a much more brute-force approach. The initial step was to shear DNA into thousands of random pieces. The second step was to sequence the DNA of each fragment. The third step was to use a computer program to align the overlapping fragments to produce a single, contiguous DNA sequence of an entire organism. The boldness of the strategy appealed to Venter virtually from the start. It was compatible with his own methods, going back to his work at NIH. It could help him forward his dream of decoding the human genome.[44] Venter soon had Smith developing his shotgun strategy under TIGR auspices. Venter deployed eight TIGR personnel and 14 of the most advanced DNA sequencing machines available to the activity. To help pay for this work, TIGR submitted its 1994 proposal to NIH. NIH rejected the proposal, saying the shotgun method would not work effectively.[45] Venter called Collins to argue his case, to no avail.[46]

In May 1995, after 13 months of effort, Venter and Smith announced their TIGR team had sequenced the first entire genome of a living organism, *H. Influenzae,* at 1.8 million letters of DNA. They published an article describing their work in *Science* two months later. Their announcement sent a shockwave through the HGP community. Even Watson, who had little regard for Venter, said it was "a great moment in science."[47] What Venter and Smith had shown was that their particular approach, propelled by new computer programs and sequencing machines, could produce results. Nevertheless, most bioscience researchers were skeptical that the technique would work on more complex organisms and certainly not on the most complex of all, the human genome. It was too much akin to relying on a computer to put together a giant jigsaw puzzle. It would force certain pieces together simply because they appeared a fit and would omit others, contended the skeptics.

Collins made clear that HGP would stay on its present course. His goal, he asserted, was to assemble the definitive "book of life." In other words, the HGP approach would yield a complete, high-quality product. The shotgun approach would err and leave gaps. Accuracy was critical where the human genome was concerned, said Collins. He saw two requirements for achieving the quality product by 2005. The first was "construction of a complete physical map for each chromosome, consisting of a series of purified overlapping fragments of DNA that would provide the raw materials for DNA sequencing. The second was for major improvements in the speed and efficiency of DNA sequencing. Unfortunately, he worried that neither requirement was progressing as he hoped."[48]

Efforts to Speed HGP

Collins was not alone in worrying about HGP's pace. Maynard Olson, who headed the HGP center at the University of Washington, Seattle, wrote a commentary in *Science* entitled "Time to Sequence." While not necessarily subscribing to Venter's approach, he said HGP should get on with the sequencing task, and do so "on time, and under budget."[49] Also, Waterston and Sulston paid Collins a visit. They were well into their research on *C. elegans,* the roundworm, an organism far more complex than the one Venter and Smith had sequenced. They "were chomping at the bit, urging Collins to let them plunge into all-out sequencing. In the right hands, they argued, the technology was good enough; the only stumbling block was money." "Just do it," Sulston urged. The result might not be as accurate as originally wished, but it would be adequate, they said. It would be a difference between 99.99 percent and 99.9 percent accuracy.[50]

Collins was not ready for such a decision that entailed a major change not favored by many HGP participants. His cautious approach earned him praise in some quarters and criticism in others. What he did do was make several new grants to HGP centers, testing novel techniques and strategies. He said he wanted to see what these pilot projects produced before shifting direction.[51]

One strategy that could be employed fairly easily to speed HGP was to get information from HGP out quicker, and seek more communication and cooperation among centers. In February 1996, the Wellcome Trust organized the first International Strategy Meeting on Human Genome Sequencing in Bermuda. In December 1992, NIH and DOE had established guidelines on sharing data and resources, which allowed researchers to keep data private for six months. The question was whether this policy had to be changed. The answer was yes. A "Bermuda Accord" was struck that stated: "All human genome sequencing information should be freely available and in the public domain in order to encourage research and development and to maximize its benefit to society." HGP participants agreed to release data in 24 hours.[52]

At the Bermuda meeting, attended by 40 leaders in the genome research community, attention was also given to other aspects of HGP scientific strategy. James Weber, director of the Marshfield Medical Research Foundation in Wisconsin, spoke, touting the shotgun approach. Most of those attending criticized the technique. "They trounced him," a Weber associate stated. "They said [the sequence] would be full of holes, a 'Swiss cheese genome.'" Weber believed the major centers did not want to change from what they were doing to an entirely different strategy. It meant, he said, "overturning their labs." Venter, the foremost advocate of the shotgun approach, was at the meeting, but said nothing.[53]

Reorientation, 1998–2001

Venter's Challenge

In January 1998, the firm Applied Biosystems, a leading manufacturer of sequencing machines, completed work on its "next generation" technology. The firm believed the advance made was so prodigious that it could assure the 2005 deadline would be met. The new machines sped the process of sequencing enormously. The company knew it could make money selling the machines to HGP and its university centers. It could do even better financially by gaining control of genome data itself and then selling the genomic information. Mike Hunkapiller, president of Applied Biosystems, sought to partner with Venter, who had the scientific expertise Applied Biosystems did not have. Venter seized the opportunity. With his shotgun scientific approach and the bioinformatic technology of Applied Biosystems, he saw his longtime goal, the human genome, now within reach. Soon, Tony White, president of Perkin-Elmer Corporation (PE), parent company of Applied Biosystems, became the third party in the alliance. He provided additional money for the venture. A new profit-making company was formed, called Celera (from the Latin for "swift"). Venter left TIGR to become president of Celera.[54] Critics noted that the entrepreneurial Venter had become wealthier with his successive moves: from NIH to TIGR, from TIGR to Celera. Venter, however, recalled he made each move reluctantly, especially the one to Celera. "I didn't want to be in business," he said. "I wanted to do science, but I wanted even more to sequence the human genome."[55]

On May 8, Venter and Hunkapiller met with NIH Director Harold Varmus, and then traveled to Washington Dulles Airport to catch Collins. They informed both men that they had a new technology and the organization to exploit it. Venter said his company would take a limited number of patents and work out license arrangements with pharmaceutical corporations and

Sequencing Lab at the Whitehead Institute for Biomedical Research.

others interested in the data. He also said he would release sequence data free of charge where appropriate.[56] Venter remembers the meeting as one in which he stressed a desire for private-public cooperation toward a common goal. He recalls Varmus, at least, as intrigued. Collins, however, has a totally different recollection of what transpired, maintaining that he and Varmus were united, and that Venter's notion of cooperation was on his terms alone.[57]

The next day, the *New York Times* broke the story. HGP now had a private sector rival, it announced. The article declared that the business "venture would outstrip and to some extent make redundant" the $3 billion public HGP. It suggested that HGP might have troubles with Congress as a consequence. Varmus quickly rebutted these statements in a letter to the *Times,* protesting that the success of Venter's new entity was not a "fait accompli" and that the feasibility of his approach would "not be known for at least 18 months."

From the outset, the media treated the Celera-HGP situation as a race between the private and public sectors. On May 9, Venter certainly acted as if he were in a race. He publicly threw down the gauntlet to HGP, announcing Celera would sequence the entire human genome in three years, at a cost of $300 million.[58]

Collins' Response

On May 12, Collins held a breakfast meeting with senior HGP staffers, center directors, and key advisers, such as James Watson. The meeting had been planned for several months and just happened to occur at this tumultuous moment.[59] It was at Watson's Cold Spring Harbor Laboratory and there was an emergency atmosphere. The *New York Times* of that morning carried an article implying the takeover of the Human Genome Project by Venter and suggested that the public enterprise might have to be satisfied with sequencing a mouse instead of a human.[60]

The individuals at the meeting were upset and angry, outraged by what they had read in the newspapers about Venter's challenge. HGP had spent $1 billion and completed only 4 percent of the human genome at this point owing to the fact very little of HGP had been focused on human sequencing by then. Most of those present had spent years on the project. How could an upstart like Venter steal their glory? He had the benefit of all the results and technology that came from the public money spent and all the public data HGP had released. But he was holding his own information to himself. What if Congress fell for Venter's claims? Would it kill the public HGP? Of course, the group believed Venter's approach would never work. It was one matter to sequence *H. Influenzae* and entirely another to sequence the

3 billion base of a human being. But Venter was resourceful and could not be underestimated. He was seen as the potential "Bill Gates of Biotech."[61]

Venter now had a gigantic bankroll from Perkin Elmer and would be getting 300 $300,000 sequencing machines that were more sophisticated than those HGP had. He would also be getting one of the world's fastest supercomputers to help him reassemble sequenced fragments. The group worried that he would not really share data, in spite of what he was saying to the media, and would seek commercially to exploit what was rightfully free to all. Watson compared Venter's assault on HGP to Hitler's march on Poland. He asked Collins: Are you going to be a Churchill or a Chamberlain?[62]

Within three days of Venter's challenge, the Wellcome Trust declared it would double its support for HGP at the Sanger Center, to $330 million, saying Sanger would take responsibility for one-third of the sequencing. Sulston, the director of Sanger, and Dr. Michael Morgan, the Wellcome Trust's program officer, stated that if NIH pulled out of the race to sequence the genome, they would lead the public effort. Speaking before a packed auditorium at the Sanger facility, Morgan declared the Trust would not only double the Sanger budget, but would challenge any patent applications on DNA sequences it regarded as contrary to the public interest. "To leave this to a private company which has to make money," he declared, "seems to me to be completely and utterly stupid." His audience gave him a standing ovation.[63]

Soon after the Wellcome Trust action, Collins brought some of the principals in HGP together for a meeting near NIH. This meeting marked the point at which Collins articulated a radical change in policy. He had been building toward this altered course for some time.[64] In December 1997, Collins had met with some of the key center directors who were engaged in the pilot projects he had funded the year before. He had discussed concerns about the way HGP was organized, the fact that there needed to be greater coordination in order to accelerate the project. From work deriving from the pilots, he had a good idea who his top performers were. The issue for him was whether/when to make a move toward a different organizational strategy. Venter helped push him over the edge of decision in 1998. This was no longer a decision on how to meet the 2005 goal Watson had set. It was now a decision to compete with Venter. That would mean a goal of 2001.

Hence, at the 1998 meeting, Collins proposed a possible reorientation in program strategy. He urged that HGP go for an early "rough draft" of the human genome. He emphasized he was not trying to change the ultimate goal, which was still to produce a near-letter-perfect assembly of all 3 billion bases in the human genome. He argued this rough draft not be seen as "a substitute." His aim was to get 90 percent of the sequence completed and made public by the end of 2001, and then fill in the gaps later. The rough draft would be useful to researchers hunting for disease genes. It would also undercut any patent position Venter or some other company might claim. Collins' new position was greeted with dismay by some HGP participants and with enthusiasm by others. In September, his NIH advisory committee gave him formal approval. Collins declared that "this was not a time to be conservative, cautious, or coast along."[65]

HGP had sequenced 5 percent of the human genome by this time. But both NIH and the Wellcome Trust were about to pump more money into the project, as the public project acquired the same machines as Celera. "The day we announced Celera," said Tony White, "we set off an arms race and we were in the arms business. Everyone, including the government, had to retool, and that meant buying our equipment." Venter got the new sequencing machines first. HGP soon followed.[66]

As HGP acquired state-of-the-art equipment, it reorganized. Up to this time, Collins had presided over a loosely coupled consortium of laboratories across the United States, which were coordinated even more loosely with a number of foreign entities. He had maintained that organizational scheme and enlarged upon it. There were now 16 major genome centers capable of sequencing, known as the G-16. The time had come to centralize, he concluded, with the support of his Advisory Council.[67]

Thus, he soon began funneling additional funds to just three centers—Washington University in St. Louis, Baylor College of Medicine in Houston, and the Whitehead Institute. The Wellcome Trust again increased funding for Sanger. DOE did what it could to strengthen its Joint Genome Institute (as its aggregate of three national labs was now called). What emerged in 1998 was a new management model for HGP that would rely mainly on five genome centers, the ones willing to "sign up" to the demanding requirements he set. This group came to be known as the G-5.[68] This more centralized approach meant that 85 percent of the work would be performed by the G-5, the rest by the remaining 11 centers, which continued in the program. But money was distributed differently, as was power to make decisions.

Collins offered Celera the chance to join the alliance, but Venter rebuffed the offer and said Collins' new schedule had little to do with reality. Venter accused Collins "of putting humanity in a Waring blender and coming up with a patchwork quilt." Collins responded by saying Venter's program was the "Cliff Notes version of the genome."[69]

Collins also changed HGP's scientific strategy. He halted mapping and went fully to sequencing. HGP was converted from an academic-style research effort into an industrial-like crash program, with laboratories operating day and night. As competition heightened, the deadline for HGP was moved up again to spring 2000, 18 months earlier than the previous aim. As the new deadline was again moved closer, the information to be attained became less complete. HGP leaders played down the competition and justified the change in terms of good science. "The best service to the scientific community," explained Eric Lander, director of the Whitehead Institute, who emerged as one of the most influential directors of the G-5, "is to deliver the draft sequence rapidly and then to circle back and perform in the course of another year-and-a-half, at most, the finishing of that sequence."[70]

Collins billed himself as the "operating manager and field marshal" of "team sequence," as he called the reshaped alliance. About half of the sequence would be produced by Washington University in St. Louis, and Sanger, working in tandem. The team at Houston would concentrate on three particular chromosomes. The Whitehead Institute would focus on one chromosome and "whatever [else] needs to be done."[71] That turned out to be a great deal, and Lander's center grew particularly rapidly and took on an assembly-line machine appearance.

Collins told his immediate staff to concentrate solely on managing closely the HGP effort. They drew up charts with milestones and interim deadlines, and monitored performance. Collins had weekly conference calls every Friday at 11:00 a.m. with G-5 directors.[72] "Signing up" meant the directors agreed to allow others in the team access to their work, virtually as they did it. It was a "checks and balances" scheme to make sure what was done under the accelerated schedule was accurate. Going directly to sequencing put tremendous pressure on the group at Washington University to assemble a usable genome-wide map at unprecedented speed and scale. To Collins' relief, Waterston and his team "delivered."[73]

The center directors involved chafed initially at some of the oversight procedures, and Collins took some of them "to the woodshed," as he put it, to obviate resistance and gain cooperation. But if HGP was to compete with Celera, which had the efficiency of doing all its work in one facility—where hierarchy prevailed, and money and technology were available and focused—HGP had to change in a big way. Center directors, who normally competed with one another for grants and glory, had to operate like division directors within a "virtual organization." The G-5 group had to subordinate individual egos to the larger goal of meeting an external challenge. Otherwise, they would fail together. Fortunately for Collins, he was backed strongly by Varmus as he reoriented HGP strategy. The centralization and leadership aspects of this strategy went against the grain of NIH culture, which was very much "bottom up." The crash project approach was precisely what the NRC had warned against in its 1988 report. But it was now 10 years later, and circumstances had changed. Varmus made sure Collins got the additional money and other support he needed to scale up and redirect his operation.[74]

Keeping Cohesion

Collins' decision to concentrate effort and push for an expedited rough draft sequence initially angered some of those earlier collaborators who felt excluded, but after private meetings with Collins, most parties concerned with HGP coalesced. Not all. Sydney Brenner, of the Medical Research

Council in England, didn't like the new policy. "Once the genome initiative got consolidated into this managed project, it became a bit like Stalinist Russia," he complained. "If you're not with us, you must be against us."[75] The key to getting agreement among various participants was the common fear that if Celera "won," they would have to go through Celera and its patent controls and expensive subscription rates to get access to genomic information. Venter said the fears of academic researchers were groundless. Trust, however, was lacking between the two sides. Whitehead/MIT's Lander had industry connections, but he made it clear that his loyalty in the genome race lay firmly behind the public genome project—what he called "the Forces of Good."[76]

One who left the HGP camp was Gerry Rubin of the University of California at Berkeley. Both HGP and Celera had projects to sequence the fruit fly *(Drosophila melanogaster)*. For Venter, sequencing the fruit fly before HGP was a way to show his critics how well his shotgun sequencing technique worked. With "an offer I could not refuse," Rubin was enticed to Venter's fruit fly team.[77] In the summer of 1999, Celera announced *Drosophila* had been successfully sequenced—in just four months, one-tenth the time it had taken to sequence the previous largest genome, which had been much less complex than the fly. Rubin's defection appalled many associated with HGP, but it showed that Celera had more than a scientific strategy and hardware. It had and could get top technical talent. Ironically, Collins had brought Rubin and Venter together at a scientific conference.[78]

By fall, the radical overhaul of HGP was an accomplished fact. With tens of millions of additional dollars that Varmus helped acquire from the NIH budget, the G-5 centers were being equipped with hundreds of new automated DNA sequencers. They were also adding new personnel to man these machines. Ph.D. students, who had been a large part of the HGP workforce and who found genome sequencing tedious, were increasingly complemented by scores of technicians more suitable for the work. The major university centers changed dramatically in style and appearance. Waterston's lab at Washington University in St. Louis employed 200 people working in shifts and operated 19 hours a day.[79]

However, a serious problem surfaced when DOE signaled a possible agreement with Celera to help it sequence the three human chromosomes for which it was responsible. NIH could not order a sister agency to stay in the fold, but did make its disagreement clear. Moreover, the Wellcome Trust contacted Lord Sainsbury, the British science minister, who held talks with Neal Lane, President Clinton's science advisor. In September 1999, Prime Minister Blair also became involved, presumably asking Clinton to intervene. Whether DOE succumbed to pressure from the White House or from NIH, the fact was that DOE dropped its potential Celera relationship before it was consummated.[80]

The entry of Blair into genome policy reflected the degree to which the issue of control of genome data was escalating to summit-level politics. There were those in both the United States and Great Britain who believed the Bermuda Accord on prompt release of DNA sequence data should become a formal international agreement. That did not happen, but the fact that the move was advocated suggests the degree to which many felt the stakes in the HGP-Celera dispute were exceptionally high. It also shows how different were the political atmospherics surrounding HGP at the end of the 1990s from what they had been at the outset of the decade.

HGP had emerged relatively quietly from the scientific community and bureaucracy. It was Big Science, but took a while to become high-visibility Big Science. Similarly, Walter Gilbert had in the early days tried and failed to get venture capital for a private genomics company. Now politicians and business executives were hyper-attentive to the implications of genome policy. The media, focusing on "the race," followed developments as an ongoing story. Venter proved highly skilled in using the media to make his case. The discoveries of disease genes along the way had added to the sense that serious issues were involved with this research. Policy makers were increasingly aware that biotechnology could well be the dominant technology of the 21st century, and who controlled that technology mattered not only in health, but also in economic competitiveness. They might not fully understand where the genome project fit in, but they assumed it was at the cutting edge. In short, the genome project was now politicized.

Efforts at Compromise

The obvious political heat and visibility of the contest, the bitter words that appeared frequently in the media, issued by both sides, led some participants to seek compromise. In late 1999, urgent discussions took place. Among those involved were Lander, for the public program, and Rockefeller University President Arnold Levine, a member of Celera's advisory board. There was the view that the approaches were complementary. Also, some Celera supporters worried that if HGP "lost," it might cause Congress to cut NIH's budget for genome research in general, an outcome regarded as negative.[81] There was definitely a threat there, as the debate took on ideological tones of government versus business. The more the debate was framed in that way, the more politicians would take sides, and there could be damage, especially to NIH. Venter seemed to be getting the better of the contest in the media. He came across as David versus Goliath, the outsider versus the establishment. Collins wished to manage science, not a public relations campaign, and he had to learn the political aspects of HGP on the job.

On December 21, 1999, the two sides met. HGP was represented by Collins, Waterston, Varmus, and Martin Bobrow, head of clinical genetics at

Addenbrooke's Hospital in Cambridge, England. Venter's group included Tony White, Celera executive Paul Gilman, and Levine. Collins brought to the meeting a draft statement of "shared principles," which he hoped to release if the meeting went well.[82]

But the meeting soured. Venter insisted on exclusive commercial distribution rights for joint data for up to five years, whereas Collins considered six to 12 months appropriate (by which time HGP would have essentially completed its sequence and made its data available to everyone). Celera also insisted on rights to various applications of the sequence, including being exclusive distributor over the Internet.[83]

In February 2000, Collins faxed a "confidential" letter addressed to Venter, White, Levine, and Gilman and signed by Collins, Varmus, Waterston, and Bobrow, reiterating the major disagreements between HGP and Celera. Collins wrote: "While establishing a monopoly on commercial uses of the human genome sequence may be in Celera's business interest, it is not in the best interests of science or the general public." Questioning whether Celera really wanted to budge from its position, Collins gave Venter one week to resume negotiations. Failing that, he stated, "We will conclude that the initial proposal whereby the data from the public HGP and Celera are collaboratively merged is no longer workable." On the eve of Collins' March 6 deadline, the Wellcome Trust released the letter to the media, presumably to pressure Celera. Instead, Celera used the letter to denounce its competitor's "slimy" and "dumb" tactics. The leak provided the media a field day and embarrassed Collins, who denied he had anything to do with the leak.[84] It also showed that Collins could not control the actions of his British partner.

In addition to many public comments condemning HGP, Celera's formal response to Collins on March 7 was that "… we continue to be interested in pursuing good-faith discussions toward collaboration," provided the company's commercial interests were protected. It saw no problem in releasing data intended "for pure research applications."[85]

The President and Prime Minister Speak Out

On March 14, Clinton and Blair issued a statement on human genome issues, including this paragraph:

> We applaud the decision by scientists working on the Human Genome Project to release raw fundamental information about the human DNA sequence and its variants rapidly into the public domain, and we commend other scientists around the world to adopt this policy.

The statement was obviously not only aimed at Celera, but other firms that were interested in taking out patents on genes. Another company, Incyte, was increasingly active. It was not pursuing the human genome as a whole, like Celera; rather, it was targeting a search for specific disease genes it saw as potentially valuable commercially. Clinton and Blair saw a possible problem in the future. However, their remarks caused another problem: a huge dip in stock price for Celera, and the biotech industry generally. That was not what was intended, and it made Venter look even more like a symbol of small private enterprise being pressed by big government.[86] The *Wall Street Journal* gave him op-ed space to plead his case as a victim.

Success

Having become part of the controversy, Clinton now sought to lead in a solution. He told Lane, his science advisor, to "fix it ... make these guys work together." Unaware of the president's action, Collins spoke to Ari Patrinos, the senior administrator of DOE responsible for that department's part of the genome project. He asked Patrinos if he could do anything to defuse the enlarging conflict.[87] For years, DOE, which began HGP, had been the junior partner in the government enterprise. Now its leadership was needed as a broker. Patrinos had a series of meetings with Collins and Venter, searching for points of agreement.[88] It was critical that the one-upsmanship cease, he made clear. The reality was that each side had certain advantages. Venter had the benefit of access to all the genome discoveries, which HGP made public. On the other hand, HGP had started earlier and had much more money. However they started, they were now in a dead heat for the "finish line." Indeed, they were racing for a finish line everyone understood was artificially constructed, in the sense that a rough draft would leave more work to do. At the same time, that finish line was probably good enough to be useful scientifically and politically.

Collins chafed at being in a "race" in which the rules were such that every 24 hours he was giving away data that benefited his competitor. The concepts of "winning" or "losing" did not fit under those circumstances, he felt.[89] Nevertheless, the politics were such he had little choice but to seek "victory" if a compromise proved impossible. Venter was urged by his business associates to avoid a truce and win the race. The benefits from being first were clear from a business perspective. But Venter saw himself as more a scientist than a business executive, and did not want to hurt NIH. Moreover, while he was confident he was ahead, he knew better than anyone the risks in his approach. Nothing was certain.[90] Under the terms Patrinos was discussing, Venter and the public project would get equal credit. The first public signs that an accord was within reach came in June when Venter and Collins appeared together without incident at an NIH cancer conference. As the final preparations were hastily laid for a White House ceremony to make the official announcement, Venter and Collins, clothed in ceremonial lab coats, appeared on the cover of *Time* magazine.[91]

On June 26, at a White House ceremony, Clinton announced that the rough drafts of the HGP and Celera human genomes were ready. Tony Blair attended via teleconference. James Watson was there in a seat of honor. Collins and Venter made a joint announcement, evincing pleasure with their share of the prize. Neither could claim a complete book of life was attained. That would take more time. According to HGP, it would be 2003 when the ultimate goal was attained. But the basic structure—this was now known, and all that remained was to publish the formal scientific papers.[92]

Unfortunately, the truce broke down in December over plans to jointly publish. On February 16, 2001, Venter published his paper on the human genome in *Science*, and at essentially the same time Collins' group published its report in *Nature*.[93] The debate over who "really" won would go on for years, but was already fading in early 2001. The consensus on the part of most observers at this point in time was that history would say both sides won, with humanity the ultimate winner.

Conclusions

The Human Genome Project is generally viewed as a governmental success. It is also seen as having had frustrations along the way, been intensely controversial, and overcome or resolved the issues that came up. These were hurdles that were technical, organizational, and political. What factors were critical in shaping and influencing the course of the program? There are probably a hundred that could be mentioned. Many are scientific or technological, such as the development of new sequencing machines. The emphasis here is on the managerial factors.

Goals

Large-scale, public, technical projects need clear, unmistakable, specific goals. The larger the projects are, the more important it is that these goals be defined and communicated to all constituencies. What a clear goal provides is a constant point of reference against which to measure, direct, prioritize, and modify actions by various individuals and organizations involved.

The major goal of HGP was clear—to sequence the more than 3 billion letters of the human genetic code. The goal was bold—it represented not an incremental decision but a discontinuous change, a leap forward in science and technology. It was estimated that it would take 15 years and $3 billion to realize the goal. While there are caveats that might be raised about timing and money, the widespread perception today is that HGP is a federal project that has worked, on time and within budget.[94]

While the ultimate goal did not change, HGP did insert an interim goal, the "rough draft" of 2000. The interim goal may well have been good science strategy; it was surely good political strategy, needed to compete with Celera. It had the positive impact of accelerating HGP's movement toward the final goal. The interim goal became as important as the final goal in achieving success, since it established HGP's credibility at a time HGP was under attack in the media and Congress. Significantly, HGP spent approximately the same amount of money to sequence the interim human genome that Celera did in the 1998-2001 period.[95] Achieving the interim goal diffused the conflict between the public and private sectors. It was a consensus goal—an arranged finish line. Once met, HGP could continue its work, in a less contested setting, toward the final goal.

Organization

Organization has to do with "who does what," the formal and informal division of labor. It pertains to the allocation of tasks and whether the parts add up to an organizational machine that helps accomplish the overall mission. Sometimes organizational arrangements stand in the way of mission success. Government bureaucracy is viewed as subject to inefficiency, because it is accountable to many constituencies and embodies values other than pure efficiency.

Venter felt that he had to leave NIH to accomplish the human genome mission. He moved from NIH to a nonprofit organization (TIGR), and then to a profit-making entity, Celera, to find the best possible base from which to accomplish the sequencing of the human genome. His own success in this respect shows that there are alternatives to government under certain conditions.

One of those conditions is timing. An earlier scientist-turned-entrepreneur, Walter Gilbert, could not attract business venture capital when he tried to set up a company to sequence the human genome in the late 1980s. When a goal is very distant, its attainment problematic, and its costs enormous, government may be the only instrument able and willing to make the huge front-end research investment necessary. When the multiple, initial technical and financial hurdles of a new field are surmounted, the private sector may enter, as it did in the human genome case.

The way government was organized to pursue HGP was not a result of careful strategic planning. Governmental involvement started through DOE;

then came NIH, which quickly asserted itself as "lead agency." While NIH was in charge, DOE retained its autonomy, and at one point almost made an arrangement to work with Celera. Keeping what became an interagency international consortium cohesive and pointing in the same direction was critical to HGP success. There were limits to what NIH, as the lead agency, could do, however, as indicated not only by the DOE possible defection, but also by the independent actions of the Wellcome Trust in England in leaking the Collins letter/ultimatum.

The organizational model of HGP for most of its project life was that of a loosely coupled international consortium. Located in six countries, this consortium had multiple sponsors and performers. There were various players engaged and they often moved in accord with individual rather than project-wide goals. However, in the early days of HGP, the mapping and sequencing tasks were viewed as so vast and technically complex as to require a large number of performers, primarily in the academic community. These performers were structured as centers—groups of researchers and technicians working with sophisticated equipment. Moreover, the first director of HGP wanted to maximize geographical spread and participation as values in themselves. He also involved social scientists, ethicists, and legal scholars, asking them to look beyond the science to its impacts.

However, the downside of HGP's structure was sensed by Collins as early as 1995 and became abundantly clear when Celera came into the picture. Venter's scientific approach and brash style made him controversial to HGP leadership and the scientific establishment generally. But his record showed that a single organization, backed by requisite money and technology, could move fast if led by the right person. Confronted by Celera, the second HGP director, Collins, concluded that HGP's organization was too loose and too uncoupled, a barrier to competing with Celera. He went from the pluralistic model he inherited and on which he built, to a more centralized model, relying on the G-5 centers. Efficiency and speed took precedence over participation. The original organizational strategy might well have made sense in the early years of HGP, when it was getting established. However, later, when much of the scientific groundwork was laid and it was confronted by an external competitor, HGP needed a very different organizational approach.

Political Support

HGP has had political support throughout its history. Had the interim goal not been set and achieved, that support might well have eroded. Goals, organization, and political support go together in government programs, one influencing the other. Politicians may understand little about the technical details of HGP, but they do think they know something about schedules and money. They react negatively to what they perceive as mismanagement, as seen in schedule slippage and cost overruns. Hence, what HGP had to do was to show results to keep the confidence of elected officials.

Luckily, HGP drew on a vast reservoir of political support that is virtually unique to NIH. Had DOE been lead agency, HGP might not have fared as well in getting needed resources. But NIH is among the most favored of government agencies, because Congress and the White House see health research as a priority. NIH, like the Department of Defense, wages war—in its case on disease, and politicians tend to worry about their own infirmities as well as those of their families. If national security helps Defense budgets, so personal security helps get money for NIH.

HGP benefited from this situation. Moreover, NIH Director Varmus proved exceptionally adept in working with the White House and, especially, Congress. Since Varmus also favored HGP within NIH priorities, he helped to shore up HGP's political support.

It should be emphasized that while NIH—and HGP particularly—had considerable goodwill in Congress and the White House, it still had to perform. The HGP spinoffs of disease gene discoveries over the years helped in this respect. The attainment of the interim goal helped even more.

Competition

Competition was a critical factor in HGP's success, but could have been its undoing. It was bureaucratic competition with DOE that induced NIH to get started with HGP. Subsequently, HGP faced internal and external competition.

The internal competition reflected the NIH bureaucratic strategy up to 1998. As noted earlier, when the goal of the HGP was announced and NIH became lead agency, NIH decided to use university-based centers as the prime mechanism by which to accomplish the sequencing goal. Universities are notoriously hard to manage, given their emphasis on freedom of inquiry. On the other hand, NIH believed the top researchers it needed were in the universities. The question was how to enlist them in mission-oriented research of this kind and get their maximum output. One answer was organization (centers) and the other was competition. The centers competed for the money in the HGP budget. The competition was important in getting the universities to maximize their effort and deliver on their promises.

NIH used peer review in managing the competition. That is, those centers that participated had to prove to reviewers, as well as NIH, that they were better than others, or would perform a specific task others could not. This enabled HGP to get academic talent working on the project that was top flight, or at least perceived as such by the scientific community. Center directors, particularly, were members of the academic elite, individuals who had established credentials and were competitive for themselves and their institutions. HGP used such competitive drives to get the most from extramural research. Non-performing centers could be dropped from the project. This system emphasizing many university centers is probably sound for a project at a scientific frontier, when technical uncertainties are limiting factors, and there is a need to explore more than one route to success. Yet internal competition can also slow down a project that has severe deadlines. There comes a point where what is a valuable form of competition early in a project can be a barrier to achievement later in its life. This is especially so where external competition becomes a dominating factor in decision making.

The external competition came from Celera. It was formidable scientifically and politically. Venter was a strong and determined rival, and the evidence suggests HGP—and the biomedical research establishment—erred for a long time in not taking him seriously. He was tenacious, skilled, and outspoken in his challenge to HGP. His shotgun approach was not valued by NIH and its peer reviewers, but one has to wonder whether it was his approach or Venter himself who was at issue prior to his sequencing *H. Influenzae* in 1995. After that event, he had to be taken seriously. Moreover, in 1998, when he got an edge through new advanced sequencing machines, he forced HGP to realize how capable a rival he was. From 1998 to 2001, HGP moved into a crash project mode and Venter became the enemy. He became the measure against which HGP performance was to be judged, for better or worse. Whether or not HGP wished to be in a race, it was in one.

Leadership

Circumstances affecting large-scale technical projects change over time. The ultimate goal may be a constant, an overall destiny. Getting there entails shifting strategies that are scientific, organizational, and political. Leadership is utterly critical—probably the single most critical factor in success. It took a certain leadership to launch HGP, and another kind to make the changes that are bringing it to a successful conclusion.

HGP had had two very different leaders. Watson was a charismatic leader, a man who will go down in the history of science for co-discovery of the double helical structure of DNA in 1953. He was the best possible person to launch HGP at a time when it was highly controversial among scientists. Few others could, by sheer personal force, have made HGP not only legitimate, but also "where the action was" in bioscience. Great projects that promise breakthroughs require recruitment of extremely able people. It is almost impossible to quantify this human dimension of projects, but there are certain projects that draw the very top people in a field to them. Having Watson at the helm made a difference in this respect. Watson was also an exceptional "scientific salesman" for HGP before Congress. The spreading of centers around the country was no doubt good science in Watson's mind, but it was also good politics, building a legislative base for HGP at the outset, when it needed it. Internationalizing HGP may have also made sense scientifically, but it additionally served Watson's purpose to make HGP a project for the world, not just the United States. Moreover, it supplemented funding of HGP. Early support of the U.S.-British Waterston-Sulston team turned out to be especially significant.

But it is not at all clear that the volatile, often abrasive Watson was the right man to implement HGP over the long haul. There are charismatic and institutional leaders, the latter following the former. Collins appears to have fulfilled the role of institutional leader well. Less flashy, much more consensual in style, Collins was able to strike an alliance with Varmus, his superior at NIH, nurture congressional relations, and develop a team approach to management that became increasingly critical as time went on.

Collins might have initially operated primarily as a "maintainer" and "augmenter" of the Watson approach during his tenure. But circumstances were such that his greatest contribution to HGP's success was his later decision to reorient the project. The process that led to this decision started before Venter's 1998 challenge, perhaps as early as 1995, when Waterston and Sulston paid him a visit and argued for a rough draft strategy that moved more rapidly from mapping to sequencing. His thinking evolved in 1996 with pilot projects to find ways to speed the project. Then came a meeting in 1997 with HGP principals in which he discussed the need to restructure HGP to meet the 2005 deadline Watson had set. Within months, Collins shifted to a crash program with a 2000 deadline for an interim goal. Perhaps he should have moved sooner toward the crash project mode, but would such a move have been possible in the NIH culture without the sense of crisis that Venter posed? What Celera did was present an external threat that empowered Collins to make big changes. Collins moved from the role of a project manager to a project leader. The bold changes he made affected science, organization, and politics.

Forces internal and external to HGP converged, and Collins acted. He did so in the nick of time and in such a way as to save HGP's credibility. It is ironic that Venter helped Collins reorient HGP. Venter created a crisis that affected not only NIH but also the bioscience establishment generally, putting into sharp question the basic government-university strategy for getting the research done. Collins transformed the loose consortium into a tight alliance with a small circle of performers and decision makers. Had Collins and others not responded, the public HGP might well have "lost"—or appeared to have done so. Appearances can be as important as reality in government, and public ridicule could have been HGP's fate.

Instead, HGP is today acknowledged a success, even as it completes the full decoding of the human genome. If Collins was empowered by external competition, Venter received vindication for his effort when he stood together with Collins at the White House victory ceremony. A negotiated finish line made both sides winners and allowed science to move ahead toward the ultimate goal, a complete genome in 2003.

Ironically, the continuing progress of HGP, and its policy of early release of data, may have contributed to the decision by Celera's parent company to change Celera's course from selling new genomic information to developing drugs. This decision forced Venter to resign as Celera's president and scientific leader in early 2002.

In conclusion, the Human Genome Project shows that relationships among government, national laboratories, industry, universities, and foreign partners are changing dramatically at the frontier of science. The Human Genome Project may well be a harbinger of the future in more ways than one. It is likely a model for large-scale technical projects in the 21st century. The implications of this case for science, policy, and administration are therefore profound.

HGP is both like and unlike the Manhattan and Apollo projects. It is alike in being a mega project that is also a breakthrough project. It is different in being transnational and involving the private industry sector as an autonomous (possibly adversarial) actor, rather than strictly as a contractor. HGP, in the present transition phase, is now consciously partnering with the private sector in looking to genomic applications in health. In some cases, joint funding is involved. There is evidence that other institutes at NIH are looking at HGP as an example of an approach they might emulate.[96] The next phase in the human genome revolution has already begun.

Implications for the Future

Most observers of the Human Genome Project's history concentrate on the contest between HGP and Celera. This makes sense in view of competition's role in the events. As we have noted, it was a critical factor in accelerating HGP's schedule. However, the record of HGP also shows the importance of partnership as instrumental in bringing about a capability to unravel the human genomic blueprint.

HGP, particularly in respect to partnership, may be a harbinger for the future in the way large-scale R&D projects are run. As noted in the previous section, HGP is both like and unlike the Manhattan and Apollo projects with which it is often compared. It is alike in being a megaproject that is also a breakthrough project. It is different in being interagency, trans-national, and involving a private foundation as a co-financer. In the present transition phase, industry is becoming involved as a financial partner in supporting research for practical cures in disease. Industry, in working with HGP, accords with "the rules," meaning companies must release findings from the HGP research in which they participate every 24 hours. Other institutes at NIH are emulating HGP's large-scale approach to management, which is a partnership model.

What HGP's approach suggests is that where very challenging objectives are involved, and talent is distributed widely, it may be necessary and desir-able to link institutions into vast research consortia. More than one-third of HGP's budget came from sponsors other than NIH. Performers included national laboratories, universities, and researchers in six countries.

Such partnerships have advantages and disadvantages. The negatives are obvious—the partners have wills of their own and may defeat or slow down the achievement of system-wide goals. There has to be a leadership structure of some kind to provide coherence, direction, and pace. The HGP model entailed a "lead agency" approach with NIH fulfilling that role by virtue of dominant funding, political support, and technical competence. While an agency may seek to lead, others may not necessarily follow. Partner-ships require leadership of one kind or another, and sometimes a form that works at one point in a project's history may not at another. A mix of sta-bility and change are essential in keeping partners together. Hence, the HGP model is one about which observers who prefer neat organizational lines, strong hierarchical management, and predictable strategy may find fault. There can be inefficiencies in partnership arrangements as consensus takes time to be forged. Nor are performers of R&D in universities or other entities always willing to go along with central decisions. Leadership often comes down to the power to persuade.[97]

Still, for better or worse, HGP does seem to be a forerunner for what is to come. It reveals a type of large-scale "network" or "system" in which the leader (an organization or person) has power that is limited, but can be enhanced. It is not "power over," but "power with."[98] Bargaining, negotiation, prodding, cheering, complaining, charming, coercing—all are techniques of management in partnership relations. These large-scale systems can include partners who are sovereign nations. That is the case with the largest science and technology project currently under way in the civil sector, the International Space Station (ISS). NASA is "lead agency" for a project involving at least 16 nations. One of the partners is Russia, which openly defied NASA in selling room on its portion of the Space Station to a wealthy "tourist," Dennis Tito. HGP thus seems more like its contemporary project,

ISS, than predecessors like Manhattan and Apollo. These were both models of centrally controlled national projects. One took place in a war setting and the other was a technological front of the Cold War.

If one looks hard at what is "new" in the way current science and technology programs are being run, the observer sees, increasingly, large-scale R&D efforts that cross agency lines, involve government-private alliances, and stretch beyond the United States. The last-mentioned characteristic is, of course, a reflection of globalization in R&D.

Looking forward, what great projects lie in the 21st century for which HGP is a possible model? One can imagine projects such as: the search for a new disease cure; a way to mitigate global warming, while still having energy to develop economically; a mission to Mars or one to divert oncoming asteroids; a technological front against terrorism; and others. Whatever lies ahead—and the unexpected is to be expected—HGP's lessons show that diverse institutions can be brought together in pursuit of bold goals that stretch beyond a decade. Partnership takes scientific vision and political will. But it also requires administrative leadership to get multiple, independent partners to adhere. It also helps if there is an urgency born of external competition and threat.

If interagency, intersectoral, and transnational partnerships are going to be the wave of the future in science and technology (and other spheres of policy), what does that say for the skills needed of individual leaders? It certainly suggests they will have to be able to grapple with increasing complexity and greater bureaucratic, political, and cultural diversity. Does current education for the leaders of tomorrow prepare them adequately? If HGP is a guide, the answer matters greatly, for the future is arriving fast!

Endnotes

1. Nicholas Wade, *Life Script* (New York: Simon and Schuster, 2001), 13.

2. Wade, 7.

3. Most of this money was spent on technology development, genome maps, and model organisms. The sequencing stage—the culmination—was a relatively small part of the overall expenditure. Correspondence to author from Francis Collins, Jan. 29, 2002.

4. J. Craig Venter et. al., "The Sequence of the Human Genome, *Science* (February 6, 2001), 1304-1351. International Human Genome Sequencing Consortium, "Initial Sequencing and Analysis of the Human Genome," *Nature* (February 15, 2001), 860-921.

5. The phases are not precise but do represent significant shifts in emphasis. For example, in preparing for the transition phase HGP funded various technology development projects. Correspondence to author from Francis Collins, Jan. 29, 2002.

6. Wade, 9-10.

7. Other factors, including personality conflicts, exacerbated the situation.

8. Interview with Francis Collins, December 4, 2001.

9. Correspondence to author from Francis Collins, Jan. 29, 2002.

10. Interview with Elke Jordan, deputy director, National Human Genome Research Institute, National Institutes of Health, July 19, 2001.

11. Francis Collins holds that HGP had many goals and the widely reported comparison raised an "apples and oranges" issue that made the public project appear less cost-effective than the private effort. Correspondence to author from Francis Collins, Jan. 29, 2002.

12. Kevin Davies, *Cracking the Genome: Inside the Race to Unlock Human DNA* (New York: The Free Press, 2001), 150.

13. Wade, Chapter 1.

14. Leslie Roberts, "Controversial from the Start," *Science* (February 16, 2001), 1182-1188.

15. Robert Cook-Deegan, *The Gene Wars: Science, Politics, and the Human Genome* (New York: W.W. Norton & Co., 1994), 10-11.

16. Roberts, 1183. Cook-Deegan, Chapter 5.

17. "A History of the Human Genome Project," *Science* (February 16, 2001), 1196.

18. Roberts, 1183-1184.

19. Roberts, 1184.

20. Wade, 30.

21. Cook-Deegan, 131-132.

22. Roberts, 1184-1185.

23. Interview with Elke Jordan, July 19, 2001.

24. Cook-Deegan, 161.

25. Roberts, 1185.

26. Roberts, 1185.

27. Interview with Francis Collins, November 30, 2001.

28. Wade, 15, 32.

29. Interview with J. Craig Venter, November 25, 2001.

30. Roberts, 1185.

31. Cook-Deegan, 328.

32. Cook-Deegan, 332-333.

33. Roberts, 1186.

34. Roberts, 1186.

35. Venter interview.

36. Cook-Deegan, 341; Davies, 69.

37. Collins interview, November 30, 2001.

38. Officially, Collins is on leave, and has been on leave since 1993. Collins interview, November 30, 2001.

39. Cook-Deegan, 343.

40. Davies, 64.

41. Roberts, 1186.

42. Roberts, 1186.

43. Collins interviews.

44. Venter interview.

45. Davies, 106.

46. Collins does not recall this phone call, which Venter remembers. Venter interview. Collins correspondence to author, Jan. 29, 2002.

47. Davies, 107.

48. Roberts, 1187; Davies, 86.

49. Davies, 86-87.

50. Roberts, 1187.

51. Roberts, 1187.

52. Davies, 87, 148.

53. Davies, 142.

54. Davies, 146-147.

55. Venter interview.

56. Davies, 147.

57. Venter and Collins (November 30, 2001) interviews. See Wade's description of the meeting, Wade, 45-46.

58. Davies, 148; Roberts, 1187.

59. Collins correspondence to author, Jan. 29, 2002.

60. Davies, 150.

61. Davies, 5; Roberts, 1187.

62. Davies, 150.

63. Davies, 151.

64. Collins interviews.

65. Davies, 162; Roberts, 1188.

66. Davies, 167.

67. Collins interviews.

68. Davies, 163.

69. Davies, 163.

70. Davies, 163.

71. Davies, 164.

72. "The Public Genome Team Races...," Newsweek (April 10, 2000), 52.

73. Collins correspondence to author, Jan. 29, 2002

74. The importance of Varmus cannot be underestimated. Elke Jordan, who served under both Watson and Collins as deputy director, notes that Varmus was an unusually capable NIH director, both internally and in relation to Congress. He made a positive difference in the life of HGP and gave it priority in his budget decisions. Interview with Elke Jordan, July 19, 2001.

75. Davies, 152.

76. The MIT center grew to 200 researchers and technicians and produced one-third of the human sequence. It became the flagship of the U.S. effort according to Davies, 165.

77. Davies, 159.
78. Collins interview, November 30, 2001.
79. Wade, 49-50.
80. Davies, 206.
81. Davies, 198-199.
82. Davies, 199.
83. Davies, 200.
84. Davies, 204. Collins interview, November 30, 2001.
85. Davies, 204.
86. Davies, 205-206.
87. Collins correspondence to author, Jan. 29, 2002.
88. Davies, 238.
89. Collins correspondence to author, Jan, 29. 2002.
90. Venter interview.
91. Davies, 238.
92. Davies, 236-237.
93. J. C. Venter et. al., "The Sequence of the Human Genome," *Science* (February 16, 2001), 1304-1351. International Human Genome Sequencing Consortium, "Initial Sequencing and Analysis of the Human Genome," *Nature* (February 15, 2001), 860-921.
94. While the United States (the National Institutes of Health and the Department of Energy) has spent approximately $3 billion, the Wellcome Trust has spent hundreds of millions in addition to accomplish the purpose. Other governments have also spent funds. There is also some ambiguity about timing. HGP began in 1986 as a DOE project, became a national project with the entry of NIH in 1988, but HGP Director Watson declared 1990 as the start date for the 15-year time clock. Hence, if one accepts the Watson timetable, HGP will be complete ahead of its 15-year schedule, in 2003. These ambiguities have relevance to the perception of success. Similarly, there were two finish lines—the interim one in 2000 and the final one in 2003.
95. According to Collins, the figure was approximately $300 million. Collins correspondence to author, Jan. 29, 2002.
96. William Schulz, "Determining Structure: 'Big Science' Protein Structure Initiative Touches Off Lively Debate," *Chemical and Engineering News* (October 15, 2001), 23-26.
97. Richard Neustadt, *Presidential Power: The Politics of Leadership* (New York: John Wiley and Sons, 1976).
98. W. Henry Lambright, *Powering Apollo: James E. Webb of NASA* (Baltimore, Md.: Johns Hopkins University Press, 1995).

CHAPTER THREE

Managing Across Boundaries:
A Case Study of Dr. Helene Gayle
and the AIDS Epidemic

Norma M. Riccucci
Professor of Public Administration and Policy
Rockefeller College of Public Affairs and Policy
University at Albany, State University of New York

This report was originally published in January 2002.

Introduction

Dr. Helene D. Gayle was director of the National Center for HIV, STD, and TB Prevention (NCHSTP) at the U.S. Centers for Disease Control and Prevention (CDC) from 1995 until August of 2001. In September of 2001, she was detailed to the Bill and Melinda Gates Foundation because of her vast experience and success at coordinating efforts across global public-private lines to combat the spread of HIV/AIDS and other infectious diseases. She has devoted her entire professional career to the public by combating such diseases.

Born on August 16, 1955, in Buffalo, New York, Helene Doris Gayle is the third of five children. She was very much influenced and inspired by her hard-working parents—Jacob, a small business owner, and Marietta, a social worker. Reflecting on the values they instilled in her, Gayle said that "both of my parents felt strongly that to make a contribution to the world around us is one of the greatest things you can do." What a presage this would be for Gayle, who would eventually go on to impact the global war against one of the deadliest diseases of the 20th century.

Gayle's parents were very active in the civil rights movement, because they, as well as their children, witnessed firsthand the impact of discrimination against African Americans in this country. Gayle's experiences here encouraged her to pursue undergraduate studies in psychology at Barnard College. Likewise, she would later pursue a medical degree at the University of Pennsylvania because she was interested in having an impact on issues affecting underserved and disenfranchised communities. And medicine—and, more broadly, public health—would provide that opportunity.

At the same time she was working on her medical degree at the University of Pennsylvania, Dr. Gayle went on to earn a Masters of Public Health (MPH) at Johns Hopkins University. Her interest in public health was sparked by a desire to be involved in the social as well as political aspects of medicine stemming from early involvement in social and political issues. Years earlier, when she was a medical student, she heard a speech by Dr. D. A. Henderson on the worldwide efforts to eradicate smallpox. That speech helped to cement her goal of pursuing a career in public health.

By 1981, Gayle had earned both an M.D. and an MPH. She was but 25 years young and about to begin a pediatric residency at the Children's Hospital National Medical Center in Washington, D.C. As a resident at Children's Hospital, she rotated on a monthly basis through all the different specialties within pediatric medicine to gain expertise as a pediatrician. Three years later, Dr. Gayle was selected to participate in the CDC's very prestigious two-year epidemiology training program, the Epidemic Intelligence Service (EIS). This program is an apprenticeship of sorts, in that the participants go through hands-on training in epidemiology. Dr. Gayle's main focus

Career Highlights of Dr. Helene Gayle

1976:	B.A. in Psychology, Cum Laude, Barnard College, Columbia University
1981:	M.D., University of Pennsylvania
1981:	M.P.H., School of Hygiene and Public Health, Johns Hopkins University
1981-1984:	Pediatric Internship and Residency, Children's Hospital, National Medical Center, Washington, D.C.
1984-1986:	Epidemic Intelligence Service, Centers for Disease Control and Prevention
1985-1987:	Preventive Medicine Residency, Centers for Disease Control and Prevention
1987-1989:	Medical Epidemiologist, Pediatric and Family Studies Section, AIDS Program, Centers for Disease Control and Prevention
1988-1989:	Acting Special Assistant for Minority HIV Policy Coordination, Office of Deputy Director (HIV), Centers for Disease Control and Prevention
1989-1992:	Assistant Director, Preventive Medicine Residency Program, Centers for Disease Control and Prevention
1989-1990:	Assistant Chief for Science, International Activity, Division of HIV/AIDS, Centers for Disease Control and Prevention
1990-1992:	Chief, International Activity, Division of HIV/AIDS, Centers for Disease Control and Prevention
1992-1994:	Chief, HIV/AIDS Division, Agency AIDS Coordinator, U.S. Agency for International Development (USAID)
1994-1995:	Associate Director, Washington, D.C. Office, Centers for Disease Control and Prevention
Feb. 1995:	Interim Director, National Center for HIV, STD, and TB Prevention (NCHSTP), Centers for Disease Control and Prevention
May 1995-Aug. 2001:	Director, National Center for HIV/AIDS, STD, and TB Prevention, Centers for Disease Control and Prevention
Sept. 2001-present:	Senior Advisor for HIV/AIDS, Bill and Melinda Gates Foundation

was on prevention of malnutrition in children in the United States and Africa.

She subsequently completed an additional year of training in preventive medicine focusing on diarrheal diseases of children in developing countries. Upon completion of her training in epidemiology and preventive medicine, Dr. Gayle joined CDC's Division of HIV/AIDS. Her early work at CDC involved examining the risks of HIV transmission from mother to child, and the risks for adolescents, college students, and U.S. racial and ethnic minorities. Knowledge gained from these types of studies served to focus the development of HIV/AIDS prevention strategies.

Dr. Gayle points out that "AIDS became the focus of my work at the CDC because it is so very central to public health and policy, and it is, in fact, a way of addressing broader public health issues related to children, women, and underserved populations throughout the world. And these are all issues that I am very committed to.... But I maintain that if we can do something about AIDS in this country, as well as in the rest of the world, then we will have moved forward as a society in dealing with much more than just a public health issue."

Dr. Gayle's work eventually took on a more international focus, as she was promoted to chief of International Activity within the Division of HIV/AIDS. In this capacity, she was involved in epidemiological research in such countries as the former Zaire, Jamaica, South Africa, the Ivory Coast, and Thailand.

Because of her outstanding achievements in the international AIDS arena, Dr. Gayle was detailed to the U.S. Agency for International Development (USAID) in the early 1990s, where she served as the agency's AIDS coordinator and chief of the HIV/AIDS Division. Working with other countries and international organizations to develop global AIDS policies, Dr. Gayle was USAID's chief representative on international HIV/AIDS issues.

In June of 1994, Dr. Gayle returned to the CDC and served as the director of the Washington, D.C. office, representing CDC on legislative, policy, program management, and intergovernmental matters. She also acted as liaison with other high-level department officials in the federal government. It was during this period of time that Dr. Gayle was asked to participate in the group that ultimately recommended the creation of a new center, the National Center for HIV, STD, and TB Prevention (NCHSTP).

Dr. Helene Gayle was in fact a key player in the effort to create this new center. Through an examination of the broader managerial and organizational functions of the CDC as they pertained to disease prevention and control, she and her working group assessed the feasibility of reorganizing and consolidating major organizational units working on HIV/AIDS and two related areas—other STDs and TB—within CDC. Integrating these activities under one structure not only improved the coordination of HIV efforts, but also provided a more integrated approach to diseases that share behavioral and biological interactions.

On September 21, 1995, Dr. Donna Shalala, then Secretary of the Department of Health and Human Services, named Dr. Gayle director of the new National Center for HIV, STD, and TB Prevention. Dr. Gayle had served as interim director of NCHSTP since its creation in February of 1995. The CDC director at the time, Dr. David Satcher, noted that Dr. Gayle was the obvious person to run the Center, not only because she helped create it, but also because of her proven track record in managing and leading efforts to prevent and control infectious diseases, in particular her successful accomplishments in combating one of the most deadly epidemics of the 20th century—HIV/AIDS. He said: "Dr. Gayle provided impressive leadership for the Center's reorganization efforts. In addition, [she] has been instrumental in providing a thorough analysis of future prevention needs and implementing organizational solutions that will improve the visibility and accountability of CDC's HIV/AIDS programs and integrate HIV/STD/TB prevention efforts."

The NCHSTP is the largest of CDC's 11 centers, institutes, and offices. It has five divisions, which are responsible for public health surveillance, prevention research, the development of programs to prevent and control

---

The Five Divisions of the NCHSTP

1. **Division of HIV/AIDS Prevention—Intervention Research and Support:** conducts behavioral intervention and operations research and evaluation and provides financial and technical assistance for HIV prevention programs conducted by state, local, and territorial health departments, national and regional minority organizations, community-based organizations, business, labor, faith-based organizations, and training agencies.

2. **Division of HIV/AIDS Prevention—Surveillance and Epidemiology:** conducts surveillance and epidemiologic and behavioral research to monitor trends and risk behaviors and provide a basis for targeting prevention resources.

3. **Division of STD Prevention:** works to prevent STDs, including syphilis, gonorrhea, chlamydia, human papillomavirus, genital herpes, and hepatitis B.

4. **Division of Tuberculosis Elimination:** works to prevent, control, and eliminate TB.

5. **Global AIDS Program:** works closely with the U.S. Agency for International Development (USAID) and other federal and international agencies to prevent the spread of HIV/AIDS throughout the world.

"Dr. Gayle has made extraordinary contributions in the fight to prevent the spread of HIV. She has demonstrated a strong commitment to public health and those who live with HIV, and will continue to effectively champion the cause through her new position."

—Dr. Jeffrey P. Koplan, Director of the Centers for Disease Control and Prevention

HIV infection, other sexually transmitted diseases, and tuberculosis, and evaluation of these programs.

As a recognized world leader in the fight against HIV/AIDS, Dr. Gayle is currently on loan from the CDC to the Bill and Melinda Gates Foundation, where she serves as senior advisor for HIV/AIDS. The foundation's major mission is to help improve the lives of people globally through health and learning. Dr. Gayle's primary responsibilities are managing and overseeing programs and policies aimed at preventing the spread of HIV/AIDS and other communicable diseases throughout the world.

When Secretary of Health and Human Services Tommy G. Thompson announced that Dr. Gayle would be detailed from the CDC to the Gates Foundation, he stated in his press release that "Dr. Gayle will provide an invaluable depth of knowledge and the ability to coordinate efforts across public and private sector lines, *and across boundaries,* to make the fullest possible use of our resources against this scourge."

Dr. Gayle looked forward to the post with the Gates Foundation, commenting, "It is my profound belief that solutions to this pandemic, both in the United States and around the world, will come only through strong public/private partnerships."

Dr. Gayle has certainly had innumerable opportunities to leave the federal service and work in the private sector as a physician, where she would

About the Bill and Melinda Gates Foundation

The Bill and Melinda Gates Foundation places a major focus on helping to improve people's lives through health and learning. It continues to look for strategic opportunities to extend the benefits of modern science and technology to people around the world, especially where poverty serves as an obstacle to participating in these benefits. It invests in partnerships with individuals and organizations that bring experience, expertise, and commitment to their own efforts to help people through better health and learning.

earn a higher salary. Yet, she opted to remain with the government because she feels that it is still an important place where she can make a positive contribution to society. She says, "I don't regret having placed a high priority on a career that enables me to make a contribution to humankind."

The Setting

It has been almost two decades since the HIV/AIDs crisis surfaced. Very early on, the U.S. Centers for Disease Control and Prevention, an agency of the U.S. Department of Health and Human Services and the lead federal agency for protecting the health and safety of Americans, became involved in the battle against this deadly disease. The HIV/AIDS epidemic continues to ravage the world's population, and the CDC is still at the forefront of the battle. As of December 2000, the CDC reports that 774,467 Americans are estimated to have AIDS, with the estimated annual rate of HIV infections in the U.S. remaining roughly constant at 40,000 since the early 1990s. In South Africa alone, statistics indicate that 4.7 million people are infected with the virus, and more than half a million were infected with HIV last year alone. Experts say that AIDS is wiping out an entire generation in South Africa—a major portion of that country's national workforce, including doctors, teachers, and engineers. "There will be, for the first time, more people in their 60s and 70s than people in their 30s and 40s," said Dr. Peter Piot, director of the United Nations AIDS program. South Africa has one of the highest rates of HIV/AIDS infections in the world. Because there is currently no cure for AIDS, the importance of prevention is monumental.

Other sexually transmitted diseases also continued to occur at high rates in the 1980s and 1990s as well. Syphilis, gonorrhea, chlamydia, and genital human papillomavirus (HPV) infection have been widespread public health concerns, and represent a serious threat to reproductive health. Moreover, certain genital HPV types are related to cervical, vulvar, anal, and penile cancers. With an estimated 340 million people worldwide being infected with an STD, the challenge for prevention is great. The largest number of new cases is occurring in South and Southeast Asia, sub-Saharan Africa, Latin America, and the Caribbean. However, over 14 million cases occur in North America. Again, it is clear that collaborative efforts to build and improve the public health infrastructure in surveillance, treatment, and prevention are imperative and cost effective.

From 1985 to 1992, the nation also experienced a resurgence of TB. One of the reasons was the disappearance of public health funds specifically targeted for TB programs, which subsequently led to the dismantling of these services. Both TB and HIV are issues that require extensive collaborations

---

Current Worldwide Statistics on HIV/AIDS

5.3 million people newly infected with HIV in 2000:
- 4.7 million adults,
- including 2.2 million women;
- 600,000 children under age 15.

80% of all adult infections have resulted from heterosexual intercourse.

At the end of 2000, 36.1 million people living with HIV/AIDS:
- 34.7 million adults,
- including 16.4 million women;
- 1.4 million children under age 15.

25.3 million reside in sub-Saharan Africa; 5.8 million live in South and Southeast Asia.

In 2000, there were 3 million deaths due to HIV/AIDS:
- 2.5 million adults,
- including 1.3 million women;
- 500,000 children under age 15.

Since the beginning of the epidemic, an estimated 21.8 million people have died:
- 17.5 million adults,
- including 9.7 million women;
- 4.3 million children under age 15.

There have been 13.2 million orphans since the beginning of the epidemic.

---

in prevention, treatment, and care. It is estimated that approximately 34.3 million people living with HIV also have Myco-bacterium tuberculosis. According to the World Health Organization (WHO), "tuberculosis kills 2 million people each year." The "breakdown in health services, the spread of HIV/AIDS, and the resurgence of multidrug-resistant TB are contributing to the worsening impact of this disease." It is further estimated that one-third of the world's population is currently infected with the TB bacillus. The overall importance of identifying those with TB, assuring access to care and drugs, and working to ensure that patients maintain their prescribed drug regimen are all crucial issues in the field of TB elimination.

Additionally, according to WHO, "since 70 percent of those co-infected live in sub-Saharan Africa, this region also bears the overwhelming brunt of the global epidemic of HIV-associated TB." The lack of sufficient surveillance, access to drugs, and public health infrastructures in this region make for what seems an insurmountable task. It is also estimated that more than 16,000 new U.S. cases occur annually.

Current Statistics on HIV/AIDS, other STDs, and TB in the United States

- As of December 2000, 774,467 Americans were reported to have AIDS:
  - 640,022 reported to be male
  - 134,441 reported to be female
  - 8,908 reported to be children under age 13
- Approximately 40,000 new HIV infections occur each year.
- In 2000, 16,377 cases of active TB among Americans reported.
- In 1999, 659,441 cases of genital chlamydial infection among Americans reported.
- In 1999, 360,076 cases of gonorrhea among Americans reported.

Source: Surveillance reports published online by the U.S. Centers for Disease Control and Prevention, www.cdc.gov.

HIV/AIDS, other sexually transmitted diseases, and TB have all proved to be devastating global epidemics in the 1980s and 1990s, and continue to represent a growing threat to public health in the 21st century. One of the people who has been most instrumental in combating these diseases worldwide is Dr. Helene Gayle. In fact, in an effort to better manage and coordinate the various activities, programs, and arsenals aimed at reducing and preventing the spread of these diseases, the CDC created, through a major reorganization effort spearheaded and led by Dr. Helene Gayle, the National Center for HIV, STD, and TB Prevention in 1995.

Let's take a closer look at the career of Dr. Helene Gayle and why she has become a recognized world leader in the fight against AIDS and other communicable and sexually transmitted diseases.

The Case Study

Dr. Gayle can be credited with innumerable accomplishments in the battle against HIV/AIDS and other contagious diseases not only in the United States but globally as well. Her accomplishments can be characterized as a combination of skills, talents, and strategies, including her expertise as a public health official, her managerial skills within the organizations she has directed, and her strong leadership skills in the external national and international communities in the fight against deadly diseases.

Reframing the Issues

In recent years, Dr. Gayle has worked very hard within the United States to reframe the issues and concerns surrounding HIV/AIDS and other STDs. She points out that in the early stages of the AIDS epidemic, there was a perception that the disease affected primarily the white gay community, which lulled people into thinking this was the only population at risk. Clearly, HIV/AIDS is not a white gay disease. In fact, today AIDS and other STDs have the greatest impact on populations of color. Dr. Gayle notes, "It is the African-American and Latino communities that are currently at the greatest risk."

Prevention messages often miss the mark in communities of color, Dr. Gayle points out. For example, in communities of color, "for far too long, the assumption was that the impact on gay and bisexual men was only among whites; this is not the case." Dr. Gayle points out that in a study of 8,700 HIV-positive men who said they were infected by having sex with other men, one-quarter of the African Americans identified themselves as heterosexual. Only 6 percent of white men, in contrast, identified themselves as heterosexual. Men who have sex with men do not always identify themselves as gay or bisexual. They may live outwardly heterosexual lives, often married with children, but continue to having sex with men. This is characteristic of men of all races, but the phenomenon appears to be more prevalent among African Americans. The phenomenon has been called having sex "on the down low" or "the D.L." She further notes that "programs for black men must address the stigma of homosexuality, which prevents many of these men from identifying themselves as gay and bisexual and may keep them from accessing needed prevention and treatment services."

In addition, needle sharing associated with injection drug use has been identified as one of the leading causes in the spread of HIV/AIDS today. In particular, injection drug use and needle sharing in African American communities has been reported to be one of the reasons for the higher rates of HIV/AIDS cases among African Americans in the United States.

The upshot is that the issues had to be reframed. One of Dr. Gayle's greatest challenges, then, has been to not only make people aware that populations of color are at the greatest risk, but to tailor and adapt the various strategies and methods for prevention to the persons (e.g., those who don't self-identify as gay) who may be less receptive and accessible to prevention messages relevant to the white gay community, yet are contributing to the rate of HIV/AIDS in communities of color. Besides reframing messages, it was also important to make sure that the appropriate messengers were also part of the equation. This requires greater collaboration and support for organizations that can effectively represent and reach communities at risk.

Creating Partnerships

Dr. Gayle stresses that linking prevention efforts with the organizations and people involved in the care and treatment of HIV/AIDS and other STDs is pivotal to success, so that there is a continuum between prevention and care. Linking and integrating the various services and strategies to assure coordination of resources, as well as cost and program effectiveness, in its efforts to control HIV/AIDS and other STDs must be accorded higher priority.

Dr. Gayle also explains that much of her work depends upon successful collaboration with community, state, national, and international partners in efforts to stop the spread of diseases such as TB, HIV/AIDS, and other STDs. As Dr. Gayle readily acknowledges, "We are not the sole players, nor will we ever have all the resources to fix all these problems on our own. Developing collaborations is key." For example, under her direction, NCHSTP works diligently to assure such coordination by developing partnerships with other agencies within its parent organization, the Department of Health and Human Services, including the National Institutes of Health, the Health Resources and Services Administration, the Food and Drug Administration, and the Substance Abuse and Mental Health Services Administration. The recently released CDC "HIV Prevention Strategic Plan" highlights the need for collaboration among government agencies, universities, state and local health departments, and community-based organizations so that relevant scientists, epidemiologists, and policy makers can come together to form a unified front in the fight against diseases such as HIV/AIDS, STDs, and TB.

Dr. Gayle with children at a community center in Maun, Botswana, that teaches young people about HIV and supports children who have family members living with HIV.

Dr. Gayle points out that collaborating with private sector organizations, in particular faith-based institutions, may be one of the most important strategies for combating HIV/AIDS and other STDs in communities of color. She notes that "it has been critical to involve and have the faith communities work with us on some of these more controversial issues because of the key role they play in helping shape opinions and attitudes and, especially in the African American community, serving as agents of social change." So developing partnerships with faith-based organizations such as churches is a key strategy in controlling and preventing the spread of HIV/AIDS and other sexually transmitted diseases in the United States as well as other countries.

Dr. Gayle is an acclaimed pioneer in the creation of community-based prevention activities, especially among minority and underserved communities. She has been particularly successful in getting disparate groups, including minority, gay, and church communities, involved so that they have a better understanding of what the government does related to HIV/AIDS and other STDs. She notes that "many of the issues around AIDS have led to a good deal of mistrust between communities at risk, as well as communities at large, and I have tried to facilitate bringing a broad cross-section of people more into the process and create more open communications among them. The AIDS epidemic has stimulated us to be much more inclusive as public health officials."

Dr. David Satcher, who is currently the U.S. Surgeon General and who directed the CDC from 1993 to 1998, commented on Dr. Gayle's extraordinary ability to work effectively in local communities. He points out that "Helene gets to know and works with people locally. I think she took the concept of government-funded programs to the local community as it has never been done before. Working and helping to plan at a local level and assuring that there are planning committees in each local community— we've never really done this before in government the way it's been done for the AIDS prevention program. It's one of the most innovative strategies ever developed in terms of involving local communities, and Helene was responsible for implementing this."

Dr. Satcher went on to say, "Another thing about Helene that makes her effective in her work with different groups or communities is that she is a likable person. She doesn't take herself too seriously, and this makes it easier for people to work with her. She has a genuine interest in other people, and people recognize this; she also has a sense of humor. And I think that all this makes for a better working relationship when you are working on difficult issues. You have to create an environment where people are comfortable, and she does this very effectively."

Working to improve access to HIV care for people in poor countries is also important for Dr. Gayle, because currently treatment for HIV is still

---

Some of the Key Policy Players in Dr. Gayle's Policy Arena

Dr. Kenneth Castro, Director of the TB Division of the National Center for HIV, STD, and TB Prevention (NCHSTP)

Dr. David Holtgrave, former Director of the NCHSTP's Division of HIV/AIDS Prevention: Intervention, Research and Support

Dr. David Satcher, U.S. Surgeon General and former Director of the U.S. Centers for Disease Control and Prevention (CDC)

Todd Summer, former Deputy Director of the White House Office of National AIDS Policy

Dr. Judy Wasserheit, former Director, NCHSTP's STD Division

---

very limited in poor countries, which bear the greatest burden of HIV/AIDS. The cost of providing antiretroviral drugs for HIV has become a particularly serious problem in developing countries, where even simple medications are out of reach for much of the population. Dr. Gayle points out that the CDC works with over 20 countries worldwide to address the issues of prevention, access, and availability of care. After years of multinational-partnered efforts, in 2001 pharmaceutical companies finally began slashing the cost of AIDS treatment drugs for Africa, which will provide great relief to those infected with the virus. However, even with lower prices, access to relatively complex antiretroviral therapy will still be limited in the short run because of weak health infrastructure.

The CDC also collaborates with private sector firms not only in the United States but also in other parts of the world, including working to set up work-site HIV prevention programs. The CDC has been involved in a program called Business Responds to AIDS (BRTA), working with major corporations for over 10 years to have employers educate and disseminate information to their workers about the causes of HIV/AIDS and how it spreads. The CDC also works with U.S. multinational corporations such as the Ford Motor Company in countries like South Africa, where education and other services are provided not only to employees but also to the neighborhoods and the communities around their plants.

In the international arena, the CDC collaborates with a number of other critical partners, including the U.S. Agency for International Development, the Joint United Nations Program on HIV/AIDS (UNAIDS), the World Health Organization, the United Nations Children's Fund (UNICEF), and the World Bank, to name a few. And, obviously, working with the countries themselves is key.

Building Relationships

One of the reasons why Dr. Gayle has been so successful at collaboration—building bridges and fostering communications between the federal
government, various communities, and global partners—is her skillful
interpersonal relations. As she herself admits, "I very much enjoy working
with people. Also, I have tried not to divorce myself from who I am, and the
many people and communities that have contributed to my sense of self.
So, I can usually see commonalities in people, [and] at the same time recognize and appreciate diversity and differences. I feel that by listening to
others and relying on my own experiences, I can find these commonalities,
which serve to break down barriers with groups."

Dr. Satcher, U.S. Surgeon General and former CDC director, said, "People
are willing to work with her because they trust her and have confidence in
her. Inside and outside of government, people have a lot of confidence and
trust in her, because they trust her motivation: She really cares about people
and helping them."

Todd Summer, former deputy director of the White House Office of
National AIDS Policy, notes that "Helene does very well at developing relationships.... She is very personable, and I have never met anyone that doesn't
like Helene. And sometimes when people [or outside groups] feel like blast-
ing the CDC, it's because of affection for her that they tone down their
words or hold their criticisms altogether."

Perhaps the key to Dr. Gayle's efficacy is her ability to foster dialogue
between and among diverse people and groups. This means, says Dr. Gayle,
"believing in what they do. If you can understand *their* position and *their*
thought processes and believe they are justified in their respective positions, you can work effectively with disparate groups and people. It is then
important to get people to see the similarities in their positions—that is, to
make them understand that we *do* all think differently, but this is part of
who we are and it doesn't make us right or wrong. When people can accept
the fact that there are other equally plausible perspectives, then you can
make some progress in your efforts to fold or incorporate these groups into
the public policy process, in this case around AIDS."

Dr. David Holtgrave, former director of NCHSTP's Division of
HIV/AIDS Prevention: Intervention, Research and Support, said that Dr.
Gayle is good at collaborating because she "has been absolutely committed
to HIV prevention not only in the United States but globally, especially in
developing countries, and she has made international HIV/AIDS work a priority of the Center. To do this really requires collaborating with the leaders of
the various countries as well as the health ministers, and then all of the
international organizations such as the World Health Organization and
UNAIDS to get that work done. This requires effective collaborating skills."

He went on to say that "Helene has extensive knowledge about how governments function, country by country, and how we function," and she believes in "really interacting with other countries, where we are truly collaborating and not trying to impose our programs on them."

The Politics of Public Health

Obviously, developing coalitions and collaborating with governmental and nongovernmental partners at community, state, national, and international levels requires a certain degree of political savvy and acumen. Indeed, because of the political as well as social challenges that have imbued the HIV/AIDS epidemic, possessing a high degree of diplomacy is essential. Her interpersonal skills as well as her technical expertise have served her well here. This latter attribute has been especially helpful in her interactions in political arenas, because technical or public health justifications are necessary for agency decisions. As she points out, "As a 'technocrat,' I have responsibilities for assisting in the formulation of public health policy, using the best available data to do so. As I help to shape the direction of research efforts for HIV prevention programs, I try to provide justification for policy options based on what we know and what we think will have the greatest positive benefit. While this seems obvious, it often isn't, because of the political considerations which underlie diseases such as HIV/AIDS."

Dr. Judy Wasserheit, former director of the STD Division of the NCHSTP, points out that Dr. Gayle "is politically very savvy and she networks well with people ... and she pays attention to the care and feeding of networks and people." Dr. Wasserheit went on to say that "Helene is very skilled in interacting with people. She is very intuitive in her understanding about how political systems and individuals work. She has a very good appreciation of this, which allows her to make the system work constructively."

Dr. Gayle has also been very successful in working with political appointees across government agencies. Dr. James Curran, former associate director for HIV/AIDS at CDC, has commented on Dr. Gayle's ability to work effectively with different political and policy players. He said: "Helene has the unique capacity to get people to work together, in part, because she is so willing to go the extra mile herself in getting the job done and, in part, because she understands not only the scientific issues but she is also able to see other people's points of view; she is able to walk in their shoes and this is a very valuable asset. It is also important that she is not politically motivated. She is committed to the public's health and not any particular philosophy of government. She is just doing her job and doing it very effectively, and this is quite laudable.... Also, she works so well with people because she likes interacting with them. People recognize this and so they like working with her.... She is very upbeat about her work, which is difficult and unusual when you are working with a fatal disease such as AIDS."

Dr. Gayle has also been successful working in a highly charged political environment, which, when working in an area such as HIV prevention, sets up a number of obstacles. Still, she has been effective, as Todd Summer points out, because "she is unflappable. Helene can take a two-by-four between the eyes and keep going. She, more than a lot of people I have ever met, is able to let a lot of things roll off her back and keep focused on what it is she is seeking to do within the limitations she faces.... She continues to push the edges," which is somewhat difficult for "an African American woman working in a predominately white male environment."

Dr. Gayle must also strike a careful balance between working in a political environment and in a government setting. That is to say, Dr. Gayle faces certain constraints as a public servant, indeed a career official, that serve as obstacles in her efforts to combat polemical diseases such as HIV and other STDs. Summer pointed out that, "Helene is a bureaucrat within a larger system. And there are limits to what she can do and what she can say. She tries to push to the end of those limits, but she is also appropriately cautious not to cross them, unless she's ready to leave the government.... When you work in government, there are always challenges against what you professionally and personally believe and what you are able to do as a government employee. And particularly in an area like HIV prevention, you rub against these limits all the time, while trying to maintain your sense of personal dignity and professional integrity in the face of bureaucratic pressures. Helene has been able to do this."

Setting Goals and Targeting Strategies

Another important aspect of her lifetime commitment to combating contagious diseases such as HIV/AIDS is having a vision. Dr. Gayle has always had a vision of what is needed to advance as well as augment existing efforts to combat infectious diseases. But, recognizing the importance of a shared vision, Dr. Gayle has always relied heavily on the input of her senior staff. As one of her division directors (the TB Division), Dr. Kenneth Castro, points out, "Helene isn't the type of person that would come in and say, 'This is my vision and you'll have to accept it.' Instead, she invited us to help develop that vision, which helped to bring all of us on board.... This way, it didn't come down from above and was forced on us."

Once a shared vision is developed, Dr. Gayle then moves to a series of actionable steps to guide her staff in reaching organizational goals. For instance, as director of the NCHSTP, her first step was to develop a broad strategic view of all the program areas—HIV/AIDS, other STDs, and TB. Setting long-term goals around what the Center seeks to accomplish in these areas is perhaps one of the most critical elements. In addition, under the lead of NCHSTP, the CDC recently finished a phase of long-term goal setting in the area of HIV/AIDS, where it seeks to reduce by 50 percent new HIV infections in the United States by the year 2005.

Besides setting long-term goals, Dr. Gayle also sees the importance of setting short-term actionable items that could be achieved incrementally. Setting small, attainable, and pragmatic goals enables her agency to reach overall goals on an incremental basis. She points out that "we try to determine what steps on the ladder will get us to our long-range goals, and then ask what are the processes and activities that we need to put in place to ensure that we will reach our goal. Measuring how well we do a particular sub-goal or short-term actionable goal isn't going to tell us whether we have reduced the spread of a given disease; but these short-term actionable goals are necessary steps in order to reach our long-term or end goal."

As Dr. Gayle goes on to say, "If our goal is ultimately to stop the spread of any of the diseases we deal with, certain processes need to be put in place. For example, we ask whether we are targeting the appropriate or correct areas for funding. If the epidemics are hitting the communities of color disproportionately, we have to ensure that we have processes in place to get the resources to those communities. So, we develop strategies around the people or communities who should be getting resources. This is an actionable step and will help us achieve our end goal of stopping the spread of a given disease."

Former Surgeon General David Satcher discussed the strong sense of vision that Dr. Gayle has for leadership of the Center and for the battle against HIV/AIDS and other STDs. In fact, he noted that "Helene has an unusual *global* vision [his emphasis] for public health, which is really critical because many of us believe that in order for public health to be successful, it must be global in perspective. It's important to think globally and then act locally, and Helene exemplifies this better than anyone I know.... She has the global vision of the problem and then she also has a vision as to how to respond to local challenges and needs."

In addition to a shared vision, a commitment to values and engendering a commitment from staff is critical to her work in the public health arena. As a public health official, particularly one involved in areas such as HIV/AIDS and other STDs, Dr. Gayle is necessarily immersed in the social as well as political aspects of medicine. But she has a serious and dedicated commitment to the goals and values of the CDC and specifically the NCHSTP, and places its mission above *all* other interests. She points out that "clearly, it's important to be realistic and mindful of the political realities but at the same time hope that our policies can be directed by our knowledge and our commitment to the health of the populations we serve. And I

Some of the values that Dr. Gayle strives to maintain for the NCHSTP and to instill in her staff include:

- Working hard to combat HIV/AIDS, STDs, and TB because it is the right and humane thing to do
- Working hard to combat HIV/AIDS, STDs, and TB not just in the United States but globally, because borders are not barriers to infectious diseases
- Acknowledging the hard work, dedication, focus, and intelligence of all the individuals who make up NCHSTP
- Recognizing the importance of collaborations across government agencies and globally
- An unyielding commitment to the battle against HIV/AIDS, STDs, and TB

hope my position would be consistent regardless of the administration in office, because it is the right thing to do from the standpoint of developing effective strategies to prevent the spread of HIV, STDs, and TB."

One representative of a community-based group points out that Dr. Gayle is so effective at her job "because, first and foremost, she has a personal commitment to the issue areas, which goes beyond her government job." Dr. Gayle, it was noted, truly has a "commitment to the health of the populations [she] serves." Her leadership in steering her Center to achieve and maintain a strong commitment to the Center's values has by all accounts proven to be successful.

Former Deputy Director of the White House Office of National AIDS Policy Todd Summer points out that "you appreciate very quickly after working with Helene that this is far more than just a job to her. She cares about the issue, she struggles within and against an environment that would probably have moved a number of people away; she's been at the CDC for 17 years, and this is a significant contribution."

The Challenges of Bureaucracy

Dr. Gayle has had to overcome a number of formidable obstacles in her work to combat HIV and other STDs, but her sheer commitment has helped her succeed. For example, Summer noted that Dr. Gayle has been very effective in "her ability to manage a system that was not designed for her to succeed." Summer was referring to the organizational structure of the CDC, where "the [various] center directors are more or less autonomous rulers of their fiefdoms." And funding for HIV programs was distributed across the

CDC's centers without very much prioritization. Dr. Gayle, Summer pointed out, had a potential battle on her hands, because as she sought to set priorities for the distribution of funding to better target the areas of need, she would have to gain buy-in from the other center directors.

Another significant barrier that Dr. Gayle faced, Summer said, was "the white boys network." Dr. Gayle is the first African American and second woman Center director at the Centers for Disease Control. Summer notes that "there is a culture [at the CDC] that is not always supportive of having an African American woman Center director. And as you can see, there aren't too many colleagues like her at CDC. So, on all levels, she is battling to try to organize funds without authority and she is battling in an environment that is not necessarily supportive of her as an African American woman and in an epidemic where congressional scrutiny ... into what [CDC] can do around prevention is always looming over her head."

Dr. Gayle agrees. She notes that being a woman and African American is often challenging. "I function in a white-male-dominated professional environment. This obviously presents many challenges. For instance, I am never sure when I walk into a room for the first time how I will be perceived. In its most productive sense, as an African American and a woman, I should not be thought of as just another statistic but hopefully as adding to the diversity that enriches our work environment and brings different perspectives, experiences, and styles of communication. I think that people who work in public health, by virtue of the issues we focus on, are often more enlightened about race and gender issues. However, many of the manifestations of racism and sexism are subtle and even unconscious based on one's lifetime experiences. Many very well-intentioned colleagues often unknowingly demonstrate an ignorance of important race and gender sensitivities."

She went on to say: "Being black and female carries some additional burdens both externally and probably internally generated as well. I hope I do a reasonable job of trying to balance those issues, choosing battles wisely and not being totally preoccupied with, but at the same time commanding respect for, my race and gender.... Not being white or male can certainly be a challenge. There are still times that because of my race and gender, people at first glance may perceive me as not being credible or competent. But I have to say that people are trying hard to get past the old way of doing business, and this ultimately creates opportunities."

Leadership: Building Trust and Confidence

Dr. Gayle's approach to leadership accounts for her vast success as a public health official within the United States and globally. As Dr. Castro stresses, "Helene is viewed as an effective leader because she ensures that we are *collectively* [his emphasis] working to achieve [the Center's] common goal." In addition, as Dr. Satcher pointed out, "Leadership means developing people's trust.... From speaking with people around the world, I learned that Helene has garnered a lot of confidence from people. And even today, I would say that she is probably the most trusted American among African countries.... She has developed a lot of credibility because of her *knowledge* and insight into public health as it relates to AIDS and also because she really *cares* about the issues, and people see this [his emphasis]. And this, to me, translates into strong leadership."

The level of confidence and trust accorded to Dr. Gayle is clearly evident in her appointment by South African President Thabo Mbeki to his AIDS Advisory Panel. President Mbeki, at the 13th World AIDS Conference held in Durban, South Africa, in 2000, caused a great stir when he suggested during his address that, while HIV is linked to AIDS, it was not the lone cause of the syndrome. He went on to say that the world's biggest killer and the greatest cause of ill health and suffering across the globe, including in South Africa, is poverty, and that poverty is to blame for the quick spread of AIDS in his country.

Hundreds of conference delegates, dignitaries, and other participants walked out on President Mbeki's opening address, suggesting that his comments were tantamount to a claim that HIV doesn't cause AIDS. Others claimed that this was a gross misinterpretation of President Mbeki's comments and that Mbeki was merely stating that HIV and AIDS are exacerbated by poverty, poor nutrition, and certain socioeconomic conditions.

Dr. Gayle at the ground breaking ceremony for the Coping Center, the first center in Botswana for people living with HIV. This center is part of a collaborative project between the Bill and Melinda Gates Foundation, Merck and Co. and the Government of Botswana.

Prior to the conference, President Mbeki had appointed an AIDS Advisory Panel to help assuage the growing public dismay and consternation that would inevitably hinder his efforts to battle HIV/AIDS in South Africa. Recognized top leaders in the field of HIV/AIDS from around the world were appointed to the panel. As Dr. Holtgrave pointed out, Dr. Gayle was appointed to the panel because of her skills in diplomacy and consensus building and her ability to build trust and confidence among people. He noted that the panel was set up to address a very difficult area of public health, which demands collaboration. And, Dr. Holtgrave went on to say, President Mbeki's comments at the World AIDS Conference threatened existing international collaborations to combat HIV/AIDS. He said President Mbeki was confident that "Helene would be able to figure out a way to keep everyone together enough so that the programs could move forward.... Helene would be able to keep the process from breaking down and becoming divisive, which is what prevents public health programs from moving forward."

Most recently, Dr. Gayle was invited to China to provide input to that country's government on developing their efforts to battle the HIV epidemic. In a country that has avoided any public attention on its growing AIDS problem, Dr. Gayle noted that if China did not address the epidemic, the United Nations estimates there could be over 20 million Chinese carrying the AIDS virus by 2010.

Another important attribute of effective leadership, which explains why Dr. Gayle is highly sought after for her skills and professional counsel, is acting responsibly, even in the face of criticism. Todd Summer notes that even when outside groups don't agree with what the CDC is doing, "Helene doesn't point fingers. She doesn't move the blame aside and say, 'Well, that's not my fault.' She takes it and goes."

Moreover, Dr. Gayle is viewed as someone who has an unwavering, steadfast commitment to the issues. Dr. Wasserheit points out that "Helene cares very deeply about what she works on, particularly HIV prevention. That level of commitment comes through, and that's an important component of leadership."

Managing Within the Bureaucracy

Dr. Gayle points out that she has always viewed staff as the backbone of her organizations and thus critical to every strategic organizational effort. In her most recent directorship of the NCHSTP, Dr. Gayle oversaw a staff of approximately 1,400 employees, and everyone of them was considered important to the mission of the Center; successfully managing her own staff members has always been seen as key to accomplishing any agency goal.

Dr. Wasserheit extolled Dr. Gayle's human resources management capabilities. She points out that Dr. Gayle is "a good manager because she has a pretty good sense of people. She's very insightful about people's strengths and weaknesses."

Dr. Gayle is a very strong proponent of open, shared leadership. "If anything," she points out, "I err on the side of providing more information, being open. And I believe the more teamwork you build, the more effective your organization will be. It builds more confidence among your staff and tends to cut down on uncertainties that inevitably occur in large organizations when information is missing or not readily available. It also increases morale and people's enjoyment of their jobs. If you don't empower your staff, it takes away people's purpose as organizational members."

Dr. Gayle further notes that "shared leadership is critical. I have an organization of 1,400 people, and if I didn't delegate and share power, we would fail as an organization. And to me as a decision maker, [shared leadership] helps me make better decisions, because it provides me with a wider range of knowledge and information."

Certainly, however, there must be an understanding of what information can be shared with staff. Dr. Gayle notes that "some information can only be shared with my senior staff, both because of the nature of the information and the relevance of the information at different levels. What may be relevant at the Center or Division level, for example, may not be relevant at other units within our organization levels."

Dr. Gayle's division directors point out that she does provide the flexibility needed to run their units. Dr. Wasserheit, former director of the STD Division, said that "I've had the luxury of tremendous flexibly and laissez faire," which, she further notes, has enabled her to run her division more effectively. Likewise, Dr. Castro, director of the TB Division, said: "Helene provides a very clear sense of direction, but then she has given me a very long leash to exercise my expertise and skills. So, in terms of style, she has been able to provide a sense of direction but also not be in the way of her senior staff. Some leaders tend to be very much hands-on. She has been appropriately hands-on when she has had to be there to represent us to the higher levels with the administration. But I feel very much at ease in that she has enabled her directors to contribute and is also very receptive to our own views.... Instead of just providing marching orders, she is very much receptive to the feedback received by her senior staff."

Dr. Gayle also stresses that risk-taking is key. "You have to be willing to take risks in leadership positions, and it means you have to take chances on the things that you believe are the right thing to do, even if it's not politically expedient. I have found that it is important not to be risk averse; taking chances and trying some things in new ways is crucial if you really want to do best for your organization and for your mission."

Dr. Castro attested to Dr. Gayle's willingness to take risks. He said, "Helene will take risks, but not recklessly. There is a balancing act here; you can't afford to take a risk that's going to bring the whole agency down." Dr. Castro pointed to a recent example of where "Helene put her neck on the line." He noted that there is a recognition among public health officials around the world that AIDS in Africa is a monumental problem with several unmet needs and that the United States is in a unique position to do something about it. Dr. Gayle, he said, "has spearheaded an effort that has resulted in resources assigned for the direct involvement of the CDC, the U.S. Agency for International Development, and other international partners to work directly with several of the sub-Saharan African countries that have an almost unmitigated AIDS problem. Her efforts have made sure we are working in partnership with the authorities there, the appropriate ministries, et cetera, to arrive at some common goals and to have us working together, shoulder to shoulder.... And this came at a high risk politically, because you could ask, 'Why should the U.S. taxpayers be spending money in Africa?' Well, from a public health standpoint, we should be, because, as Helene has passionately striven to demonstrate, these diseases don't stop at our borders and neither can our intervention efforts."

In sum, Dr. Gayle has been a world leader in efforts to prevent and contain the spread of infectious diseases such as HIV/AIDS. She has devoted her entire career to this. By examining her extraordinary work in the national and international arenas, we can discern what it takes to be a successful, effective manager and leader in the public service.

Lessons Learned about Effective Managerial Leadership

What are some of the factors and attributes that contribute to or characterize Dr. Gayle's success in the fight against deadly diseases such as HIV/AIDS, other STDs, and TB? Some of the factors of effective leadership correspond with Robert Denhardt's findings (1993). The following represent a summary of several lessons to be drawn.

Lesson 1: Developing Integrative, Targeted Strategies

The issues or concerns being addressed by an organization and its leaders need to be continually identified and reassessed so that there is a clear understanding of what responses and strategies can be mounted to help

remedy the problems or concerns. Once the issues are clearly identified or
reidentified, linking and integrating organizational resources and strategies
to develop solutions is key.

In the case of Dr. Gayle and the NCHSTP, reassessment of the populations most affected today by HIV/AIDS led to a finding that people of color,
in particular African Americans and Latinos—and not white gays, as popular wisdom might have it—are at the greatest risk of contracting HIV/AIDS
today. The next step was to link with the individuals, organizations, and
community groups involved in the prevention and treatment of HIV/AIDS
to help prevent it from spreading among all populations at risk. This, as
noted, requires developing and then working closely with various coalitions, which serves to leverage other resources and other key players in
combating such diseases.

Lesson 2: Developing Broad Coalitions

A vital aspect of effective managerial performance is collaborating
within and across governmental agencies, as well as with private sector
organizations. No policy maker operates in a vacuum, and so success
hinges on the extent to which government leaders develop and nurture affil-
iations and networks with community, state, national, international, and
private sector partners. Perhaps even more important is a clear recognition
of the types of resources that need to be leveraged.

For example, in the domestic arena, Dr. Gayle has found that not only are
other governmental agencies instrumental in combating infectious diseases,
but so, too, are faith-based and other community organizations. In her vast
number of years studying these issues, Dr. Gayle has found that community-
based organizations may be the most effective in helping to stop the spread
of infectious diseases. Therefore, she has targeted organizations to develop
community partnerships, including churches and other established organizations as important resources in helping to combat such diseases as HIV/AIDS.

In the international arena, Dr. Gayle has found that it is critical to work
closely not only with global leaders, but particularly with private sector
firms based in the countries being ravaged by the AIDS virus. Thus, lever-
aging the appropriate resources and players for the clearly identified problem or concern is key to effective management in government agencies.

Lesson 3: Possessing and Demonstrating Interpersonal Skills

Good interpersonal skills were consistently named as a key element in
Dr. Gayle's ability to effectively achieve her goals, and they cut across many

of the other factors attributable to successful managerial performance. Qualities such as honesty, integrity, and uncompromising commitment to one's work and agency mission significantly affect a manager's ability to be successful. In addition, a good sense of humor and the ability to appropriately inject humor can make a difference in terms of effective communication and ultimately cultivating linkages with individuals or groups.

As many noted, Dr. Gayle's outstanding interpersonal skills helped to build good working relationships across national and international boundaries and created an environment where people were comfortable addressing difficult issues such as HIV/AIDS. And her interpersonal skills go beyond good communication skills to include strengths in facilitating, coaching, moderating, and coordinating. Perhaps one of the NCHSTP division directors said it best when she said that Dr. Gayle "is politically very savvy and she networks well with people ... and she pays attention to the care and feeding of networks and people.... Helene is very skilled in interacting with people."

Lesson 4: Exercising Political Skills

It seems axiomatic that political skills are critical to effective performance in government. The environment, by its very nature, is highly political. And so a high degree of diplomacy and political astuteness is essential. Dr. Wasserheit points out that Dr. Gayle "is very intuitive in her understanding about how political systems and individuals work. She has a very good appreciation of this, which allows her to make the system work constructively."

Effectively working with different political and policy players requires political savvy and good interpersonal skills. But, as was pointed out by several people, effectiveness depends on acting politically but not being politically motivated. As Dr. Curran succinctly stated, Dr. Gayle is "committed to the public's health and not any particular philosophy of government." She has not let politics get in the way of her commitment to fighting the battle against the spread of infectious diseases.

Lesson 5: Possessing and Exercising Technical Expertise

Possessing technical expertise is critical not only because of the knowledge necessary for the substantive aspects of a policy field such as public health, but also because it provides credibility when interacting with other agencies, community groups, or policy players. The ability to engender trust and commitment from the very people, groups, and organizations that must be relied upon to achieve one's goals heavily depends on expertise.

However, technical expertise alone may be insufficient. Drive and dedication are also key. As seen here, Dr. Gayle not only has technical expertise in the epidemiology of infectious diseases, but she is also personally and professionally committed to combating them. Her life's work has been devoted to this issue, particularly around HIV/AIDS, and she has not let anything or anyone deter her in her efforts. Her dedication has been repeatedly praised and identified as one of the most important factors in her successful achievements.

Lesson 6: Setting a Vision

Having not just a vision but a *shared* vision of what is needed to advance and further develop existing efforts to combat infectious diseases is vital for effective managerial performance in government. Dr. Gayle sought out and welcomed input and participation from her senior staff, not only because of the substantive value, but also because it helped establish a sense of ownership and commitment on the part of senior policy makers and managers.

Lesson 7: Fostering Pragmatic Incrementalism

Ensuring that everyone is on board facilitates another important factor in effectively leading and managing a government agency: developing pragmatic incremental goals. Dr. Gayle recognized the importance of not only developing long-term goals, but also setting short-term actionable steps that could be achieved incrementally. Setting small, attainable goals enables her agency to reach overall goals and at the same time provides a sense of accomplishment and satisfaction. The ability to witness the positive outcomes associated with one's work provides a tremendous sense of reinforcement and job satisfaction and also helps to further workers' commitment to achieving long-range goals.

And, as Dr. David Satcher, the former Surgeon General and former director of the CDC states, Dr. Gayle's *global* vision for public health is critical, because for public health to be successful in the United States, it must be global in perspective. "It's important to think globally and then act locally, and Helene exemplifies this better than anyone I know," said Dr. Satcher.

Lesson 8: Committing to Values

A commitment to values requires a serious dedication to the goals and values of your agency, placing them above all other interests. In essence, it requires *valuing* the values. Dr. Gayle formally enumerated for her agency and staff a set of values that she herself strives to maintain for her agency and works hard to instill in her staff. These values include working unyieldingly to combat infectious diseases in the United States and globally because it is the right and humane thing to do; acknowledging the hard work, dedication, focus, and intelligence of all the individuals who make up the NCHSTP; and recognizing the importance of collaborations globally and across government agencies and communities.

Lesson 9: Empowering Staff and Sharing Leadership

Sharing leadership responsibilities empowers staff. This, in turn, is likely to enhance workers' investment in their work, enhance the work's significance, promote self-determination, and increase workers' motivation and satisfaction. In addition, empowerment not only redistributes power, but it also provides a mechanism by which accountability or responsibility for outcomes is placed with individuals or teams. By making the workplace more participatory, democratic, and accountable, empowerment creates an organizational culture that promotes a sense of commitment to goal attainment and, ultimately, significantly enhances organizational productivity.

Empowering her staff comes naturally to Dr. Gayle, who has a very open, participative style of management. This has proven to be effective for her organization, where experienced, highly trained workers, with medical or social science doctoral degrees, run the various units of the NCHSTP. She has found that by empowering her staff, they have developed a vested interest in the work of their individual units and in the integrated efforts of each unit in achieving the overall agency goals. Most importantly, Dr. Gayle emphasizes that empowerment and shared leadership are not "one-shot" processes but a way of organizational life aimed at discovering and utilizing the full potential of every member of the organization.

Lesson 10: Taking Risks

Taking responsible risks is also a critical management strategy that can promote effective managerial performance. New ideas and innovation tend to be the byproducts of risk taking, and so taking responsible risks—risks driven by a sense of ethics, honesty, and legal responsibility—is an effective managerial strategy. So, too, is encouraging staff to take risks, while working with them to help them understand the reason for mistakes and reducing their recurrence. Effective leaders also ensure that risk taking is not punished.

Dr. Gayle has found that taking risks is crucial for achieving your agency's mission. As Dr. Castro stated, "Helene will take risks, but not recklessly." Responsible risk taking can foster positive change and lead to successful organizational performance.

Lesson 11: Exercising Management and Leadership Skills

Certainly, all the factors mentioned above are important attributes of effective leadership and managerial performance, which requires flexibility, openness, dedication, commitment, and patience, to mention only a few characteristics. Effective managers and leaders in government also must have the ability to plan, organize, communicate clearly, motivate staff, and set realistic goals. They must also be honest, fair, understanding, expert in their field, and knowledgeable of the politics surrounding the environments within which they operate. And as Dr. Gayle clearly exhibits, they are goal-oriented and exhibit good interpersonal skills. Finally, an effective leader is able to create followership, which connotes not mastery but synergy. It is a relationship marked by trust, confidence, and an *intertwining* of interests.

Conclusions

In recent years, there has been a resurgence in efforts to promote greater efficiency and trust in government services. Beginning with the National Commission on the Public Service—which sought to rebuild public trust in government—to more recent efforts aimed at reinventing government (e.g., under the National Performance Review and the Government Performance and Results Act of 1993), there has been widespread interest in identifying ways to improve government service.

This study looked at various characteristics that are associated with effective managerial performance in government. Building on earlier studies and focusing on one high-level career executive in government, Dr. Helene Gayle, a host of factors were identified. By examining the work of Dr. Gayle, a recognized global leader in public health and the fight against HIV/AIDS, other sexually transmitted diseases, and tuberculosis, we have a better understanding of the various tools, skills, and strategies government executives can employ in their efforts to improve public services to the American people.

Most important, the jobs of government executives are highly complex. They operate in environments marked by great uncertainty and ambiguities, particularly around political, social, and economic issues. Their ability to work effectively involves mastering these environments as well as the groups, agencies, and institutions that comprise them. Managing within and across the boundaries of such environments, not only within the United States but globally, requires management and leadership skills that transcend the traditional bureaucratic, rule-bound approaches to incorporate creativity, innovation, and risk taking. It is perhaps this more progressive style of leadership and management—exhibited by Dr. Helene Gayle, for example—which may ultimately characterize managerial effectiveness and excellence in government.

Dr. Gayle is one of the public health officials who has worked tirelessly to assure that the boundaries to engage in disease prevention inside the United States have been enlarged, allowing agencies such as the CDC to more actively participate in global disease prevention. Her efforts to better understand, prevent, and control the spread of HIV, other STDs, and TB have been recognized worldwide, and after almost 20 years of unfailing commitment, she continues to wage the battle.

Bibliography

Altman, Lawrence K. 2000. "AIDS Surges in Black and Hispanic Men." *New York Times,* January 14.

Denhardt, Robert B. 1993. *The Pursuit of Significance: Strategies for Managerial Success in Public Organizations.* Belmont, Calif.: Wadsworth Publishing.

Doig, Jameson W. and Erwin C. Hargrove. 1987. *Leadership and Innovation.* Baltimore: Johns Hopkins University Press.

Elmore, Richard F. 1980. "Backward Mapping: Implementation Research and Policy Decisions." *Political Science Quarterly* 94 (Winter): 601-616.

Lynn, Laurence E., Jr. 1987. *Managing Public Policy.* Boston: Little, Brown and Company.

McNeil, Donald G., Jr. 2000. "Agencies Urge Use Of Affordable Drug For HIV in Africa." *New York Times,* April 6.

Recesso, Arthur M. 1999. "First Year Implementation of the School to Work Opportunities Act Policy: An Effort at Backward Mapping." Vol. 7, *Education Policy Analysis.*

Terry, Larry. 1995. *Leadership of Public Bureaucracies.* Thousand Oaks, Calif.: Sage Publications, Inc.

CHAPTER FOUR

Leading a Cabinet Department: Donna Shalala at the Department of Health and Human Services

Beryl A. Radin
Professor of Government and Public Administration
School of Public Affairs
University of Baltimore

Portions of this report were originally published in October 1999 and November 2000.

Part I:
Managing Decentralized Departments

Background

Few public agencies are as complex as the U.S. Department of Health and Human Services. The management challenges posed by this public organization have worried administrators and policymakers since the Department was officially created as the Department of Health, Education and Welfare in April 1953, converting the Federal Security Agency (an agency that contained a range of programs) to a cabinet-level department.

Today, HHS manages more than 300 programs, covering a vast array of activities in medical and social science research; food and drug safety; financial assistance and health care for low income, elderly, and disabled Americans; child support enforcement; maternal and infant health; substance abuse treatment and prevention; and services for older Americans. The range of these programs means that the activities found within the Department affect the health and welfare of nearly every American.

The $350 billion budget for Fiscal Year 1999 was implemented by 59,000 employees. HHS is the largest grant-making agency in the federal government, providing some 60,000 grants per year. It is also the nation's largest health insurer, handling more than 800 million claims per year. The Department's programs are administered by 11 operating divisions in both headquarter locations as well as 10 regional offices.

The complexity of HHS has created a set of management challenges for the Department secretaries over the 45 years of the Department's life. One of the challenges has been the definition of the role of the Office of the Secretary and its relationship to the operating components of the agency. For at the same time that the Secretary is the official "head" of the department and held publicly accountable for the actions of the programs within it, the Congress and the public have frequently focused on the operating components when specific action is demanded. Thus the Department is expected to respond to two sets of expectations that call for inconsistent strategies: *centralization* in the Office of the Secretary and *decentralization* in the operating programs.

The Historical Functions of the Office of the Secretary

When the federal government's involvement in social programs increased dramatically in the 1960s, new attention was focused on the operations of the Department of Health, Education and Welfare. To that point, the Department—like the Department of Defense—operated much like a collection of separate entities. Some described the Department as a

feudal system where power and authority were found in separate components, with the head of the "kingdom" operating more like a titular leader
rather than one with actual control.

By the mid-1960s, however, the Office of the Secretary had emerged as
a force within the Department. The span of activity grew wider as the federal government became a more important force in the society. Building on
two processes—controlling the budget process as well as the determination
of departmental positions on legislation—the Office of the Secretary grew
and played a centripetal role of molding together the separate forces within
the program components and reaching for a common set of policy goals
within the Department. For the most part, the assistant secretaries in the
Department were used primarily as staff offices whose role was to help the
Secretary knit together related functions in the operating agencies.

Management efforts within the Department reflected an approach that
emphasized control, monitoring, consistency in operations and approaches,
and clarity about lines of authority. From that time on, most Secretaries of
the Department have searched for management systems that provide policy
leadership as well as offer a way for them to oversee departmental administrative matters and programs. In a few cases, efforts at management reform
have accentuated attempts to identify interdependencies and shared issues
across program elements. Most efforts, however, emphasized modes of control of the separate elements within the Department.

This past agenda drew on several strategies. In some cases, the attempt
to control the program components was done through manipulation of the
organization structure, moving program components into new configura-
tions in which they were required to work with previously separate and
autonomous elements. For example, most of the Department's health programs were moved into a newly configured Office of the Assistant Secretary
for Health in 1968. More frequently, however, the control agenda was
achieved through formalized processes of budget development, planning,
policy analysis, personnel, procurement, legislative development, public
affairs, and legal advice by the general counsel. Through the years, various
management techniques (such as the Planning, Programming, and Budgeting
System, known as PPBS) became the instrumentality for the processes. In
some cases the control agenda was achieved by focusing on the substance
of specific policy initiatives.

A report issued by the General Accounting Office in 1990 provides a
depiction of the approach that was predominant until 1993. This report on
management in HHS was one in the GAO series of management reviews of
major departments and agencies. The intent of the report was to assess the role
and effectiveness of the Office of the Secretary in managing the Department
and to identify ways in which departmental management processes and
structures could be improved. GAO focused on the lack of what they called

"an effective management system within the Office of the Secretary" (USGAO, p. 3). According to GAO, a management system should be able to identify issues, define goals and objectives, develop strategies, create monitoring systems, oversee operations, and receive feedback on performance. In its analysis, GAO wrote that the efforts within the Department did not go far enough and that HHS was not able to create a system that actually required the operating programs to respond to the will of the Secretary. GAO found that the lack of departmental strategic planning was a "key element missing" from the HHS system.

Although the GAO report did acknowledge some of the forces and constraints that made it difficult to encourage central management in HHS, it was clear that the GAO analysts sought ways to overcome these difficulties. GAO also argued that it was possible to differentiate between two types of planning—strategic and operational—and to cast the role of the Office of the Secretary in the strategic planning mode which would set the framework for the operational planning role performed by the program units.

The report pointed to some systems that had moved in the preferred direction but noted that "No secretarial management system has stayed intact long enough to provide stability to the Department's basic operations." (USGAO, p. 3) At the time the report was written, a senior level advisory body called the Management Council was in place, providing a bi-weekly venue for the senior staff of the Department to meet with the Secretary. In the past, Department-wide planning processes such as PPBS and CAMS (the Cooperative Agency Management System) had attempted to provide a Department-wide perspective. Creation of the Executive Secretariat—an office that circulated policy proposals to appropriate parties within the Department—provided a mechanism for clearance of policy positions and documents (especially regulations).

The Study: Approaches During the Clinton Administration

Donna Shalala, Secretary from January 1993 to January 2001, adopted a conscious management strategy that is very different from those attempted in the past. She began with the assumption that the Department contains many decentralized elements and that it is not possible to change them. She described the Department as composed of many units that have their own history, needs, cultures, and constituencies. She used the professional credibility of the subunits within the office (especially those dealing with the health world) as an important source of public and political support. She downsized the Office of the Secretary and delegated many different functions to the operating components (this general approach was clearly rationalized by the reform strategy of Vice President Gore's National Performance Review). At the same time, she attempted to devise processes that emphasize coordination and identify areas in which crosscutting approaches are essential. Her efforts represented an attempt to change the ways in which the Department is managed and, as a result, to improve the internal and external effectiveness of its operations.

This research sought to explicate the dimensions of Shalala's strategy through interviews with agency heads as well as through analysis of written materials such as guidelines and instructions that detail the behavior that is expected. It examined the relationship between the Secretary and her agency heads and their perceptions of the process and how they operated within this set of expectations. The analysis includes general patterns of behavior and the ways that traditional control processes (especially the budget process) play out in the decentralized environment.

The research sought to sort out the balance between responsibilities at the program unit level and the role of the units within the Office of the Secretary. It also focused on the institutional capacity within the Department to make the determination of the balance.

These subjects served as the basis for interviews with nearly 20 top officials in the Department in 1999.

The HHS Reality

Despite efforts that spanned several decades, the strategies that had been employed by past secretaries over the years were not able to deal with the predictable realities of the Department's external environment or with predictable internal dynamics. These are forces that any Secretary must confront. The external environment challenges management in many different ways: the diversity and size of operating programs; the reality of vague and difficult goals; fragmented accountability structures and program authority; different program responsibilities; controversial issues; and diverse constituencies. The forces that emerge from internal dynamics include multiple policy perspectives, conflicting policy approaches, staff-line competition, and "gaming" filtering units. This study suggests that the flexible strategy that was employed by Secretary Shalala was more effective in dealing with these forces than efforts that had been tried in the past.

External Forces
- *Diversity and size of operating programs.* The large number of programs contained within the HHS umbrella represent a very diverse array of objectives, cultures, and approaches. Each of the components within the Department has its own history, needs, and approaches. Attempting

to homogenize them within a centralized unit—even for planning purposes—dilutes their strengths and their unique values.

- *Vague, difficult goals.* The Department's program embody goals that are
  often contradictory, vague, not unified, and difficult to measure. Efforts
  to find goals and objectives that link separate programs too often result
  in situations in which controversies embodied in the programs are
  ignored or posed in highly abstract forms.

- *Fragmented accountability structures.* The accountability structures that
  frame the programs within the Department mirror the fragmented
  nature of the American policymaking system. Units within the Department
  are responsible to a number of separate budget, oversight and authorizing congressional committees which represent different perspectives
  on programs. Some of these committees and subcommittees have
  established very detailed expectations for the implementation of programs under their control. They are also subject to the expectations that
  are defined by the Executive Office of the President, particularly the
  Office of Management and Budget and the domestic policy staff, which
  often differ from congressional expectations.

- *Fragmented program authority.* Some of the programs within the Department have more in common with programs found in other departments
  or agencies than they do with other HHS programs. The congressional
  predilection to fragment program authority has created a crazy quilt
  array of program responsibilities across the federal government.

- *Different program responsibilities.* HHS has responsibility for programs
  that contain a wide range of administrative and policy mechanisms.
  Some of the programs that are implemented by HHS actually require
  Department staff to perform the work or deliver the services. Others
  involve providing funds (either as block grants, discretionary grants, or
  other forms) to others, particularly states and communities, who would
  deliver the services.

- *Controversial issues.* Many of the policy issues that are contained
  within the HHS portfolio represent some of the most controversial
  domestic policy issues in the society. Issues such as government expenditures for abortion, welfare reform, and financing of health services
  evoke a variety of views and reflect very different perspectives on politics
  and policies. While the Department may seek to take a clear position
  on such issues, the external forces work in different directions. In
  addition, the Department's role involving these issues may be as a
  funder of programs that are delivered by other levels of governments,
  not as the actual deliverer itself.

- *Diverse constituencies.* The diversity of programs within the Department is paralleled by an even more diverse set of constituencies that
  follow the details of decisions involving their concerns. Constituency or

interest groups focused on a specific set of programs often represent very different approaches to those programs. The Department acts as a juggler, attempting to deal with multiple perspectives on a program area. In such a situation, ambiguity rather than clarity often serves the Department well.

Internal Forces

- *Multiple policy perspectives.* The controversies found within the society sometimes have been reflected within the Department itself. In the past, individuals appointed to top political roles represented diverse policy and political agendas. It was not uncommon to have a Secretary committed to one perspective on an issue and a Deputy Secretary or Assistant Secretary to a very different approach. When this occurred, it was difficult to reach agreement on policy directions, and loyalty to a single agenda defined by the Secretary was difficult to achieve.
- *Conflicting policy approaches.* At times the diverse program components within the Department represent different approaches to the same policy problem. When there is not agreement on the most effective way to address policy issues, various program elements may be charged with quite different (indeed, sometimes conflicting) approaches. For example, health research agencies may develop effective treatment forms that are not reimbursed by the agencies charged with financing services. This evokes conflict among the units for the preeminent role on the issue.
- *Staff-line competition.* The growth of an active and large Office of the Secretary staff, with its various components, led to competition between the program units and the Office of the Secretary for influence and the Secretary's ear. Program units sometimes perceived that the role of the Office of the Secretary was to second-guess the decisions of the operating components and to overturn their recommendations. As the Office of the Secretary grew larger in size, the various staff units had increased ability to monitor the program unit decisions more closely and to substitute their own technical judgment for that of the operating unit staff. This led to practices in which program units sought ways to avoid interacting with the staff components and, instead, learned how to minimize their impact on the program.
- *Gaming filtering units.* The creation of filtering units (that is, units that are established to filter information and package decision memos before they reach the Secretary) did not guarantee that decisions would be more effective or provide a way to represent varying perspectives within the Department. At times the program units found ways to bypass these efforts or bring them into the process very late in the game.

About Donna Shalala

Donna Shalala is the longest serving Secretary of Health and Human Services in U.S. history. She is currently President of the University of Miami, a position she has held since June 2001. She joined the Clinton administration in January 1993 and then led the administration's efforts to reform the nation's welfare system and improve health care while containing health costs.

In her time as Secretary, the Department guided the approval of the Children's Health Insurance Plan, raised child immunization rates to the highest levels in history, led the fight against youths' use of tobacco, and crusaded for streamlined processes for approving new drugs to treat AIDS and other diseases. A column about her in *Government Executive* magazine touted Dr. Shalala because "she cares about management. She has built a strong team at the top of the Department, and has taken care to replenish the ranks below as well. ... She has a finely honed sense of the desirable and the practical in large institutions."

Dr. Shalala also redefined the role of HHS Secretary, partnering with businesses and other private sector organizations to extend the Department's public health and education mission. She appeared in a "Milk Mustache" advertisement to help promote osteoporosis prevention, threw the season-opening pitch for the Baltimore Orioles as part of a campaign to delink baseball and smokeless tobacco, and appeared in an online chat on the WNBA's website to discuss breast cancer prevention. An avid athlete and sports fan, Dr. Shalala was the first season ticket holder for the league's Washington Mystics.

She served as the Chancellor of the University of Wisconsin-Madison from 1987 to 1993. Prior to the University of Wisconsin, Dr. Shalala served as president of Hunter College for eight years, and as an Assistant Secretary at the Department of Housing and Urban Development during the Carter Administration. From 1975-1977, she served as Treasurer of New York City's Municipal Assistance Corporation, the organization that helped rescue the city from the brink of bankruptcy.

An acknowledged scholar of state and local government and finance, Dr. Shalala earned her Ph.D. from the Maxwell School of Citizenship and Public Affairs at Syracuse University in 1970. She has also served as a Peace Corps volunteer in Iran.

While serving as Chancellor of the University of Wisconsin, Dr. Shalala administered the nation's largest public research university and spearheaded the $225 million program to renovate and add to the university's research complex. In 1992, *Business Week* named her one of the top five managers in higher education.

Study Findings

In some ways it is difficult to generalize from the HHS experience because the management of the Department reflects many unique personal attributes of the Secretary and relationships within the administration. Secretary Shalala's tenure in the Department was very unusual. Secretary Shalala completed eight years in office, far beyond the experience of any other Secretary. Continuity and great depth of understanding of policy, political, and management issues were possible as a result of longevity in office.

In addition, the Secretary's past experience played an extremely important role in the process of defining management strategies. This included both previous federal experience in the Department of Housing and Urban Development as well as her years as the president of two universities. While quite different from HHS, these experiences gave her at least two sets of skills: first, familiarity with the operations of federal cabinet agencies, and second, comfort and ease in thinking about management in an organization with very diverse and autonomous units. It is also important to acknowledge that she had a personal and professional relationship with both the President and the First Lady that extended over some years.

But despite these unique elements, there are a number of findings that are of interest beyond this situation and provide a case for an alternative approach to the strategy that had been often tried. They include attributes found in the political appointees themselves, the organizational framework that defined the Department, the management strategies and approaches that were undertaken, and the response to external pressures.

The HHS Political Appointees

The team that was assembled in HHS at the beginning of the Clinton administration was composed of individuals who were experts in their fields, loyal to the Secretary, and able to operate in a highly collegial fashion. Although some of those individuals did not stay in their positions throughout the two terms of the administration, persons who had similar characteristics succeeded them.

Knowledgeable individuals. The top appointees in the Department were—with few exceptions—individuals who are viewed as experts in their area of responsibility. Staff brought administrative, research, and programmatic knowledge of the program areas with which they were charged. As such, most of them were able to command respect from the constituency groups with whom they dealt as well as from the career staff in the agency. This familiarity with the issues also supported a longer-term commitment to an action agenda that led to terms of service that extended beyond the typical 18-month tenure for political appointees.

Loyalty to the Secretary. While appointees of the President, all of the top staff in the Department were selected by the Secretary with the approval of the White House. There did not appear to be any instances of divided loyalty or situations in which political appointees were responsive to a different agenda than that generally defined by the Secretary (although there were disagreements between some individuals and the White House that resulted in resignations). This created a situation in which there was a personal commitment to achieve a common agenda.

Collegiality and openness. The personal relationships that developed between top staff in the Department appear to be important to the strategy that was undertaken. This was reinforced by social events and opportunities to discuss issues of the day. While not all of the senior staff were close friends, they developed a sense of being part of a team effort. New members of the staff were welcomed into the group, and there was little indication of a newcomer vs. old timer dichotomy.

The Secretary cultivated a sense of openness within the Department and made herself accessible to staff. This became a model for other senior staff, who were expected to function in the same way within their own units.

The Organizational Framework

All leaders approach their organizations with assumptions about the agency for which they are responsible. Secretary Shalala's approach to HHS as an organization contained several elements:
- an emphasis on the program units as the heart of the Department;
- an assumption that staff units are not there to control or second-guess the program units;
- an organizational structure that seeks to minimize hierarchy and reduce layers of accountability.

Program units as the centerpiece. While some Secretaries of HHS have sought ways to build a perception of the Department as a single entity, Secretary Shalala did not move in that direction. Rather, there was a clear sense that the program units—usually called the Operating Divisions or OpDivs—were the heart of the Department. They are units that perform the work of the Department and are responsible to their own constituencies as well as congressional committees and subcommittees. Specific responsibilities that had traditionally been located in the Office of the Secretary (such as personnel and procurement) were delegated to the OpDivs.

Staff units as value added. Although strong individuals were appointed to head up the staff units—usually called the Staff Divisions or StaffDivs—their role was sometimes defined as running operations that are value added to the Department. Their value was of two types: first, advising the Secretary on those issues which are on (or should be on) her decision plate,

HHS Organization Chart (1999)

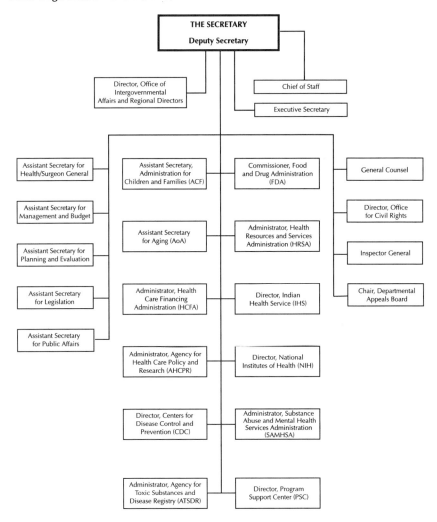

and second, serving as a resource for the OpDivs when the program units choose to call on them. Although there continued to be instances in which some tension arises between the program units and the Staff Divs, this tension was relatively rare and significantly less than was experienced in the past. The reduction in conflict followed decreases in the size of the units within the Office of the Secretary during the Clinton administration, and there was a concerted attempt to pull out some operating responsibilities that had been lodged within some staff units.

Flat organizational structure. During the first term, a new organizational structure was put into place that embodied the preeminence of the operating units. Until 1995, the program units found within the Public Health Service reported to an Assistant Secretary for Health (called OASH—the Office of the Assistant Secretary for Health). Although some of the units traditionally bypassed this intervening level and in practice dealt directly with the Secretary, the OASH played a formal decision role within the Department, particularly as it involved the budget development process. The change in the structure removed this level and defined the role of the Office of the Assistant Secretary for Health as a staff unit.

The flattened organizational structure more clearly represented the Secretary's management view. This set of decisions was rationalized by the organizational advice that emanated from the Vice President's National Performance Review, which advocated flat organizations built around efforts to empower line officials.

At approximately the same time, the Social Security Administration was separated from the Department, minimizing the number (and size) of the program units responsible to the Secretary. The departure of the Social Security Administration cut both the Department's budget and its staff in half.

Management Strategies and Approaches

The management strategies employed within HHS under Secretary Shalala signaled a clear move away from traditional command and control approaches. The focus within the Department was on substantive policy issues rather than on formal management processes. While the budget process continued to be relatively formal, it did not communicate a central control agenda; indeed, the process was highly collaborative and transparent. The decision-making modes employed invested in high levels of interaction and a consensus model. Information exchanges rather than control was emphasized within the Department.

A focus on substantive issues, not on management processes. With very few exceptions, the Office of the Secretary's strategy for interaction with the program units highlighted specific policy initiatives or policy concerns. Each year the Secretary established a small number of initiatives or themes that represented either Departmental or administration priorities. In many instances these initiatives called for collaborative efforts across separate program components, reflecting the reality that a number of important issues actually cross bureaucratic lines. In both FY 1998 and 1999, teams were created around each of the initiatives that had been proposed the year before, with specific agencies charged with chairing or co-chairing the effort. Each team was asked to define the goals of the initiative, the interagency cooperation required, and to signal the issues that required the attention of the Secretary, the Deputy Secretary or the Chief of Staff.

Traditional Roles of the Office of the Secretary

- Provide Direct Services to the Secretary
- External Affairs
- Policy Direction
- Advising the Secretary
- Program and Policy Coordination
- Services to the Department

The budget process as a collaborative and transparent enterprise. Perhaps the most highly institutionalized decision process within the Department centers on the budget. Even in this instance, there were few situations in which the budget office in the Office of the Assistant Secretary for Management and Budget attempted to second-guess the budget requests developed by the operating program components. Instead, the budget office provided strategic advice on the construction of OpDiv budgets. The budget is developed by the program components on the basis of themes or specific initiatives to be highlighted by the Secretary.

Opportunities for dialogue between the operating divisions and the Office of the Secretary about the budget took place at several points. Each OpDiv presented its request and summarized its management and program focus in a venue called the Budget Review Board. It was chaired by the Assistant Secretary for Management and Budget with participation by the Assistant Secretary for Planning and Evaluation, the Assistant Secretary for Health, and the Assistant Secretary for Legislation. The Board helped define the issues in the budget and through discussion assisted the OpDivs in determining what aspects of the request should be emphasized as the budget is presented to the Secretary. The heads of the operating programs were queried about their requests and asked to indicate how those requests mesh with the Secretary's initiatives.

Approximately a month later, the budgets were presented to the Secretary and the Deputy Secretary in a setting that included all of the senior staff within the Department. All of the agencies had an opportunity to review each other's budgets and comment on areas that are of shared interest. When these presentations were concluded, all of these individuals were asked to prepare a budget for the entire Department by voting on allocations—an exercise that emphasized the importance of looking at the submission from the perspective of the Secretary. The Secretary imposed the constraint of an overall budget amount, and senior staff made their recommendations within this constraint.

While changes were sometimes made in the original OpDiv submissions, for the most part the budget that was sent to the Office of Management and Budget (OMB) represented the requests proposed by the program units. This approach minimized the conflict among programs for resources when they operate with limited resources. While OMB frequently recommended cuts, in a number of instances the Secretary was successful in appealing them to the OMB Director or to the President. As such, budget conflict rarely occurred within the Department and a unified position was submitted to OMB. The transparency of the process minimized the practice of OpDivs end-running to OMB. Instead of battling inside the Department, the battle was moved to the Executive Office of the President.

Modes of decision making. Collaboration and collegial values underlay the decision-making process within the Department. Decisions were frequently made as a result of interaction between relevant players and a consensus approach was utilized. The exchanges were personal and the interactions required a significant time investment. Transparency and openness characterized the decision-making process. Meetings were held only on an as-needed basis, avoiding a perception that such sessions are required for their own sake. There is little evidence that the senior staff in the Department operated collectively as the Secretary's cabinet although individuals were constantly engaged in exchange with the Secretary and Deputy Secretary about policy issues.

To some extent, the collegiality supported what has been described as a lack of bureaucracy within the Department. Compared to the past, there was minimal exchange of paper, and OpDivs searched for ways to solve their own problems.

The "no surprises" ground rule. The most important ground rule that was well entrenched in the Department was the "no surprises" rule. The autonomy that has been provided to the OpDivs carried with it an expectation that the program heads would let the Secretary, the Deputy Secretary, and the Staff Divs know when important issues were coming to the surface. This expectation was characterized as one of reciprocity: Except in rare instances, the Office of the Secretary will not second-guess the OpDiv if it is aware of the emerging issues.

The major formal mechanism for assuring this was found in the operations of the Executive Secretariat. This office acts as gatekeeper for the Office of the Secretary and seeks to facilitate ways for information to flow to the Secretary. The Executive Secretariat decides who gets involved in issue discussions either in person or through memoranda.

Reliance on information exchange. Because the Secretary chose to avoid regularly scheduled meetings that might serve as a formal management council, several other mechanisms were developed within the Office of the Secretary to facilitate exchange of information. The Deputy Secretary held quarterly management meetings with each of the OpDivs, providing a venue to review a range of administrative and policy questions relevant to

Integrative Mechanisms Which Link Office of the Secretary and Operating Divisions

Formal Processes
    Executive Secretariat
    The Budget Process

Issue Focus
    Secretarial Initiatives
    Tobacco Work Group
    Food Safety Council
    AIDS Steering Committee
    Minority Initiatives Steering Group

Regular Feedback Mechanisms
    Deputy Secretary Quarterly Management Meetings
    ASMB Management Lunches
    ASPA Weekly Conference Calls

Response to White House Requirements
    Y2K Work Group
    The National Performance Review

the program unit. Representatives of each of the Staff Divs sat in on these meetings and, periodically, other OpDivs were invited to participate by the OpDiv under review. The Deputy Secretary used these meetings as a way to hold the OpDiv heads accountable for program performance. The meetings also served to build (indeed, to institutionalize) a set of expectations about specific program or policy goals.

Several of the Staff Divs also held regular meetings with their counterparts in the operating agencies. For example, public affairs and legislative staff from each of the OpDivs participated in exchanges (e.g. conference calls and meetings) that were organized by the Office of the Assistant Secretary for Public Affairs and the Office of the Assistant Secretary for Legislation. Other Staff Divs (such as the General Counsel and the Office of the Assistant Secretary for Management and Budget) also had formalized or less formal relationships with their counterparts in the program units.

While some of these exchanges took place face-to-face, technology made it much easier to keep in contact with individuals who may be located outside of Department headquarters. (For example, the Centers for Disease Control is located in Atlanta and the Health Care Financing Agency is in Baltimore). The ease of devising list-serves for e-mail communication made it very simple to facilitate the exchange of information across a very large organization.

Responding to the External Environment

Although it is clear that the Secretary established management dimensions and processes for the Department that emphasized decentralization and autonomy for the program units, external pressures also had an impact on the balance between centralization and decentralization in HHS. There were a number of instances in which the Secretary, Deputy Secretary, or other parts of the Office of the Secretary played a pivotal role, moving toward some level of centralization. Chief among them were directives that came to the Department from the White House. These included the National Performance Review, Y2K planning, and the Minority Initiatives effort. Administration initiatives—particularly those related to management questions—tended to push toward centralization (or at least direct activity organized by the Office of the Secretary). In each of these cases, however, there was an attempt to respect the expertise and autonomy of the operating units and to differentiate between operating responsibilities and a more general guidance or facilitating role that was assumed by the Office of the Secretary.

In some cases the Congress looked to the Secretary to respond to specific issues. Members of Congress search for whoever they believe can assist them and usually write to the Secretary when they have concerns about specific programs or individual policy decisions. At the same time, in its appropriating, authorizing, and oversight roles, the Congress tends to deal directly with program units.

Attention from the White House and the Congress often led OpDivs to go to the Department for assistance in strategizing an effective response to queries or criticisms. Two of the Staff Divisions—the Office of the Assistant Secretary for Public Affairs and the Office of the Assistant Secretary for Legislation—are especially sensitive to the pressures from external sources and seek to protect the Secretary (as well as the Department as a whole) from negative press or political reactions.

Conclusions and Recommendations

The management approach that was put into place in the Department of Health and Human Services is, without doubt, only one of a variety of administrative strategies that can be employed in public agencies. The choice of a strategy depends on a number of variables—the personality, skills, and experience of the leader, the tasks that are to be performed, and the expectations of the players in the external environment. While the Shalala HHS approach may not be the only way to manage a large and diverse organization, it does provide an alternative example to the traditional command and control strategy often suggested for such agencies.

The Department that was operating during the Clinton administration was led by a Secretary who was extremely comfortable serving as an advocate for the program units and as a supporter of their agendas, and who relied on personal relationships and policy discussions instead of formal bureaucratic processes to arrive at decisions. She was not interested in establishing an Office of the Secretary that saw its role as second-guessing or micro-managing the program components. She was at ease developing a general direction for the Department through a strategically defined set of policy initiatives. She relied on staff whom she trusted and respected.

In addition to the programmatic diversity contained within the Department, it is also important to acknowledge that many of the programs for which HHS is responsible depend on others for implementation. HHS staff actually delivers some of the services that are contained in the Department's portfolio. But state, local and other organizations have significant levels of discretion over the implementation of other programs. In that sense, attempts to establish an expectation that any federal agency—and particularly the Office of the Secretary can control the details of program operations can only be viewed as unrealistic.

The Shalala HHS approach, however, did have some shortcomings. The autonomy provided to the Operating Divisions meant that program units were not always able to take maximum advantage of learning from one another. The bottom-up approach is dependent on recognition of interdependencies between programs. Most of the crosscutting efforts within the Department were of relatively short duration. While there was a recognition that some of these efforts should move into more institutionalized and permanent status, given the informal nature of relationships in the Department it was not easy to move in that direction.

The system put in place was flexible enough to build in the ability to respond to demands for centralization as well as decentralization when issues emerged from public concerns or crises, articulated by the Congress, the White House, and the press. It also was robust enough to respond to the different perspectives that emerged when individual actors looked at issues from a political rather than a programmatic lens. Indeed, the conflicts that surfaced were rarely a clash between career and political staff perspectives. Rather, they represented conflicts between one set of political actors whose responsibilities focused attention outside the Department and another set of political actors who emphasized the details of the programs for which they are responsible.

Despite the success of the Shalala strategy, an underlying uncertainty about the identity of the Department does remain. It is not clear what makes HHS a Department or what elements are viewed as essential to the identity of the Department as a single entity. One could imagine a situation where additional program elements in the Department would be spun off, following the model set by the creation of a separate Department of Education and a separate Social Security Administration. The arguments that would be used to oppose such a move are not always convincing, particularly in the face of a strong constituency that wants a separate identity for their programs.

The Shalala administration demonstrated that shared values, personal relationships, and professional respect do provide the basis for a corporate identity. But it is not at all certain that these will continue when a different set of individuals assumes office. Yet the experience of flexibly managing HHS as a largely decentralized department does attest to the possibility of adopting a management strategy that is an alternative to the traditional centralized mode.

Implications for the Future

The HHS experience under the leadership of Donna Shalala provides a number of lessons for future leaders of HHS as well as others who are faced with the management of decentralized departments.

Management style should be tailored to the individual strengths and predilections of the leader. As such, it is not possible to establish a single measure of management effectiveness. Rather, the particular approach that is used will be idiosyncratic to the individual involved. These individual preferences will also have a direct effect on the role of the top officials in the organization. For example, the role of the Deputy Secretary and the Chief of Staff within the organization will be defined by the personalities, background, and interests of the Secretary and second-tier officials.

The appointment of top officials in the organization is crucial. When the leader of the organization has the ability to select his or her own team, those individuals are likely to be most effective in operating as a unified group. Loyalty to the top official in the organization does not preclude loyalty to the President (or other top political actors). In addition, selection of top officials with expertise and knowledge of the field for which they have responsibility provides the base for management approaches that emphasize discretion and delegate to specialized units.

Units with responsibility for implementing programs are the core of the organization. Staff units (such as those in the Office of the Secretary) should be relatively small in size and always aware that they are present to support the "work" of the organization. Efforts to constrain the ability of the program units to carry out their responsibilities should not be devised simply as a way to control their action.

A focus on substantive policy outcomes should be predominant; institutionalized management processes should be viewed as a means to policy ends, not as ends in themselves. The creation of teams of staff around specific policy issues provides a focus that highlights policy goals. In addition, the team approach allows for flexibility and response to emerging issues.

The internal budget process can be used as a method of highlighting shared goals and values. While operating within an environment of limited resources, the budget process can be used to facilitate information exchange and to identify crosscutting programs and approaches. This approach provides a solid basis for a unified departmental budget request.

Internal management strategies cannot be insulated from external policy, management, or political pressures. No matter what management approach is used by an agency leader, he or she must always assume that external forces are likely to create demands that modify those plans. As such, it is not surprising that most organizations have a mixed portfolio, combining both centralized and decentralized management efforts.

Part II:
Managing Across Boundaries

Background

Public organizations that are in operation at the beginning of the 21st century exhibit characteristics that are quite different from those organizations that were found during most of the 20th century. A snapshot of such organizations—particularly those operating at the federal government level— provides a picture that is without a clear visual focus. It is often difficult to ascertain which aspects of the organization are in the foreground of the picture and which aspects are in the background.

This creates a real challenge for a new Secretary of a cabinet department. Not only are these organizations extremely complex, but they are increasingly charged with the implementation of a variety of policies and programs, employing a range of instruments to carry out those programs. Increasingly federal organizations do not actually carry out the service delivery function themselves but, rather, rely on others (both actors in other levels of the public sector as well as those in the private and nonprofit sectors) to carry out the mission of the organization. The combination of complexity and involvement of others creates a sense of increased uncertainty for top managers, who must respond to constantly changing circumstances.

The ambiguity and conflict that is a characteristic of contemporary organizations is often masked by their formal structures. While specialized units have been brought together under a common umbrella or framework, one needs simply to scratch the surface of those organizations to recognize that it is often illusory to think of those umbrellas as an accurate way of describing what actually goes on within the organizational structure.

Mechanisms are required that allow a cabinet official to be able to act relatively quickly to new problems, to avoid establishing management processes for their own sakes, to focus strategically on a specific set of policy or program goals, and to deal with a variety of actors both inside and outside the department. In addition, the cabinet Secretary often needs to develop procedures that are time limited and crafted to deal with a specific issue.

While some degree of complexity has characterized federal organizations over their history (and formal structures have never really described what happens inside an organization), the extent of this complexity has increased over the past decade. Most recently, the determination to flatten organizations, reduce hierarchies, and devolve responsibilities for implementation of programs to others has contributed to this situation. As a result, the techniques and approaches that have been used in the past to manage large public organizations require rethinking.

In the past, management of these organizations relied on two major approaches: tinkering with organizational structure and adopting centralized processes as control mechanisms.

Changes in Organizational Structure

Modifications to the organizational structure have traditionally been used as a way of linking programs or units together or to limit the autonomy of specific units. The reorganizations that emerge from this strategy provide a mechanism for those charged with the management responsibility within a large umbrella agency to minimize fragmentation and establish consistencies across program units. The assumption has been that centralization will solve most problems.

Although some reorganization efforts have been openly devised as methods of controlling what are viewed as maverick or runaway agencies, most of these efforts have been promoted on the basis of increasing efficiency or providing approaches that would achieve policy or program effectiveness. In addition, agencies are constrained by Congress in their ability to make major changes in structure solely on management grounds.

Centralized Management Processes

Traditionally a series of internal management processes have been used to highlight consistencies and efficiencies within large agencies composed of multiple and diffuse units. The budget process is most commonly used to play this role, providing a way for the top offices of a department or large agency to establish command-and-control mechanisms that minimize the autonomy of units in their search for fiscal resources. Units have usually come to centralized budget offices as supplicants for those resources. Similarly, both the personnel process and the acquisition process have been employed to achieve this purpose, providing mechanisms in which a centralized unit in the large organization plays a controlling role, limiting the discretion of the smaller units. Over the years, the growth of staff units within the top reaches of federal agencies has been a response to this urge.

By the end of the 20th century, however, the limitations of both of these strategies have been acknowledged by many who have responsibility for federal management reform. The various efforts that have been associated with the reinvention movement (the National Performance Review and other reform efforts) have moved the pendulum away from reform that increased centralization and emphasized a command-and-control approach to management. As Osborne and Gaebler have described it, organizations have adopted the "steer, not row" approach to management.[1]

Increasingly, those who have employed structural reorganization strategies recognize that these efforts may have less to do with substantive achieve-

ments than with symbolic action. Moving a unit around within a larger organizational framework may have little impact on the way that the unit actually does its work. Similarly, the attempt to manage large-scale federal
organizations through centralized units has neither been very effective nor
has it comported with the fragmented decision-making process that characterizes the American political system. While the press and some legislative
critics focus on the role of the Secretary or the top organizational leader in
an agency, decisions related to resources (particularly the budget) and legislative authority are made in the context of the specialized units within the
umbrella organization. At the same time, there are times when some centralization of specific functions is the only effective way to address problems.

Thus, in this context, to continue to rely on the traditional modes of
achieving a corporate identity in large-scale federal agencies seems to be
foolhardy. While these strategies have not been completely rejected, an
array of new approaches have been developed as alternative ways of managing these structures. The tools available to deal with these issues usually
lie within the Office of the Secretary of a department—that is, in the staff
rather than line components of the department. Some of the techniques that
have been employed are not new but, because they are used in a context
of decentralization, take on a different meaning than they did in the past.

Rather than emphasizing structural centralization or command-and-
control strategies, these approaches have sought to find a way to define a
role for top management in the context of decentralized, flat, and devolved
organizations. While the majority of the energy and work of these organizations is done in the decentralized units, there are times when it is important to find a way for the top management to become involved in activities,
playing a coordination or crosscutting role.

The HHS Experience under Donna Shalala

Since its creation in 1953 as an amalgam of several existing agencies,
the U.S. Department of Health and Human Services (originally the
Department of Health, Education and Welfare) has struggled with the
appropriate balance between centralized functions in the Office of the
Secretary and autonomy to the various agencies and bureaus contained
within its boundaries. Over the years, the pendulum has swung back and
forth between emphasis on centralization and decentralization as either
implicit or explicit management strategies.[2]

Donna Shalala, Secretary from January 1993 to January 2001, adopted a
conscious management strategy that was very different from those attempted
in the past. As described in Part I of this chapter, she began with the assumption that the department contains many decentralized elements and that

change has to be self-generated within those elements to be effective. She described the department as composed of units that have their own history, needs, cultures, and constituencies. She used the professional credibility of the subunits within the office (especially those dealing with the health world) as an important source of public and political support. She downsized the Office of the Secretary and delegated many different functions to the operating components. At the same time, she believed that the Office of the Secretary can play a leadership role in stimulating change in the submits.

The reorganization that accompanied the movement of the Social Security Administration (SSA) out of HHS in 1995, halving the department's staff and budget, reinforced the Secretary's own style. The structure that was devised created a flat organizational structure, which represented the Secretary's personal management view. These efforts coincided with the activities of the Vice President's National Performance Review, which advocated flat organizations built around efforts to empower line officials.

A number of examples have emerged from this management style that illustrate a modified way of managing a very large federal department. Some of these examples illustrate efforts at institutionalizing processes that both respect the autonomy of the decentralized units but, at the same time, provide a role for the Office of the Secretary and the top management of the department. Still other examples reflect specific policy or program issues that require the department to play a role, either because of external pressure or because of conflicts between approaches taken by units within the department. Not all of these examples illustrate totally new approaches to management. Interagency groups are clearly not new. But because they are employed in a department which is largely decentralized, they have tended to be taken more seriously than similar efforts in the past.

The seven case studies that have been included in this analysis highlight four types of crosscutting mechanisms: mechanisms for problem solving; mechanisms for coordination; mechanisms for information sharing/team building; and processes to balance a bottom-up and department-wide perspective. These cases include the role of the Office of the Secretary in improving human subjects protection; strategies for addressing racial and health disparities; the HHS Data Council; preparation for Y2K; Management Issues Lunches; the Budget Review Board; and the Government Performance and Results Act process.

They also illustrate the potential of the Office of the Secretary in a variety of roles. These examples indicate that it is possible to devise ways for the Office of the Secretary to become involved in the department's decision process without resorting to command-and-control approaches. The roles that are illustrated include seeking long-term solutions, broadening an issue, serving as a facilitator, encouraging bottom-up efforts, and translating technical issues to generalist language.

The challenge for the department is to provide a way to relate to each program unit individually and, at the same time, allow for the creation of an approach that makes sense for the department as a whole.

The Case Studies

Crosscutting Mechanisms for Problem Solving

Broadening an Issue and Playing a Neutral Party Role: The Role of the Office of the Secretary in Improving Human Subjects Protection

Early in 2000, attention was drawn to the role the federal government may have played in the death of a patient at the University of Pennsylvania as a result of an experimental gene transfer intervention during treatment. The main concern of the press was focused on the actions of the researchers at the University of Pennsylvania. But the fact that the research had been funded with federal dollars made it clear that it was important to examine the regulations that were in place to protect individuals who were subjects of clinical research.

This examination soon showed that the existing policies constituted a problem. Both the National Institutes of Health (NIH) and the Food and Drug Administration (FDA) had existing policies that were found to be inadequate, developed on the basis of different definitions and schedules, and that varied in terms of their enforcement efforts.

The HHS role in this area flowed from the growth in public funds appropriated to NIH for biomedical research after World War II as well as the statutory responsibility given to the FDA for regular clinical research associated with bringing drugs, vaccines and other biologics, and medical devices to market. Protection of human research subjects accompanied this effort, ensuring that human research subjects are protected from unreasonable risks, participate of their own free will, and make their decisions only after they have been informed fully about the potential risks and possible benefits of their participation. These efforts developed from the Nuremburg Code—the principles that were established following World War II in response to Nazi experimentation on human beings during that war.

The instrumentality for implementing the regulations that flowed from these principles is the Institutional Review Board (IRB). These bodies are established and operated by universities, hospitals, and other institutions that receive research awards from the federal government or other sponsors. They are responsible for reviewing proposed research protocols and informed consent statements before subjects are recruited and clinical research begins, as well as continuing oversight of the projects throughout their life cycle.

Case Study: Human Subjects Protection

Organizations Involved	**Office of the Secretary:** Office of the Assistant Secretary for Planning and Evaluation Office of Public Health and Science **Agencies:** National Institutes of Health Food and Drug Administration
Problem/Issue	Responding to a public crisis and reviewing departmental human subject protection policies and procedure
Lead Organization	Office of Public Health and Science
Time Dimension	Short term/long term
Accomplishments	Broadened issues Clarified policies
Role of the Office of the Secretary	Planning role Limited operational role

Although the public's concern about the effectiveness of these policies focused on the death at the University of Pennsylvania, there was already concern about the capability of the IRBs to carry out the responsibilities that were given to them. A series of three reports was issued in 1998 by the HHS Office of Inspector General (OIG), pointing to some of the problems associated with protection of human subjects and highlighting the demands and pressures on the IRBs that made it difficult for them to carry out their role. The OIG asserted that it was time for a fundamental reexamination and reengineering of the HHS oversight process in this area. In addition, in its report to the President, the National Bioethics Advisory Commission called for improvement in the accountability of IRBs and new techniques to ensure implementation of protections at the local level. Concern was voiced about the procedures used to manage financial conflicts of interest so that research subjects are neither misled nor coerced and that efforts would be made to assure that investigators and sponsors of research did not share financial interests in the research.

Two components within HHS shared responsibility for the IRBs: the NIH Office for Protection from Research Risks (OPRR) and the FDA. OPRR oversees IRBs operated by HHS awardee institutions (largely research and academic institutions) while FDA oversees IRBs that review clinical research related to products it regulates, irrespective of whether that research is ongoing at HHS awardee institutions or other sites.

Following the issuance of the OIG reports, both OPRR and the FDA stepped up the pace of their inspections of human subjects protection activities at research institutions within their areas. These activities reinforced the OIG conclusion that the IRB system is under considerable strain. However, while all of the HHS components agreed that persons who volunteer to be human subjects must be afforded the maximum protection from unnecessary risk, they did not agree on the specific steps that should be taken to deal with this problem. The two major units involved in this policy area differed in their approach to the issue and did not share a common strategy for dealing with the IRBs.

While there were significant actions taken in both the NIH and the FDA, until the death at the University of Pennsylvania there was no defined role for an overall department perspective that would be taken by the Office of the Secretary. The public concern about the specific research—gene therapy research—provoked a concern from the department's Deputy Secretary that resulted in involvement of the Deputy Assistant Secretary for Science Policy in the Office of the Assistant Secretary for Planning and Evaluation. That involvement meant that a department-wide perspective was developed that both broadened the scope of the immediate crisis issue and also created a permanent venue that was able to deal with cross-cutting issues.

A number of actions were taken at this point. A working group was established that focused on specific problems that were related to gene therapy. Plans for a series of conferences on safety were actually already in place, but both the NIH and the FDA needed to raise issues that crossed their organizational lines. The scrutiny of the activities disclosed that there were shortcomings in the monitoring of studies. While FDA subscribed to an international protocol on monitoring, the guidelines that were established did not require drug companies to monitor their gene therapy research. Shortcomings were also found in NIH's monitoring of studies.

The department perspective also emphasized the need to move out of the specific arena of gene therapy research. While those problems were severe, they were not unique. The structural problems in IRBs were a significant part of the gene therapy situation. As past reports had indicated, the IRB system was strained, operating without adequate resources or without appropriate stature on campuses. The analyses pointed to the possibility of focusing on the revenue stream that is available to reimburse awardees' expenditures for the indirect costs of research. This stream—often called "overhead"—was viewed as a potential source of funds for improvement in human subjects protection. The department strongly urged research institutions to strengthen their local efforts to protect human research subjects, to give their IRBs the standing and resources needed to do their job properly. This approach highlighted the reality that human subjects protection is a shared responsibility among the federal government, research institutions, IRBs, investigators, and sponsors.

As the issue moved beyond the program units to the Office of the Secretary, the approach emphasized strategies that were largely in agreement with the reports of the OIG. These included recasting federal requirements (highlighting a "just-in-time" approach for awardee institutions and reengineering the federal oversight process); strengthening continuing protections (emphasizing the role of the Data and Safety Monitoring Boards); and enacting educational requirements (making informative materials more readily available to the research community). The new approach also highlighted the need to help insulate both researchers and IRB members from financial conflicts of interest that threaten their independence.

HHS also determined that the human subjects component of the NIH OPRR should be elevated to the Office of Public Health and Science (OPHS) within the Office of the Secretary. Even before the death at the University of Pennsylvania, a decision was made to take this action. A new office was created—the Office for Human Research Protection (OHRP)—on the basis of advice from the National Bioethics Advisory Commission as well as the Advisory Committee to the Director of NIH. The director of the office was selected on the basis of a national search and a public advisory committee was created to help guide the OHRP and the department overall.

To some extent, the creation of this office recreated a more centralized approach to health policy issues. Yet the change continued to emphasize the important role of the program units. Until 1995, all of the public health units in the department were placed under the umbrella of an Assistant Secretary for Health. Theoretically, at least, both NIH and FDA reported through that Assistant Secretary (although they did operate as very separate and discrete units even when they reported to that Assistant Secretary).

The role played by the Office of the Secretary in this policy area has two aspects. The first was largely a planning function played by the Deputy Assistant Secretary for Science Policy. Once that planning opportunity was completed, the issue was handed to the program agencies as well as the new office. Both of these players—the program units and the OHRP—played an operational role, with the program units working closely with the Office of the Secretary to develop a shared strategy.

There are a number of challenges that are illustrated by this case:
- Many policy areas reflect different constituencies and definitions of work by the program units.
- Crisis problems are often a result of systemic issues and cannot be dealt with as unique phenomena.

- It is important to keep operational responsibility in program units even when the Office of the Secretary is involved.

Responding to a White House Initiative and Crafting a Department Response: Strategies for Addressing Health Disparities

In June 1997, President Clinton announced an initiative on race. That initiative was described as a critical element in the President's effort to prepare the U.S. to live as one country in the 21st century. Each cabinet department was asked to respond to this challenge. The HHS focus highlighted problems related to disparities in health outcomes. Although life expectancy and overall health has improved in recent years for a large number of Americans, not all Americans were included. Because appropriate health care is often associated with an individual's economic status, race, and gender, a number of gaps were found in the health conditions of many racial and ethnic minorities. The effort sought to emphasize the underlying causes of higher levels of diseases, including poverty, lack of access to quality health services, environmental hazards in homes and neighborhoods, and the need for effective prevention programs tailored to specific community needs.

In addition to the White House interest in the issue, both the Secretary of HHS as well as the Surgeon General had already been concerned about the problem. It also resonated with various elements within the society, particularly with community groups and with the Black and Hispanic congressional caucuses. But while there was a convergence of interests on the topic, there was no agency or individual within the department that had played a department-wide public leadership role on the topic. While the Surgeon General could use his bully pulpit role to stimulate attention to the problem, the real ability to respond to the issue was found in the decentralized program units within the department and with various health groups within the society that had essential roles in the health delivery system.

Prior to the HHS reorganization in 1995, there might have been a response to this challenge through the Office of the Assistant Secretary for Health (a unit which contained all of the public health agencies). In reality, however, that office would have been confronted with the same problems that faced the department in 1997—program autonomy and competing agendas. Some way had to be established to highlight the overall department concern about the issue and to develop a strategy that acknowledged the importance of actors both inside and outside of HHS.

The strategy that was devised included both a department-level response as well as a response from the individual program units. The locus for the efforts is found in the Office of the Assistant Secretary of Public Health and Science, through the efforts of a deputy assistant secretary whose responsibilities highlight these issues. Each agency within the department was asked to identify priorities within their program portfolio to address six areas in which

Case Study: Strategies for Addressing Health Disparities

Organizations Involved	**Office of the Secretary:** Office of the Assistant Secretary for Planning and Evaluation Office of Public Health and Science **Agencies:** All
Problem/Issue	Responding to a White House directive that highlighted disparities in health outcomes often associated with race
Lead Organization	Office of Public Health and Science
Time Dimension	Short term/long term
Accomplishments	Developed department-wide focus; reviewed program portfolios
Role of the Office of the Secretary	Kept agenda before participants

there are health disparities among racial and ethnic minority populations: infant mortality, diabetes, cardiovascular disease, cancer screening and management, HIV/AIDS infection rates, and adult and childhood immunization.

Within the Office of the Secretary, the Assistant Secretary for Health/Surgeon General and the Assistant Secretary for Planning and Evaluation served as co-directors of an effort that reviewed the status of the department's goals to eliminate health disparities; consulted with minority communities and the scientific and research communities; and reviewed and recommended efforts related to the department's resources and programs.

Two committees were established that represented a cross-section of agencies to look at health and customer service concerns that impact minority populations. The departmental Minority Initiatives Steering Committee was designed to provide policy direction and guidance for key minority health initiatives (these include the Asian American and Pacific Islander Action Agenda, the Hispanic Agenda for Action, the Historically Black Colleges and Universities Initiative, and the Tribal Colleges and Universities Initiatives). This steering committee was chaired by the HHS Deputy Secretary and included the Assistant Secretary for Health/Surgeon General, the Assistant Secretary for Management and Budget, and the heads or deputies of HHS program divisions.

In addition, a departmental Minority Initiatives Coordinating Committee was established, comprised of senior agency staff who report directly to agency heads or their deputies. The group works within the context of the steering committee policy directives and draws together the actual work of all four minority initiatives to avoid duplication and foster interagency cooperation on strategies to improve the health status of minorities. The department's approach was a three-pronged effort:

- Dialogue (broadening and strengthening its partnerships with state and local government, national and regional minority health and other minority-focused organizations, and minority community-based organizations)
- Research (attention to improvements in monitoring and developing the local and national data necessary for determining priorities and designing programs and research on ways to improve interactions and interventions in minority communities)
- Action (a number of new projects were designed to test different models for reducing disparities in specific minority communities).

Program units within the department responded to the effort with a range of programs and new policies. Community coalitions were established in 18 states, funded by the Centers for Disease Control and Prevention, to help address racial and ethnic disparities in the six target areas. More than 30 community coalitions received funding for planning and will compete for implementation funds in the future.

In February 2000, a new Coordinating Center for Research on Health Disparities was proposed at the National Institutes of Health. The center would be in the Office of the NIH Director's Office of Research on Minority Health. This center was designed to facilitate the development of an NIH-wide Strategic Plan for Research on Health Disparities that would bring together each institute, center, and programmatic unit of NIH in a collaboration to better understand the causes of health disparities. This had been a longtime recommendation by the Congressional Black Caucus. To some extent, this office represented a centralization of functions. But more importantly, it served to provide symbolic attention to this set of issues.

In addition, the department took other steps:

- Publicized the first state-by-state look at risks for chronic diseases and injury for the five major racial and ethnic groups
- Collaborated with Grantmakers in Health (a consortium of foundations concerned about health issues) on a national leadership conference to generate ideas and identify action steps for the racial and ethnic health disparities initiative
- Developed an information World Wide Web site for the initiative to be used by interested media and communities
- Organized internal work groups in each of the six areas that are looking at HHS's existing programs and making recommendations

- Solicited public input about the issues from a series of regional meetings regarding Healthy People 2010, a set of overarching disease prevention and health promotion goals being pursued by the department
- Reviewed departmental data collection systems and made recommendations on how to improve data collection for racial and ethnic minorities.

There are several challenges that are illustrated by this example:

- This is an issue that required programmatic attention across the department and could not be dealt with by a single body.
- Past reorganizations can leave a void in the way that program units relate to one another.
- A number of program areas did not see this issue as a part of their responsibility.
- This issue not only involved actors inside the department but required action by a number of groups outside of the department.

Crosscutting Mechanisms for Coordination

Responding to the White House and Creating a Crosscutting Venue: The HHS Data Council

In March 1995, HHS was asked by Vice President Gore to develop a departmental response to issues related to promotion of health care applications of the national information infrastructure. The Vice President highlighted four different areas: data standards, privacy, enhanced health information for consumers, and telemedicine. Although the department already had work underway in each of these areas, the request asked for consolidation of ongoing efforts into a coherent strategy coordinated with other agencies, with attention to private sector and state roles in achieving more effective use of an information infrastructure for health care applications.

The White House request spawned a department-wide information policy initiative, handed to a department-wide committee to develop. That group not only focused on the four areas specified by the Vice President but also broadened the scope to focus on the department's own information system policies, moving away from categorical program-specific activities to a more integrated and cohesive approach to these issues.

By December 1995, the Secretary created a permanent, formal body that was constituted to reflect the reorganized HHS structure. That group would address the full range of health and nonhealth data and privacy questions identified by the working group.

The Data Council's charge was to coordinate all HHS health and nonhealth data collection and analysis activities through a data collection strategy, coordination of activities, data standards and policy, and privacy policy activities. Membership on the council consisted of all assistant secretary and agency administrator level HHS officials who have a direct reporting

Case Study: HHS Data Council

Organizations Involved	**Office of the Secretary:** Office of the Assistant Secretary for Planning and Evaluation Also others **Agencies:** All
Problem/Issue	Responding to the variety of data systems and policies and facilitating coordination across them
Lead Organization	Office of the Assistant Secretary for Planning and Evaluation Program
Time Dimension	Long term
Accomplishments	Creating a venue to deal with issues
Role of the Office of the Secretary	Broadening to include generalist concerns

relationship to the Secretary, the HHS Privacy Advocate, and the Secretary's Senior Advisor on Health Statistics. It is co-chaired by the Assistant Secretary for Planning and Evaluation (located in the Office of the Secretary) and a rotating program head. Each member was asked to appoint an alternate to attend when the top official is not available and a staff contact person to handle communications about Data Council business. Staff for the council is provided by the Office of the Assistant Secretary for Planning and Evaluation.

The Council developed a six-item agenda that would guide its work:
- Develop a department-wide data collection strategy, including coordination and integration of surveys and oversight of surveys and general statistical analysis
- Coordinate HHS and inter-departmental health data standards activities, including the implementation of the Health Insurance Portability and Accountability Act
- Serve as HHS liaison for the National Committee on Vital and Health Statistics
- Serve as a focus for HHS issues relating to privacy of health and social services information
- Provide a forum for coordination of health and human services issues raised by the expanding national information infrastructure activities

- Provide a forum for coordination of HHS responses to external requests for HHS action on issues related to health and social services data.

As the Data Council evolved, its mandate became more complex. The passage of the Health Insurance Portability and Accountability Act of 1996 called for the department to develop standards that not only met the new expectations about electronic transmission but also made privacy protections. This latter responsibility required the Data Council to work closely with the National Committee on Vital and Health Statistics, the department's public advisory committee on health data, standards, privacy, and health information policy. In addition, the Data Council was also asked to respond to the need for data to be presented in a form that would provide information on race and ethnicity.

To accomplish these tasks, the Data Council organized itself into a number of working groups. These included the Survey Integration Work Group, the Joint Working Group on Telemedicine, the HHS Privacy Committee, the HHS Committee on Health Data Standards, the Working Group on Racial and Ethnic Data, and the Working Group on International Health Data Collaboration.

To a large extent, the meetings of the Data Council and the working groups were dominated by individuals who focused on the technical aspects of data collection, largely in health. The meetings did provide a forum for individuals with data responsibilities across the department to share concerns and provided a forum for the exchange of ideas. The agenda that was before the group reinforced this technical tendency.

While the forum did meet these needs, it also had a down side. Because the health focus of the group so dominated the agenda, there was minimal participation in the deliberations from the human services element in the department. For example, rarely did data issues confronting the Administration on Children and Families come before the data venue.

The Data Council members also found it difficult to translate their concerns to the budget process. Some participants in the process observed that a data strategy approach had not emerged from the council deliberations. A "wish list," rather than a set of priorities and issues that could be viewed in operational terms, was developed. As a result, data staff found that the budgets that emerged did not provide them with resources for data collection or with policies that allowed them to move to the next levels of electronic technology. The technical staff who dominated the Data Council were not able to translate their concerns in a way that prompted interest by the budget planners at either the individual program unit level or at the departmental level.

By 2000, steps were taken to address these problems. Individuals from the human services side of the department became more involved in the meetings, and Data Council meetings were used to help data staff understand the intricacies of the budget process. Some of this occurred as a result of increased involvement of individuals from the Office of the Secretary. While the operational aspects of data issues would continue to be the responsibility of the program units, the presence of staff from the Office of the Secretary helped to broaden the issues and move the activities of the Data Council from a highly specialized focus toward a more generalist orientation.

There are a number of challenges that are illustrated by this example:

- It is difficult for technical staff to find a way to relate to generalist processes such as the budget process.
- An organization this large and complex has a diversity of data systems that make it difficult to operate in a unitary fashion.
- The complexity of the assignment given to the group was extremely difficult and actually increased over time.
- There is a variability of interest in these issues by various program units.

Avoiding a Crisis and Establishing Department-wide Norms: Preparation for Y2K

There are few management issues that commanded the attention that was given to the federal government's efforts to avoid any computer crisis when January 1, 2000 arrived. Although there were some efforts within HHS to plan for the technical conversions that were necessary to prepare for the transition, the attention to the issue was located at a fairly low level in the department. It was not until the White House focused on this challenge that the HHS Deputy Secretary became involved. At the same time, members of Congress held a series of hearings on Y2K issues, focusing public attention on problems that might emerge if the federal agencies were not ready for the conversion.

The President's Management Council (PMC) began a government-wide effort that was orchestrated out of the White House and the Office of Management and Budget (OMB); a President's Council on Year 2000 Conversion was established and subgroups were formed to focus on the issues and problems that would be confronted by federal agencies. The HHS Deputy Secretary chaired the group that focused on transition issues in the health care system.

The initial effort to prepare for the Year 2000 was originally viewed as a computer problem. As time went by, it was soon realized that the problem was much broader because of so many system interdependencies and computer functions in devices other than computers (such as medical devices and card key entry systems). By the beginning of 1999, being ready for Y2K was the highest priority in the department.

The Deputy Secretary's involvement focused on the dimensions of the issue as a problem that cut across the department. He was particularly concerned about keeping continuity of health care intact when the due date came. This would not only involve the department's own computers but

Case Study: Y2K

Organizations Involved	**Office of the Secretary:** Deputy Secretary Assistant Secretary for Management and Budget **Agencies:** All
Problem/Issue	Responding to public and congressional pressure and the need to coordinate departmental responses to Y2K
Lead Organization	Deputy Secretary
Time Dimension	Short term/long term
Accomplishments	Established department-wide norms to avert crisis Identified longer-term issues
Role of the Office of the Secretary	Conscience, reminder of problems Convened meetings Facilitated resources

also systems that were found in hospitals and other aspects of the health care system.

Efforts were developed at three levels. The first involved the department's own systems (payments and other mission-critical priorities). The second highlighted the work of the partners involved in carrying out the work of the department (state agencies and other partners). And the third level involved the program sectors themselves, assuring that the missions of the department's programs could be accomplished (e.g., assuring an adequate supply of pharmaceuticals).

Working closely with the Office of the Assistant Secretary for Management and Budget, in 1998 the Deputy Secretary convened biweekly meetings with representatives of the program units. In most instances, the Chief Information Officer of a program unit attended the meetings and, in a number of cases, the program head attended. During these meetings, each element in the department was required to report on what it was doing to prepare for January 1. Following each meeting, a graph was prepared that presented the percentage of compliant Y2K mission-critical systems by program unit. The team's task was to collect and provide information on mission-critical systems, facilities, telecommunications, business continuity and contingency plans, and outreach efforts.

In addition, meetings were held with outside groups that were partners in carrying out HHS program responsibilities. Devolution of responsibilities to state and local governments as well as private and nonprofit groups meant that HHS would not be able to carry out its program mandates unless these groups were ready for the conversion. These included businesses, public service agencies, trade associations, and consumer groups.

The specific tasks required for each program unit varied, depending on the technical systems in place, the structure of the program (if it depended on others to carry out operations), and the level of resources required to make the change. The most complex tasks involved conversion of millions of computer codes within the Health Care Financing Administration, work with field offices and tribal contacts by the Indian Health Service, and systems in place at FDA and the Administration for Children and Families. In addition, the Program Support Center (the unit charged with implementation of payroll and other financial systems) was in the middle of changing to new computer systems. Given these challenges, efforts were made to focus on agencies with problems.

Although the precise requirements were diverse, the participants in the process recognized that the department would sink or swim as a single unit. During the initial meetings of the department's Y2K team, individuals appeared reluctant to share information, fearing the legal and proprietary problems that might emerge. A number of the program units found the biweekly meetings difficult and were frustrated by the complexity of the task and the time requirement to address the problems. Yet these program staff knew that the issue was of importance to the Secretary and the Deputy Secretary and that involvement of management from the top of the department was essential. As the sessions continued, the participants began to see that they could learn lessons from each other by discussing their experiences.

Before it left the department to become an independent agency, the Social Security Administration had begun its compliance activity. While it was in advance of some of the other department units, it was making these changes on its own, and there was not an opportunity for others to learn from SSA. No other part of the department had picked up on the SSA experience.

Involvement of top management also facilitated the ability of the program units to make successful requests for additional resources required to deal with the conversion. The President's Council on Year 2000 Conversion was able to put pressure on OMB to assure access to funds outside the regular budget process, and some of the program units received emergency support for conversion activities. The Assistant Secretary for Management and Budget (ASMB) acted as the conduit for these funds. By October 1999, all of the program units had 100 percent compliance in their Y2K mission-critical systems.

As January 1, 2000, neared each of the program units and the Office of the Secretary established Day One Centers to monitor the status of the department's systems as well as those in the health care sector and in the states supporting HHS programs. These centers provided around the clock secure operations capable of receiving reports from the program units, public health organizations, other federal agencies, the pharmaceutical industry, and health care organizations. If required, the centers were able to analyze the reports quickly and provide accurate and timely information to the White House regarding the status of health care and human service sectors. The department also participated in the publication of a booklet for consumers that addressed specific patient and consumer concerns about the delivery of health care after January 1, offered suggestions for what individuals could do to prepare for the transition, and provided the consumer with a list of resources for additional information. In addition, technical assistance was provided to state partners, especially by ASMB staff.

As it assessed its preparatory activities for the Year 2000 conversion, HHS reported that it remediated 284 mission-critical systems, 890 non-mission-critical systems, 146,051 data exchanges, 6,225 telecommunication devices, 3,727 HHS-owned or -managed facilities, and 26,217 HHS-owned medical devices. HHS also hosted six international U.S. Information Agency-sponsored Y2K groups to promote an international exchange of information and provide U.S. expertise. The preparation resulted in a largely problem-free experience. In effect, there were no problems for any of the HHS systems nor in the nation's health care or human service system.

Although the department-wide activities were focused on Y2K compliance, the actions that were taken to prepare for the transition created a better understanding of how the department's diverse computer systems work and about the people who operate them. The Y2K effort required each organization in the department to inventory and audit its existing installed base of hardware and software. Systems were identified as mission-critical, high impact, obsolete, or in need of upgrades and redesign. In addition, the lessons learned through the year 2000 efforts contributed to an understanding of policy, procedure, and security issues that will be addressed by the components in the department in upcoming years.

Several challenges are illustrated by this example:
- Political and public attention to the issue can put severe pressure on agency decision-makers to respond.
- It is difficult to move issues from technical dimensions to the broader policy system.
- There is often variability in the capacity of program units to respond to an issue and, as well, variability in the intensity of the problem across the department.

- Concern about the demands and an initial lack of trust involves the direct involvement of the Deputy Secretary.
- A crisis environment can be used to broaden the issue and focus on long-term responses.

Crosscutting Mechanisms for Information Sharing/Team Building

Creating an Informal Management Forum: The Management Issues Luncheon Meetings

During the first years of the Clinton administration, the HHS Deputy Secretary scheduled regular meetings that involved all of the individuals within the Office of the Secretary who had some form of management responsibility. Following the reorganization of the department in 1995, a decision was made to broaden those meetings to include individuals from the program units with major management duties.

Beginning in mid-1996, meetings were held to provide a venue for individuals concerned with management of the large, complex department to discuss issues and exchange ideas in an informal setting. The Assistant Secretary for Management and Budget served as the convener and chair of the sessions. In addition, the meetings were viewed as opportunities to prepare for and follow up on meetings of the President's Management Council, the Chief Financial Officers Council, and other government-wide management groups.

Despite the prominent role of the ASMB, the group evolved into a highly interactive body with program unit participants taking responsibility for the activities. The meetings (usually held on a monthly basis) followed a common format. Opportunities were given to participants to make announcements and provide updates on current developments; a few topical issues were discussed, usually on the basis of presentations from the appropriate department staffer; and time was provided for members to raise issues that were on their minds. Minutes were not taken of the discussions and, since decisions were not actually made in this setting, there was no formal codification of the discussion (even when there was an agreement among the participants).

The individuals invited to participate in the sessions were the top management officers in each organization—usually a deputy in that unit or the individual who served as the executive officer. Most of the parties involved in the meetings were career staffers, with a few political appointees where relevant. Attendance at the luncheons was very good; rarely did those who were invited send a subordinate staff member.

During the first several years of the luncheon meetings, the agendas included updates on the budget, discussion of labor management partnerships, the quality of work life strategy, pass-fail performance management

Case Study: Management Issues Lunches

Organizations Involved	**Office of the Secretary:** Assistant Secretary for Management and Budget **Agencies:** All
Problem/Issue	Responding to the need for senior leaders in the department to discuss major management issues
Lead Organization	Assistant Secretary for Management and Budget
Time Dimension	Long term
Accomplishments	Established safe haven for participation and discussion
Role of the Office of the Secretary	Facilitated exchange of views Provided information on current developments

systems, human resource planning studies, and updates on the strategic plan and performance plans required by the Government Performance and Results Act (GPRA). In addition, individuals were invited from other agencies to give presentations on the National Performance Review and flexiplace and telecommuting policies.

By the end of 1997, planning groups were organized, composed of participants in the sessions. These groups included teams focusing on human resources/organization development; GPRA/strategic planning; systems/information technology; and financial management. Each of the groups was asked to elect a chair and develop a list of possible issues or actions that would serve as an action agenda for the Management Issues Luncheon meetings. These groups presented their proposed action agenda at the January 1998 meeting, highlighting specific ways to address the issues or actions identified and a tentative timetable for dealing with them. Each planning group took responsibility for each monthly meeting during 1998. In addition to the planning group reports, discussions were also held on credit card expansion; travel policies; early out and/or buyout authority; electronic commerce; audits; department-wide employee surveys; and developments in the Public Health Service Commissioned Corps.

At the end of 1998, participants were asked to evaluate the meetings in more than an anecdotal fashion. The responses indicated that these meetings were addressing the needs of the participants as management officials.

The evaluation included the following comments about the Management Issues Luncheon meetings:

- "They brought to focus issues that are relevant and of concern throughout the department."
- "They provided an opportunity to meet and network with counterparts in other operating and staff components."
- "They had a specific topic to focus on, as well as an opportunity for discussion on subjects of current interest. All subjects had relevance to issues on which I normally work."
- "The luncheons provide an opportunity for management officials in the various operating divisions to get to know each other, which makes doing business with them outside the meetings much easier."
- "They allowed operating division managers to see how other operating divisions are addressing issues that we all have to address and provide information on relevant topics."

Participants were also asked for recommendations for future meetings:

- "Allow at least 15 minutes of "peer time" at each meeting for discussion of whatever is on people's minds."
- "Ask the Assistant Secretary for Management and Budget to report each month on the previous month's important activities of the Secretary and Deputy Secretary."
- "Continue topic focus but leave time for budget status, Hill updates, GPRA status, etc. Invite knowledge outsiders (or insiders) to make brief presentations on these subjects."
- "We don't always take full advantage of opportunities to discuss some of the issues more broadly. Some topics clearly deserve more attention than we have been giving them."

During 2000, responding to these suggestions, sessions focused on Census 2000, the HHS Distributed Learning Network, and problems involving fiscal management practices at the Centers for Disease Control (CDC). In all of these meetings, the participants found it useful to talk about management issues as ideas, treating them on a conceptual level.

Several challenges are illustrated by this example:

- The tradition of dealing with the Office of the Secretary management office in a top-down fashion is difficult to break.
- The top management officials in the program units have few opportunities to discuss issues in a "safe" environment.
- A non-decision venue provides a way to allow program officials to understand the department-wide perspective, moving beyond "stovepipes."

Crosscutting Processes to Balance Bottom-Up and Department-Wide Perspectives

Replacing Centralized Budgeting with a Collegial Process: Recasting the Budget Review Board

For many years, predating the Clinton administration, the budget process within the Office of the Secretary had been the vehicle for exerting a strong, centralized Office of the Secretary perspective. Both program and staff units within the department presented their budget requests in the early summer of each year to a board composed of top officials from the Office of the Secretary. Members of the Budget Review Board (BRB) have traditionally included the Assistant Secretary for Management and Budget (serving as the chair), the Assistant Secretary for Planning and Evaluation, the Assistant Secretary for Legislation, and the Assistant Secretary for Health.

Prior to the 1995 reorganization, the Assistant Secretary for Health developed a budget that included all of the public health components (including the NIH, FDA, and CDC). After that reorganization each of those components presented its own budget individually to the BRB, joining the non-health units within HHS. The head of each of the program units within the department explained the policy issues facing that agency and how the budget requested would improve the health and well-being of the nation. In the past, the agency heads often came to the BRB as supplicants, requesting expenditure authority that may or may not have been approved by the BRB and the Secretary. This was the first stage of a very complex process, moving from the BRB to the Secretary and then to OMB. The "pass-back" from OMB could then be appealed by the Secretary, first to the OMB Director and then to the President. That was the budget that eventually was presented to the Congress. If a program unit did not receive its request, it was common that the agency (or its constituency) developed an end-run strategy, working around the Secretary and advocating increases in the budget in other decision venues.

The process that was put in place by Secretary Shalala was built around her acknowledgment that the department is a highly decentralized and diverse organization. She comfortably served as an advocate for the program units, supporting their agendas, and relied on personal relationships and policy discussion to transmit her own perspective. Thus the BRB's approach changed over the eight years, moving away from a centralized control strategy to one in which the Office of the Secretary acknowledged the need for autonomy and discretion within the program units.

At the same time, however, the BRB meetings were organized to help program units construct their budgets in an effective manner, emphasizing themes or specific initiatives highlighted by the Secretary. The staff work for the meetings was done by the Budget Office within the Office of the

Case Study: Budget Review Board

Organizations Involved	**Office of the Secretary:** Assistant Secretary for Management and Budget Office of the Assistant Secretary for Planning and Evaluation Office of Public Health and Science **Agencies:** All
Problem/Issue	Modifying centralized budgeting to be more collegial
Lead Organization	Assistant Secretary for Management and Budget
Time Dimension	Once a year
Accomplishments	Created collegial process Established forum for balancing competing values
Role of the Office of the Secretary	Defined parameters and framework for discussion

Assistant Secretary for Management and Budget. The staff in that office is organized to parallel the structure of the department. While ASMB has tried not to be overly directive in its guidance and to give program budget managers some freedom in how they develop their justifications, it found that this may result in inconsistencies in the presentation of information.

The BRB helps define the issues in the budget and through discussion assists the program units in determining what aspects of the request should be emphasized as the budget is presented to the Secretary. The heads of the operating programs are queried about their requests and asked to indicate how those requests mesh with the Secretary's initiatives. Representatives of program units other than the one presenting its budget are encouraged to sit in on these presentations. When specific elements are to be included in the budget documents—such as the annual performance plans required by the Government Performance and Results Act—those elements are also discussed in the presentations. In calendar year 2000, the members of the BRB spent more than 60 hours reviewing the agency budget requests. The discussions that took place during the BRB sessions did not result in a collective recommendation; rather, they involved an exchange of information between participants.

Later in the summer, the budgets were presented to the Secretary and the Deputy Secretary in a setting which included all of the senior staff within the department. All of the agencies had an opportunity to review each other's budgets and to comment on areas that were of shared interest. The program unit heads were expected to sit in on each other's presentation to understand the activities of the department as a whole. When these presentations were concluded, all of these individuals were asked to prepare a budget for the entire department by voting on allocations—an exercise that emphasized the importance of looking at the submission from the perspective of the Secretary. This process gave them some sense of competing values that characterize the programs in the department and allowed them to develop a sensitivity to the overwhelming demands on the budget that will finally emerge from the department. The Secretary imposed a constraint of an overall budget amount and senior staff made their recommendations within this constraint. Not everything that was requested by the program units appeared in the final budget.

The Secretary had four primary sources of inputs to inform her budget decisions: the briefing materials provided by ASMB staff, the program presentations at the Secretary's meetings, the results of the ballot vote, and ASMB recommendations on aggregate budget levels. The final budget represented a melding of the Secretary's priorities and program requests from the agencies. This approach minimized the conflict among programs for resources when they operate with limited resources. While cuts are frequently recommended by OMB, in a number of instances the Secretary was successful in appealing them to the OMB Director or to the President. The unified position within the department contributed to this success. As such, budget conflict rarely occurred within the department and a unified position was submitted to OMB. The transparency of the process minimized the practice of program agencies end-running to OMB. At least in some cases, instead of battling inside the department, the battle was moved to the Executive Office of the President.

This example illustrates several challenges:

- It is not easy to move away from the tradition of central budgeting.
- It is difficult to get beyond the narrow interests of program units.
- It is possible to define a department-wide budget.
- It is possible to make cuts in program unit requests that are understood by top program staff and more or less committed to by them.

Moving to Shared Perspectives and a Common Language: Developing the Performance Plans Required by the Government Performance and Results Act

After the passage of the Government Performance and Results Act 1993, the HHS response to the requirements of the legislation was found within the separate program units within the department. This strategy

Case Study: Government Performance and Results Act

Organizations Involved	**Office of the Secretary:** Assistant Secretary for Management and Budget **Agencies:** All
Problem/Issue	Responding to requirements of Government Performance and Results Act
Lead Organization	Assistant Secretary for Management and Budget
Time Dimension	Long term
Accomplishments	Developed common language, shared perspective
Role of the Office of the Secretary	Developed analytic reports that highlight shared programs and crosscutting goals Played facilitating role

acknowledged the size and decentralized nature of the department. While charged with the implementation of approximately 300 programs, the size and disparate functions of these programs lent themselves to a decentralized approach to program management and performance measurement.

Although the specific requirements of the legislation did not go into effect until 1997, several of the HHS program agencies decided to devise pilot projects (a possibility included in the law) that might serve as demonstrations or examples for others. However, there was limited attention to these pilot efforts within other parts of the department since the two major requirements of the legislation—a five-year strategic plan and annual performance plans—were not immediate demands.

In 1996, work began seriously on the HHS strategic plan, led by the Office of the Assistant Secretary for Planning and Evaluation (ASPE). Although a staff level work group had been formed in early 1994 to develop a department-wide plan and provide technical assistance to the program units as they developed their own plans, these efforts were disrupted by the health care reform initiative and reinvention activities. The guidelines that had been established for that staff-level work group called for a two-part plan—a department-wide part with broad, crosscutting goals and objectives and agency-specific plans to supplement the crosscutting goals.

In the fall of 1996, concerns were expressed about the strategic plan that was emerging through this process. Its critics argued that the plan lacked vision and a strategic focus. The two-level approach was thought to create multiple layers and a large number of goals, objectives, and strategies that were uncoordinated, duplicative, and did not flow from one another. It was described as the product of a staff-level process, resulting in goals, objectives, and strategies that satisfy major program and constituent interests but fail to articulate a vision or priorities. As a result of these criticisms, the Secretary and Deputy Secretary decided that a document would be written by a few top staffers in ASPE and circulated within the department before it became final. Thus a bottom-up approach was replaced by a document developed in a top-down fashion.

While this document did present a picture of a unified department, held together by six overarching goals, the strategic plan did not easily fit into the fragmented decision-making structure that is a part of the HHS reality. Both appropriation and authorizing committees in the Congress focus on specific program areas, not on broad goals. Even the staff of OMB scrutinizes only specific elements of the department's programs since a number of separate budget examiners have responsibility for specific program areas. And the approach did not seem consistent with the management approach taken by the Secretary and Deputy Secretary.

In part in reaction to the more centralized ASPE process, the Office of the Assistant Secretary for Management and Budget—the unit within the Office of the Secretary that was given responsibility for the development of the annual performance plans required by GPRA—developed a strategy that emphasized the unique nature of the individual HHS program components. Because the performance plans were attached to the budget submissions, their development was clearly a bottom-up process.

During the first several years of the process, the role of ASMB was that of a gentle facilitator, attempting to provide opportunities for representatives of program units to raise questions and discuss their experiences. The annual performance plans that were devised were very different from one another. While most of the program units made some reference to the themes established by the strategic plan, their performance plans—as their budgets—emphasized quite diverse goals and objectives.

While the deliberations within the congressional appropriations process did not indicate that members of Congress were focused on the problems that stemmed from the diversity of these documents, there was strong criticism of the HHS submissions by the General Accounting Office and by the Republican leadership in the Congress. The model of decision-making that was employed by these critics assumed that HHS was managed as a centralized, command-and-control department. While this model was not realistic for a department the size and scope of HHS (nor did it comport with the Secretary's personal approach), there was a danger that the criticism of the GPRA submissions could cause problems for the department.

Thus the staff of ASMB was faced with a dilemma: how could it respect the diversity and autonomy of the program units and, at the same time, find ways to address the critics who sought a unified, single document? In addition, there clearly was a range of GPRA-related competencies within the department, and it would be useful for program unit staff to find ways to learn from one another.

The strategy that was employed within ASMB contained several aspects. The ASMB staff developed a performance plan summary document that did provide a more unified picture of the department. It focused on the linkage between program unit goals and objectives and departmental initiatives and the HHS strategic plan. It highlighted crosscutting areas, drawing on the individual performance plans to illustrate shared areas. It set out the HHS approach to performance measurement and the close relationship between the department's budget development process and the GPRA performance plans.

In addition, the ASMB staff held a series of conference calls that provided an opportunity for program unit staff to discuss issues, share experiences, and develop a collegial (almost collective) approach to the task. These calls (and some face-to-face meetings) were constructed to provide methods of active rather than passive involvement in the process.

Finally, the ASMB staff worked closely with a subgroup of the GPRA program unit staff to develop a standardized format which all program components agreed to use for their FY 2001 performance plans and their FY 1999 performance reports. This format established a consistent "order of presentation" of information required by the law and OMB for performance plans and reports. While the program units followed the standardized format to make certain that they met all of the requirements of the law, significant flexibility remained to ensure that the units were able to tailor their performance plans and reports to meet their individual needs. Some components chose to present certain types of performance information at the agency level; others chose to present information at the program or goal level. For the reader who was required to assess all of the HHS performance plans, this shared format painted a picture of some level of consistency across the program units and did make the job of reading the documents somewhat easier.

There are several challenges that are illustrated by this example:

- Analytic efforts seem to provoke a tendency for the Office of the Secretary to fall back on past centralized practices.
- It is possible to move to a sense of the department as a whole through facilitating rather than controlling strategy.
- Public attention and legislative requirements can evoke a set of external pressures to develop a department-wide perspective.
- It is important to find ways to respect the individual cultures and approaches of program units.

Conclusions and Recommendations

The examples that have been presented indicate that a department as large and diverse as HHS is able to craft a role for the Office of the Secretary without relying on traditional modes and approaches to make its views known. This experience should be useful to other cabinet Secretaries. While the experience of HHS does have some unique aspects, the lessons that can be drawn from these examples reach beyond this single federal department.

Indeed, the examples seem to fit with the fragmented nature of the external decision-making institutions in the U.S. government to which federal agencies are accountable, especially the structure and processes found within the Congress. Cabinet officials can expect to be required to respond to emergent problems and issues that are not a part of their own agendas. These items emerge from both internal and external demands.

While the Office of the Secretary may no longer emphasize a command-and-control role within a department, it does have other roles that are extremely useful to a cabinet Secretary. The units within the Office of the Secretary have the ability to move program units to seek longer-term solutions than those that may emerge from a crisis or immediate set of demands. They have the ability to broaden an issue beyond a narrow solution. The units in the Office of the Secretary can serve as a facilitator, encourage a bottom-up process within the department, and can help technical staff translate their concerns to be able to communicate to less specialized staff.

The units within the Office of the Secretary have the ability to help program unit staff move beyond their specialized and specific concerns and escape from what are called their "stovepipe" perspectives. In addition, these units can devise patterns of participation that draw on staff who move beyond narrow representational roles.

There are a number of characteristics of these examples that should be emphasized:

- Traditional management techniques take on a different meaning when they are used in a decentralized agency. This is especially illustrated by the activities undertaken by the Management Issues Lunches.
- The Office of the Secretary is able to respond to crises or perceived crises in ways that are effective. Both the human subjects example and the Y2K experience indicate that involvement of the Office of the Secretary allows the department to look beyond the crisis and to define approaches that provide longer-term change. The Deputy Secretary can play an important role in this regard.
- Office of the Secretary involvement provides a vehicle to broaden an issue and move it beyond a narrow constituency. This is particularly important in programs that involve partnerships with others (e.g., state and local governments, tribes, nonprofit organizations). This

dynamic was found in the racial disparities example as well as the human subjects case.

- The Office of the Secretary can play an effective role as a facilitator. It can create venues that provide a setting for collegial exchange of views and a low-key way to develop collaborative strategies. This was found in the Management Issues Lunches, GPRA, and the Data Council. This is not a traditional role for the Office of the Secretary, but it can act to facilitate the active involvement of program units.
- The Office of the Secretary can be an effective participant in efforts that are clearly bottom-up. This is illustrated by the Budget Review Board activities as well as the GPRA effort. Designing settings that allow program officials to share information in a non-threatening role can avoid a narrow compliance attitude.
- The Office of the Secretary may be able to create modes of interaction between technical/specialist staff and generalist managers. This was found in the Data Council activity.
- Budget processes can serve as the centerpiece for many of these efforts. The budget process can be structured in a way that avoids turning program units into supplicants. The BRB example indicates how those units can be empowered during the budget process.

The crafting of a particular crosscutting approach depends on several variables, which can lead to a range of approaches. These include a broad problem-solving approach; an ad-hoc, time-limited effort; an approach that is specifically designed to avoid traditional hierarchical bureaucratic behavior; and an approach that is developed around existing decision processes. Thus a cabinet Secretary might examine:

- *The clarity of the external mandate that provokes the activity.* Specific directives from the White House or the Congress create a sense of immediacy, and these mandates are easily communicated to the participants in a time-limited fashion. While the Office of the Secretary may move the immediate demand to seek longer-term solutions or broaden the issues, it is required to first deal with the mandate.
- *The breadth of the required participants.* If an effort involves only a few program units, then it can be targeted at those units. If, however, it involves a wide range of program and staff offices, then it takes on a less direct strategy. In these cases, the Office of the Secretary may decide to play a facilitating role.
- *The time frame involved.* Some efforts stimulated by the Office of the Secretary involve short time frames. Often these efforts are quite ad hoc in nature and do not move into institutionalized processes. Others, however, may begin with short time demands but are turned into longer term agendas.

It is possible to devise ways for the Office of the Secretary to become involved in the department's decision process without resorting to command-and-control approaches. Care must be taken in the way that program units are treated; they must be respected, not tolerated. The examples of cross-cutting and coordinating mechanisms that have been presented suggest that these new approaches to management within the Office of the Secretary must be applied with modest expectations. Not all areas are appropriate for an active Office of the Secretary role, and it is important to work hard to avoid preempting the program units. At the same time, these approaches do provide a way for a diverse agency to develop a corporate identity in which the whole is greater than the sum of the parts.

Appendix:
Leading the Department of Health and Human Services: A Conversation with Secretary Donna Shalala and Deputy Secretary Kevin Thurm

During the fall of 1999, The PricewaterhouseCoopers Endowment for The Business of Government hosted a seminar with Department of Health and Human Services (HHS) Secretary Donna Shalala and Deputy Secretary Kevin Thurm. Endowment Executive Director Mark Abramson and Professor Radin moderated the discussion with Secretary Shalala and Deputy Secretary Thurm. Excerpts from the discussion are presented below.

Secretary Shalala, it's now been almost seven years since you assumed the position of the Secretary of HHS. As you reflect back on the beginning of your term, what were your initial reactions to the department?
Secretary Shalala: Let me start with my experience with the presidential transition. We all received transition books. I quickly concluded that the transition team didn't have a clue about managing large institutions. In fact, they recommended the exact opposite of the management structure we developed. The transition team recommended that I institute two new undersecretaries, one to manage the health part and one to manage the welfare part, and thus install two new heavy bureaucracies to get control of the department. Of course, we chose to do just the opposite.

So that was my initial introduction to the department. I knew a little bit about the department because I had actually headed the transition when they pulled education out of the department during the Carter administration. I knew how cabinet agencies were organized because not only had I been a student of government, but I had been at the Department of Housing and Urban Development when Secretary Pat Harris first came in and I had seen that transition. So I knew some things.

I also knew what President Clinton's priorities were. My expectations were that we were going to try to do some very big things very fast and it was extremely important that I totally focus on recruiting the best team of people that I could bring in. I also worked to produce a list of short-term things that we could do to demonstrate our ability to actually produce real outcomes in the department, as well as some long-term initiatives which the President wanted to do, including welfare reform and health care reform.

So my initial reaction was that I had these transition books that made absolutely no sense because they wanted me to add bureaucracy, to add political control, to centralize, and it was just the opposite of what I wanted to do.

One of the things that you need in a department is an effective deputy secretary. Deputy Secretary Thurm, can you describe your job?
Deputy Secretary Thurm: In doing the job that I have now, I had the great advantage of having served as the chief of staff of the department. First, the deputy secretary must be in line with what the secretary wants in that role. While there are some standard things that deputy secretaries do, it becomes pretty clear that the position is to fill the role the secretary wants. The two of you must be able to communicate effectively with each other about what that role is.

Second, as I think is the case in most departments, the deputy secretary is the chief operating officer and is essentially in charge of day-to-day decision-making on management issues. The job is also to work closely on policy issues that require the secretary's attention, to guide these issues through the department and to work closely with the chief of staff and executive secretary on these issues. My colleagues and I decide when these policy issues need to come to the secretary's attention.

Third, based on the priorities that have been identified by the President, Vice President, and the secretary, the deputy secretary has to make sure that those priorities are focused on and develop processes for making sure that progress happens. I also run quarterly meetings on the secretary's initiatives that cross-cut the department.

Finally, I want to stress that continuity matters and Secretary Shalala's staying power has mattered a lot in the effective management of the department. The Secretary has recruited excellent people and insisted that we work together and that there would be consequences for people who didn't play by the rules. This is really important, and I think that my colleagues within the department have really stepped up to the tone set by the Secretary's leadership.

One of the themes and one of the major findings in the Radin report is that the department has really avoided or at least minimized traditional bureaucratic and management processes and structures. What was the reaction of longtime HHS career people to the kind of approach that you put in place?
Secretary Shalala: Well, we made some strategic moves at the beginning that were very important. The White House asked me how many political appointees we wanted to keep as we were going through the transition, and I said basically none except for two individuals. We kept David Kessler at the Food and Drug Administration and we asked Bernadine Healy to stay through the transition at the National Institutes of Health.

But everybody else was going to go. That meant that for a relatively short period of time, we had to lead the department with the senior civil servants, pulling them in to both the way in which we wanted to manage the department and making them know that we thought that their contributions were valuable. We worked hard to make them feel comfortable. It meant that I personally got to know senior civil servants who were three to four levels down in the department. We sent them very clear messages about their value and that we weren't going to separate the political appointees from the senior civil servants in the department.

Our members of the Senior Executive Service knew that I taught in the field and that I had considerable respect for the federal service because I had been Scotty Campbell's student (Scotty was the first director of the Office of Personnel Management in the Carter Administration). That helped initially, but it was really when we pulled them in after the political appointees arrived that made the difference. I was not insecure about very large meetings. We never had a meeting just with political appointees. In fact, during the summer we encouraged people to bring their interns to our decision-making meetings because large meetings mean that everybody has a chance to participate and to interact.

Can you describe the relationship between the Secretary and the Inspector General (IG)? In many departments, they do not get along, but in HHS the two of you appear to have developed a very productive working relationship.
Secretary Shalala: When I was an Assistant Secretary at the Department of Housing and Urban Development (HUD) and absolutely new to the government, I had a very good experience with the Inspector General. Chuck Dempsy, one of the legendary Inspectors Generals in government at HUD, took me under his wing. The first thing I did when I got the job as Secretary of HHS was to call Chuck and tell him that I had a vacancy in the IG position and I needed the best person in the country. He said, "Well, the best person is out in Hawaii and I don't think you can get her, but you can try." This was how Chuck recommended June Gibbs Brown to me. I called June up and she said, "I'm not sure I want to move, but I've heard good things about you, so why don't I come out and talk to you."

The White House, as you would expect as part of the personnel process, had some ideas about IGs. The department was not only complex, it was a dangerous place from my point of view, with huge issues about fraud and waste in the system. I wanted a pro and the best person I could possibly recruit.

I could offer the HHS Inspector General two things. First, I told June that I wanted an IG that would keep her independence and that I would respect that independence. I actually had once read the act establishing the Inspector General. I was aware of the relationship between the IG and the Congress and the kind of independence needed. But I also wanted someone who would help me to anticipate problems in the department and who would see herself and her senior team as members of the senior manage-

---

Donna Shalala on Managing in a Large University

I think you should know that I come from a nonhierarchical management experience because I come from higher education. I think it is important to know that even within this highly decentralized organization that is very carefully and accurately described as the Department of Health and Human Services, I personally have far more control than I ever had in a major research university. In my mind, HHS is really command-and-control management compared to the kind of power that I had as chancellor of a great research university where power was shared with deans, the alumnae, the football coach, and students. That is really nonhierarchical.

---

ment team of the department. I told June that we would work hard to find that balance.

The second thing I promised was real resources. I was convinced that unless we were prepared to do a full-court press, we would not get what we have now achieved, and that is an actual change in the behavior of the health care industry. And I had some ideas about how to get some serious resources for the IG.

To show you how much confidence I had in the IG, when I did finally recruit June I turned the entire security force that protected me over to her office. I feel that I was able to recruit the person I consider the best Inspector General in or out of government — a real professional. She has coached me as part of the process, and I think we both have kept our word.

She has helped us. It all depends on the way you think about the IG office. As we are developing new polices, I will frequently ask June to help us anticipate what kind of protections we need to build into new legislation. So I try to get June to work on the front end with us. I don't interfere in the decisions she has to make or in the reports she has to make to Congress, but we do give each other a heads up and she helps me to manage the department.

In following a decentralization strategy, the question comes up as to why you need the department. Could you both describe whether there is an overriding corporate culture at HHS and how you would define the whole of HHS? Is it more than the sum of its parts?
Secretary Shalala: I would argue that it is more than the sum of the parts and that you have to understand the multiple cultures in the department to be able to manage it. The National Institutes of Health (NIH) have a very different tradition from the Health Care Financing Administration. It's not

much different from managing a very large research university in which the law school people are very different from the medical school people, who are different from the liberal arts people. But no one would suggest that there is not a clear identity for the university itself.

None of the parts of the department would get very far without being part of a larger whole. In fact, I have argued from the beginning that it was a mistake to spin off the Social Security Administration. I think it gets buried without being at a cabinet level and having an advocate at the cabinet table.

Every single part of the department is more powerful because of their ability to work with another agency or with multiple agencies in the department. In general, being part of a larger cabinet-level department gets them to the cabinet table, to a congressional committee chairman, in a way that would not happen if they weren't part of a larger whole. So I think it actually elevates some of their critical issues and gives them more power as part of a larger whole.

I am not uncomfortable with the fact that people identify with the agency they are in. But the way this town works, they are better off in a powerful cabinet department if they really want to move issues or get out of trouble in some cases or get a decision at a high enough level.

The secretary has to be very secure to have very powerful agencies under her. But we also have processes to rein them in, when necessary, to reduce the amount of traditional end running to the Hill, and to have appropriate kinds of discipline. From the public's perspective, they don't know one agency from the other. They need services that often require more than one agency working together. So we think about it both at the level of the individual citizen, as well as at the level of power needed to operate in Washington.

Deputy Secretary Thurm: I think I would add one further reflection, which is that there are both agency cultures, such as the NIH culture, but there also are institute cultures. The National Cancer Institute views itself as different from the National Institute on Drug Abuse and so on. People identify essentially with the level closest to them. You ask people where they work, and it's going to be an institute at NIH or a center at one of our other agencies.

Secretary Shalala: For agencies in our departments, you have to convince them that you are value added if you're from the Office of the Secretary. They have to see you as being able to deliver something that they can't deliver on their own. They've got to see this group bringing together something that they can't get on their own. I think that is extremely important.

Deputy Secretary Thurm: It all depends on where you are sitting, because people in the agencies are always wondering about the Office of the Director, what value is added there. Everybody is always looking up. What's the value added by the Office of the Secretary? What's the value added by the

Donna Shalala on the Government Shutdown

During the government shutdown in 1995, we paid a lot of attention to the morale of our personnel. We communicated with them. I remember that somebody said to me that we don't have anything specific to tell our employees at that moment. I said that doesn't make any difference. I told my staff to just send out a piece of paper from the Secretary that says we care about them.

When our employees were at home during the shutdown, we suggested that our supervisors call their employees at home just to check in with them and to see whether they were all right. Then we made a move that turned out to be symbolic to our whole administration. It was just before Christmas and you might remember that we had only half our payroll money, so it looked like we could give our people only a very small check. We figured out, however, that we didn't have to take all of the deductions out of their check; that meant that every HHS employee got almost a full check before Christmas. They didn't anticipate that. There were stories on television that people in other departments were getting $7 checks before Christmas. We tried to take care of our people. That made all the difference in the world in terms of morale and the kind of signal that we wanted to send our employees.

people down the street at the White House or the Old Executive Office Building? What do they know about what we do? It depends on where you are sitting in the relationship.

We've talked about the deputy secretary position and we've talked about the Inspector General. There is one other key job — the chief of staff. Can each of you comment on the role of the chief of staff and the role of your own chief of staff?

Secretary Shalala: Well, first of all, I hadn't a clue because we had not had any chiefs of staff when I was in government during the Carter administration. We had had executive assistants in those days. So I didn't have a clue. Kevin is the only person who can answer that question, because he is the person who had to work through both the roles of the deputy secretary and the chief of staff.

Deputy Secretary Thurm: First, I benefited during the transition from a briefing that my predecessor gave. She was upfront about the way the department worked and the processes that they had used. She started me thinking about the kinds of issues that we would need to think about. It was very helpful to me. There is no position description you can pull off the shelf for chief of staff.

Second, we asked the Secretary what she wanted. We walked in with few people at the beginning. We tried to do everything we needed to do and do it quickly and identify key priorities. We worked out the role of the chief of staff in those early days. The relationship between the chief of staff and the deputy secretary is crucial to getting people to manage below the level of the secretary, consistent with the secretary's priorities. It is an important relationship to work on and to be clear about.

Our chief of staff — the way we defined it early on — was essentially focused on providing immediate services to the secretary, such as scheduling for the secretary. Scheduling is very important because where the secretary spends her time reflects the issues that she would like to identify with. Other functions include staffing issues, preparing briefings, and providing decision-making support to the secretary.

The chief of staff is also the liaison to other federal departments and agencies on behalf of the department and to the White House, which is a crucial role. The office oversees the political appointment process so that we could ensure that we do this as quickly as possible and consistent with the Secretary's wishes and identify people and move them through.

Working with the deputy secretary, the chief of staff identifies the issues that go to the secretary to resolve conflicts within the department. If we are unable to resolve them, we work to sharpen the conflicts to make them clearer for the secretary to decide. There is also a scanning function that is done with the executive secretary: identifying issues that need to be brought to the secretarys' attention and creating processes to resolve them so that you are not reading about them in the next day's paper.

Endnotes

1. David Osborne and Ted Gaebler, *Reinventing Government: How the Entrepreneurial Spirit is Transforming the Public Sector* (Reading, MA: Addison-Wesley Publishing Company, 1992).

2. See Part I of this chapter.

Bibliography

Miles, Rufus E., Jr., 1974, *The Department of H.E.W.* (New York: Praeger Publishers).

Radin, Beryl A., 1992, "Policy Analysis in the Office of the Assistant Secretary for Planning and Evaluation," HHS/HEW, in Carol H. Weiss, editor, *Institutions for Policy Analysis* (Newbury Park, CA: Sage).

Shalala, Donna E., 1998, "Are Large Public Organizations Manageable?," *Public Administration Review*, July/August, Vol. 58. No. 4.

United States General Accounting Office, February 1990, *Management of HHS: Using the Office of the Secretary to Enhance Departmental Effectiveness.* (GAO HRD-90-51, Washington, D.C.: GAO).

CHAPTER FIVE

Leadership for Change:
Case Studies in
American Local Government

Robert B. Denhardt
Professor
School of Public Affairs
Arizona State University

Janet Vinzant Denhardt
Professor
School of Public Affairs
Arizona State University

This report was originally published in September 1999.

Introduction

In his book *The Pursuit of Significance*, Robert B. Denhardt profiled a number of important public sector leaders who have been involved in transforming their communities or agencies into streamlined, high-performance organizations.[1] Based on a series of interviews in Australia, Canada, Great Britain, and the United States, he identified five characteristics associated with the work of these "revolutionary" public managers—a commitment to values, service to the public, empowerment and shared leadership, "pragmatic incrementalism," and a dedication to public service. Several questions raised in response to this research suggest areas for further investigation.

First, while *The Pursuit of Significance* explored the values that these managers held to be important, questions have been raised about the methods that they employed in changing their communities and organizations. Specifically, some have asked whether there is a model for successful organizational transformation that can be identified and followed by public managers hoping to lead change in their organizations. Or, at a minimum, is there a specific set of activities that public managers should undertake that will allow them to approach the question of organizational change in a systematic and comprehensive fashion?

Second, some have suggested that leadership is dependent on the "fit" between the leader and a specific set of circumstances at a particular time. This raises the question of whether individuals successful in one place through employing a particular set of values and methodologies could successfully manage organizational transformations in other settings using a similar approach. In other words, do the characteristics identified in *The Pursuit of Significance* reside with individuals, or are they only found where there is a fortuitous mix of leadership, followership, values, culture, and other circumstances? Or, to put the issue more practically, what adjustments do managers need to make to adapt their change efforts to new settings? Moreover, is there a model or set of guidelines that might instruct the change process?

Our purpose in this research is to test these ideas through a detailed analysis of the work of three local government executives known for their success in guiding widespread and highly successful organizational changes in their communities. Specifically, in this research we will develop case studies of the recent work of three public managers previously profiled in *The Pursuit of Significance*. Through these case studies of public managers who have successfully led change in more than one community, we can ask whether the strategies they employed previously are "transportable" and to what extent alterations need to be made based on the specific circumstances faced by those who are leading change in public organizations.

Among those managers included in *The Pursuit of Significance* was Robert O'Neill, then city manager of Hampton, Virginia. O'Neill is now county executive of Fairfax County, Virginia, and is trying once again to make major improvements in the quality and productivity of his community. Another city manager profiled earlier was Phil Penland, formerly of Deland, Florida, and now city manager of Altamonte Springs, Florida. Penland is another who has sought significant improvements in quality and productivity in both communities where he has served. A third city manager, Jan Perkins, previously city manager of Morgan Hill, California, and now city manager of Fremont, California, is once again engaged in a dramatic transformation of her city government.

In this report, we will examine the question of leadership for change in American local government from three perspectives. First, we will profile the change activities of each of these three city/county managers as they have sought to transfer a set of values and a methodology for leading change into a new setting. Specifically, based on several days of interviews in each community, interviews that involved the city or county manager and eight to 10 other managers, elected officials, or employees well positioned to observe the manager's change activities, we will present case studies of the way in which each of these managers has sought to lead change.

Second, cutting across the three specific cases, we will examine the process of leadership for change. We will present lessons that we think can be drawn from the experiences of these managers (and their direct commentaries on leadership in local government), lessons that hopefully will suggest a methodology for leading change in American local governments. We hope that this set of guidelines, based in practice, might instruct other managers as to how to move carefully and systematically through the change process and how to adapt general models of organizational transformation to the specific circumstances in which they find themselves.

Third, we will examine several key lessons that emerged in the course of our study. What are the most important lessons that grow from their experience? How might these lessons be employed by other managers seeking to enhance the quality and productivity of their organizations? And what kinds of personal and professional commitments will be required to lead change in a positive direction?

The Case Studies

The communities we visited were quite different in geography, demography, and political culture. The managers we interviewed had different tenures, used different approaches, and focused on different issues. Yet each of the three had been successful in leading change. In this section, we will present a brief overview of the three cases, hoping to provide the background necessary to understanding the more general processes of leadership. In the next two sections, we will focus on the ways in which these different managers went about the change process, looking first at a model of leadership for change, then examining the lessons that other managers might draw from the work of these managers.

Robert O'Neill, Fairfax County, Virginia

Robert O'Neill was widely heralded for his innovative approach to leading change at the local level while he was city manager of Hampton, Virginia, through the 1980s and early 1990s. In 1997, O'Neill was hired as county executive of Fairfax County, Virginia, a county of nearly a million people in the Washington, DC area. O'Neill arrived in Fairfax at a difficult time. The county had just been through a fiscal crisis. The culture of the organization was one that seemed content with operating on a day-to-day basis, largely reacting to the board of supervisors. (Fairfax County is governed by an elected Board of Supervisors consisting of nine members elected by district, plus a chairman elected at large.) Moreover, the county government was organized in a fairly traditional top-down structure, with communications across departmental boundaries being relatively rare.

In the eyes of his employees, O'Neill had several strikes against him, resulting in a healthy skepticism about his tenure. First, he was seen by many employees as coming from a fairly small jurisdiction compared to Fairfax County (Hampton has a population of about 140,000). Second, bolstered by newspaper accounts that O'Neill was coming to "cut out waste," employees feared layoffs by a potential "hatchet man." Third, O'Neill immediately faced several difficult issues that had been before the board for some time before his arrival (for example, the elimination of compensatory time for senior managers and the possible reorganization of several units in county government). Taking on these issues early in his tenure did not necessarily endear O'Neill to county employees.

On the positive side, however, O'Neill immediately started meeting with employee groups, engaging in a variety of conversations, meetings, and brown bag luncheons in all areas of the county. His message in these meetings was contained both in his words and in his actions: he wanted to open communications with employees, he wanted to listen to what they had to say, and he expected to involve them in major decisions facing the county. Similarly, he began a seemingly endless series of meetings with people in the community, including business groups (such as the Chamber of Commerce), civic organizations, and neighborhood associations. In fact, those close to O'Neill marveled at his capacity to be in meetings from early in the morning until late at night throughout the week. Finally, O'Neill undertook a fairly systematic effort to establish close working relationships

About Robert O'Neill

 Robert O'Neill was appointed county executive of Fairfax County, Virginia, in August 1997. In January 2000, he was selected as president of the National Academy of Public Administration. Mr. O'Neill served as city manager of Hampton, Virginia, from 1984 to 1997. He also served as assistant manager for administrative services for Hampton, Virginia. From 1981 to 1984, Mr. O'Neill was director of management consulting services, Coopers & Lybrand.

In addition to serving as its president, Mr. O'Neill is a fellow of the National Academy of Public Administration. In 1996, he received the National Public Service Award presented by the American Society for Public Administration and the National Academy. He has served as president of the Virginia Local Government Management Association and vice president for the Southeast Region of the International City/County Management Association.

He received a master's degree in public administration from the Maxwell School of Citizenship and Public Affairs, Syracuse University, in 1974 and a B.A. degree from Old Dominion University in 1973.

and even personal relationships with the 10 members of the Board of Supervisors. Among other things, he established regular meetings with each of the members of the board and also began a practice of calling each member on Sunday evening prior to each Monday board meeting. (A staff member noted that, in order to make this work, you have to learn such things as which members watch the *The X-Files* and which go to bed early!) In any case, members soon learned that O'Neill was someone with whom they could discuss issues and someone who wanted much the same things for the community that they did.

Among the early moves O'Neill made, several were particularly striking in terms of the process of leading change. First, there were several opportunities that presented themselves in which major personnel changes occurred. While O'Neill didn't seek major changes in his executive management team, a large number of department heads (nearly half) resigned within the year following O'Neill's appointment. There is no evidence that anyone was directly fired, but rather that a generation of department heads hired many years ago simply reached retirement age together and found this a convenient time to leave the county. Whatever the reasons for the retirements, O'Neill was presented with the opportunity to hire a number of new people in key positions. (We should note, however, that these appointments were not people "handpicked" by O'Neill. Rather they emerged through a highly participatory process involving many members of the management team, members of the board, and occasionally representatives of the community at large.) In many cases, however, rather than replacing those who retired, O'Neill used the retirements to restructure the organization, particularly where he felt that the previous organization reflected the strengths and weaknesses of a particular individual rather than the most efficient way of doing business. (In addition to the reorganizations, there are also now fewer deputy county executives, so that department heads have more direct access to O'Neill rather than going through a deputy in charge of several areas.)

Second, O'Neill began placing a greater emphasis on community involvement, using his own involvement in the community as a model. While some Fairfax agencies, like planning and human services, were in the community every day, O'Neill felt that more intense and widespread community involvement was appropriate. So throughout his tenure, he has placed a high priority on personally reaching out to the community, including the development community, professional groups, and civic organizations. In his meetings with these groups, O'Neill tries to open lines of communication and, according to a staff member, doesn't speak to audiences but rather encourages significant dialogue. He listens very carefully to what people say and, as that staff member reported, typically comes back with a long list of items for follow-up. O'Neill has also encouraged departments throughout the county government to play a more involved role in the community, but what has been key so far is the personal model he has established himself.

Third, O'Neill's major effort at internal organizational change has been the establishment of a series of task forces to look into key issues in the organization: Development of a Vision Profile, Compensation and Gainsharing, Piloting the Competition Model, Department Head Evaluation System, Employee Involvement, Flexibility in Personnel Classification, Employee Communication, and Leadership Development. Designed by O'Neill but given board approval in the FY1999 budget, each of these task forces consists of between 20 and 40 county employees selected "diagonally" from across the organization. That is, each group includes people from across the various departments and from the top to the bottom of the organization, though each is chaired by a member of the county executive's staff.

Where it seemed appropriate, a skilled facilitator was brought in to help the groups work through their tasks, but, in all cases, O'Neill encouraged (indeed almost required) a broad effort to communicate fully with county employees on the work that was being done. For example, the task force on compensation identified a set of problems, then took these problems to focus groups of employees just to ask, "Are these in fact the right problems for us to be working on?" More recently, that same group has been making a series of presentations to employees on its key proposals. The various task forces are expected to conclude their work and bring forward a series of proposals over the coming several months.

While it remains to be seen what the task forces will produce in terms of specific substantive recommendations, what is most interesting from our standpoint is the message that is implied in the process O'Neill designed. Not only was O'Neill seeking solutions to some important organizational problems, but he was communicating to those in the organization that they would be expected to go about their work in a different way. The message to employees was that everyone should communicate with one another across departmental boundaries and up and down throughout the organization. Through the task forces, O'Neill was modeling a set of behaviors that he thought would be important to the organization, and he was doing so in a non-threatening way. O'Neill put it this way: "If we can keep the strength of the specialties we've developed, but also develop flexibility, responsiveness, and adaptability—if we can build an organization that has both those sets of strengths, then that's what we want to do."

Bob O'Neill's tenure in Fairfax County provides great insight into one way that a local government manager can bring about substantial change. In this case, the goal has simultaneously been to address some important organizational issues and to model a new way of doing business in the county. The goal is to address some important concerns, but also to establish a new culture, one in which openness and involvement and widespread communication are the norm, not the exception. A month or two into the work of the task forces, during a particularly engaging discussion, a county employee leaned over to O'Neill in a meeting and said: "This is what you did this for, isn't it?"

Phil Penland, Altamonte Springs, Florida

Altamonte Springs is a predominately middle class suburban community in the Orlando metropolitan area. Known as a center for retail shopping (especially at the Altamonte Mall), the city has an especially high level of commercial development, and, despite a generally middle class population, it has an especially large number of multi-family dwellings. Phil Penland has been city manager of Altamonte Springs for approximately 16 years, having previously served as city manager in nearby Deland. Over the course of his tenure in Altamonte Springs, Penland and the city have developed a reputation for innovation and excellence that is the envy of other local governments in the area. Indeed, the *Orlando Sentinel* recently referred to Altamonte Springs as the "premier" city government in the area. Phil Penland's role in creating a solid governmental foundation and then encouraging an extraordinary degree of creativity and innovation is undeniable.

About Phillip D. Penland

Phillip Penland has been the city manager of Altamonte Springs, Florida, since May 1983.

He began his career in public service in 1974 as the assistant city manager of Deland, Florida, and in 1975 was promoted to city manager.

Mr. Penland holds a bachelor's degree in political science from the University of Central Florida. He was instrumental in creating the Local Government Leaders in Public Policy Forum program at the Harvard University John F. Kennedy School of Government.

In 1988, he was recognized as the Public Servant of the Year by the Greater Seminole County Chamber of Commerce.

Descriptions of Phil Penland's work in Altamonte Springs tend to center on two or three especially important or signal efforts that helped set a tone or establish the culture of change and innovation that dominates the city of Altamonte Springs today. Early in his tenure Penland became convinced of the need for Altamonte Springs to develop a core identity or a more clearly defined "downtown," as opposed to its image as centering around the Altamonte Mall, a large enclosed shopping center. Working with the city commission and with business and civic leaders, Penland was able to create a Community Redevelopment Agency that employed tax increment funding to create a bright and sparkling downtown. The area that became the center of Altamonte Springs actually began with an overgrown drainage basin. Over time the basin became a lake, surrounded by walkways and innovative decor, and boasting shops, restaurants, and an increasing number of office complexes. With the new "downtown," Altamonte Springs began to take on an identity and cohesiveness that had been lacking in the community prior to that time.

Penland's work on this project and others early in his tenure was important not only for its impact on the community, but also because it deeply affected his own relationship with the city commission and the community. Having moved to the council-manager form of government a couple of years before Penland arrived, Altamonte Springs was in the throes of significant change. Penland saw the time as an opportunity to make things happen. The demographics of the community were changing, the form of government was changing, so change might be possible in other areas as well. With the support of the Orlando newspaper, whose editors were firm believers in the council-manager form of government, Penland and Altamonte Springs began receiving recognition for the important work they were doing and for an increased quality in the level of governmental services. In turn, the city commission began to develop increasing trust in Penland and his staff, a spirit of trust and confidence that continues at a very high level today.

Internally, Penland and Altamonte Springs were among the very first local governments in Florida or elsewhere to undertake a substantial quality improvement program. With the help of Florida Power and Light, Altamonte Springs began what became the EPIQ program (Excellent People Improving Quality). Basically a quality circles program, though with some variations, the EPIQ program attracted a huge percentage of the city's employees to participate in groups addressing issues ranging from work process improvements to quality of work life concerns. The recommendations these teams have produced vastly improved the quality of the city's work.

What is amazing is that the quality improvement program was not only highly successful in its early days, bringing forth a large number of important ideas that were ultimately implemented, but that the program continues at a high level of activity and involvement many years later. Interviewees largely attribute the program's continuation to two factors: 1) the large number of really good ideas that have come forward, and 2) continued active and vocal support of the program by the city manager. Indeed, the program has been so successful over the years that Penland and Altamonte Springs have resisted the temptation to jump to other fads and have continued along the quality path. Penland himself is seen as an advocate for the program—one staff member even describing his support for the quality program as "rabid." Indeed, as reported by one staff member, Penland regularly challenges his employees: "If you give 110 percent and you are a member of a quality team, your supervisor will notice, your department director will notice, and I will notice. And will that give you a leg up in moving through the organization? Yes, it will—because it will say you are interested in your work team, you are interested in your work, and you are interested in bettering yourself."

What's especially interesting is that the approach to problem solving used in the groups and task forces involved in the quality program have become a part of the normal way of conducting business in the city. Penland remarked: "The teams did such good work, such fantastically good work, that the approach came to be part and parcel of who we are. We are constantly reinventing ourselves. We are constantly entertaining change. We don't have to use the buzzwords. Our teams just find a better way."

The culture of quality that has been created in Altamonte Springs is matched by a strong commitment to "customer service." The city regularly undertakes a citizen survey designed to ask citizens about the quality of services they receive, but also to ask about the overall quality of life in the community and how the community can become a place people really take pride in. As part of the survey process, focus groups of citizens are brought together to discuss their views of city government. As they talk, department heads listen from behind a one-way glass. (The citizens know this.) Additionally, all departments are encouraged to develop systematic means of soliciting citizen information about the quality of services. For example, both fire and police officers keep a record of those with whom they interact, whether in an arrest, an emergency medical call, or just a chance encounter. A customer contact card is sent to a random sample taken from among these people, and their comments about the quality of their interaction with the city are noted. Finally, employees throughout the city are encouraged to know enough about various events in the city, so that anyone a citizen talks with has at least some information about what's going on in the city and how services can be accessed.

Perhaps more important than the individual efforts in quality service mentioned here is the fact that Penland and his top management team seem to have created a "culture" of innovation within the city, a culture that is accepted and indeed applauded by citizens, commissioners, managers, and staff throughout the city. People are encouraged to look for innovative ways to approach their work, they are encouraged to try out new ideas (knowing they will be supported even if their good faith efforts fall short), and they are rewarded for their contributions to improving the quality and productivity of city government.

The culture of innovation, a constant interest in change, and the value of exploring new ideas were mentioned most frequently by respondents when we asked about the hallmarks of the city. But almost as many respondents commented on another pervasive aspect of the organization's culture: a firm commitment to ethics. The city has done many of the formal things recommended to improve the level of ethical behavior in the city (i.e., developing an ethics policy), but perhaps more important, ethical behavior is constantly stressed throughout the organization. Penland talks constantly about ethics and, indeed, no one joins city government without hearing, as part of their new employee orientation, Penland's "lecture" on the importance of ethics. The manager and the top management team are careful to set a good example themselves (Penland insists that he and the top management team be "unfledging models for ethical behavior"), but also to encourage and celebrate attention to the ethical aspects of everything city employees do. "We talk about it a lot," Penland remarks. "If you talk about something a lot, people come to understand that it's important."

Phil Penland's work in Altamonte Springs provides important information with respect to the process of leading change, but is especially important to our research here in that it allows us to see how change and innovation can be institutionalized over a long period of time. Altamonte Springs didn't merely change during the first years that Phil Penland was city manager—though significant changes did occur during that period. The city continues to grow and to change, and indeed the city's interest in change and innovation seems as strong today as ever before, perhaps even stronger. The key message that has become a key to "the Altamonte way" is that change is all around us and if government wants to keep up, we are going to have to find new and better ways of doing things each and every day.

Jan Perkins, Fremont, California

Fremont, California, is a relatively young city, created through joining five unincorporated areas into one jurisdiction about 45 years ago. Yet it is a large and diverse community of nearly 200,000, the fourth largest in the Bay Area. Jan Perkins came to Fremont as assistant city manager in 1992 after serving as city manager of Morgan Hill, California. After about 10 months, the manager she worked with was fired, and she became acting city manager, then city manager.

At that time, Fremont, like many other California cities, was suffering from both economic difficulties and from the state's efforts to pull back the property tax as a source of local government revenue. Yet, while city employees were being laid off and services were being curtailed, citizen demand for quality public services remained high. More important, however, in Perkins's mind, was the fact that citizens had lost confidence in their government. They didn't feel they could trust the government to do the right thing and to do it well. For both these reasons, Perkins and other city officials in Fremont recognized that something dramatically different had to be done. Under these circumstances, change and innovation were not luxuries; they were necessities.

The change process started early in Perkins's tenure, as one of her council members proposed bringing in an outside consultant (for a half million dollars) to diagnose what might be done. Especially since a neighboring city had just done exactly the same thing and failed to adopt a single recommendation, Perkins felt that greater benefits could be obtained by working with those within the city to figure out how the quality and productivity of the city might be improved. A facilitated workshop session, involving top elected and appointed officials, was devoted to understanding "what we do, how we do it, and why we do it." From there, the question became "How can we do it better? Or, more specifically, how can we become fast and flexible, customer oriented, focused on results, and engaged in important partnerships internally and externally?" Over the past five years, Perkins has led a dramatic change in Fremont's city government, a change built around delivering high-quality services to citizens, creating an internal culture built around continuous and employee-driven improvement, a highly collaborative

About Jan C. Perkins

Jan Perkins has been the city manager of Fremont, California, since September 1994. She was selected by Fremont in 1992 as the associate city manager and became the interim city manager in September 1993.

Ms. Perkins has close to 25 years of experience in city government and management. She began her career in public service in Michigan local government in 1975 after completing her masters degree. She was the assistant city administrator/ community development director of Adrian, Michigan, before becoming the assistant city manager of Grand Rapids, Michigan. She then became the city manager of Morgan Hill, California, before moving to Fremont.

Ms. Perkins holds a bachelor's degree in sociology and a master's degree in public administration from the University of Kansas. She was also awarded a certificate from the Program for Executives in State and Local Government from Harvard University in 1987.

approach to decision making and problem solving, and the creation of partnerships within the city and with surrounding communities.

The city's interest in customer service was given initial impetus by complaints from local developers about how long it took to get permits and other approvals to undertake construction in Fremont. In a time when economic development was a key issue, these concerns were heard loud and clear and the permitting process was significantly improved. Similar concerns were raised in other areas, to the point that Perkins and her top staff began concentrating on developing a serious philosophical commitment to service quality, as well as providing employees with the tools to carry out that commitment. In part, Perkins describes the philosophy as the Nike slogan: "Just do it." That is, the message to employees was that if they saw a way in which the citizens of Fremont could be better served by city government, they should take action. "Just do it." But the philosophy also reflected an approach similar to the Nordstrom's department store service philosophy: We are not only interested in the transaction—the specific product or service being delivered. We are also interested in building a relationship, a relationship between customers and the business or, in this case, between citizens and government.

Movement in this direction was aided by making change a positive force in city government. In part, selling the idea of change was not hard, because the need for change was clear. Certainly the city council saw the need and encouraged the city manager to spread the message. And she did.

Perkins recalls, "I just kept persevering. I was sounding the same theme all the time. I kept encouraging groups to take on (improvement) projects. When they did, they would get great feedback. And that was really important." The message now seems to be spread through the organization, to the point that one front-line employee told us that what is new is that Perkins has created an atmosphere where change is encouraged. "Try things," she told us. "If it doesn't work, back off a little, but keep on trying." (The fact that this comment came from a front-line employee is itself significant, for another part of the change has been to encourage people *throughout* the organization to be open to taking some risks and trying new things.)

The city's capacity to innovate has also been aided by a much more collaborative approach to decision making and problem solving, an approach cutting across traditional organizational boundaries. Whatever their positions, employees are encouraged to think of themselves as representatives of the city and to do what is necessary to provide citizens with the answers they need. For example, if a planning department employee sees a street light malfunctioning, that employee should take action, rather than just passing off the problem as one for the street maintenance people to discover and correct. Similarly, any employee receiving a phone call about any topic is encouraged to "own" that question until it has been satisfactorily answered.

This attitude is also supported by a strong emphasis on partnerships (or collaborative problem solving) at many different levels in the organization. Early in the process of labor negotiation, for example, both labor and management recognized issues that were important to consider though they extended beyond the traditional concerns for wages and working conditions. Perkins created joint labor management committees to consider these issues through a structured problem solving process known as "interest based bargaining." This collaborative process encourages participants to identify their basic interests (before jumping to solutions) and then to engage in collaborative problem solving to find a way to accommodate the varied interests represented. Interest-based bargaining was so highly successful in labor management relations that the same approach has been encouraged throughout city government. Training in the process has been offered to all employees of the city, and interest-based bargaining has become a standard way of doing business in Fremont.

The same approach to building partnerships through collaborative efforts is used as the city relates to citizens and to other nearby governmental entities. City employees don't just inform citizens about what is going to be done to them, they also go out and ask citizens what they want, then balance those interests with those of the city. But even beyond that, city employees and citizens engage in interest-based problem solving, even around issues of how to design a process to involve the public. The city engineer told us, "We do more than tell them what we are going to do. We go out now and involve them in the design of the process itself. The process is laid out by the people involved." Perkins describes the shift in thinking as a shift from government as a "vending machine," in which you put your money in the slot and take out the product or service (though occasionally not getting what you want and kicking the machine!), to a "barn raising," in which many people come together to combine their efforts to produce a product or service that all can feel good about.

Building partnerships with other governmental entities is also important. Perkins recognizes that, in many areas, citizens don't care which department of city government delivers the service, they just want the service delivered in a timely and responsible fashion. Extending that logic, citizens may not even care which local government (or school board or hospital district) delivers the service. So, she reasons, if you are interested in improving public confidence in government, you would do well to work closely with other cities and other agencies. For this reason, Fremont has taken the lead in creating intergovernmental partnerships of all types, many evolving from an annual "Elected Officials Summit," which brings together representatives from various cities in the region, as well as people from the school district, a hospital district, water districts, etc.

Jan Perkins describes the change process in Fremont as involving waves of change, each wave building over time the quality of the city's work. Wave I involves recognition of the need to change, building trust and relationships internally, specifying the mission, vision, and values of the organizations, gathering "low hanging fruit"; and beginning education and training around these concerns. The key question here is "Why do we do what we do?" Wave II involves deepening knowledge and skills, improving work processes, reforming the administrative system, building trust and relationships eternally, and exploring more entrepreneurial activities. The key question here is "How can we best serve our customers?" Wave III involves rethinking the organization's structure, making the boundaries between departments more permeable, providing seamless service delivery, and deepening trust and relationship both internally and externally. The key question here is "Who does what?" Finally, Wave IV involves partnerships with other agencies and groups, integration of the community's vision and the organization's vision and creating inter-dependencies between the community and the organization, steering and rowing, and asking the question, "What is next?"

Steps in Leading Change

The case studies presented outline the particular accomplishments of the three local government managers whose work we examined. What is obvious, of course, is that each of the three took on quite different tasks—from compensation to downtown revitalization to the development process—yet each was successful not only in that particular area but in creating an attitude or culture in which change is not only accepted but valued. What is striking, however, is that, despite the differences, each of these managers used a similar "methodology" in bringing about change. They did certain things in a certain sequence. In our view, detailing these steps or elements in the change process should be useful in understanding and bringing about change in other local governments. In this section, therefore, we will examine a model of change suggestive of the steps undertaken by these managers to lead change in their communities. In the next section, we will look at some of the key lessons that these managers and their staffs shared with us concerning the change process in local government today.

Based on this research, we would argue that public managers who are successful in leading change in their organizations do undertake similar specific and largely sequential activities. The steps we will outline should not, however, be taken as discrete in the sense that one step must be fully completed before another is undertaken. Rather the steps are often overlapping and iterative, more like what Jan Perkins referred to as waves of change. But with this caveat, we would suggest that public managers interested in leading change must:

- assess the organization's environment and the need for change.
- plan strategically, though pragmatically, for change.
- build support for the change process both through conversation and through modeling the change process in their own behavior.
- implement specific changes, but in doing so encourage a broader positive attitude toward change and innovation.
- institutionalize the change.

Assess the Organization's Environment and the Need for Change

The first thing each of the managers whose work we analyzed did upon coming into the community was to try to learn about three areas: the governing body, the organization, and the community. Their key advice in this stage was straightforward: You have to listen, listen, listen! You have to listen to the governing body. You have to listen to your employees. And you have to listen to the community.

Obviously, managers moving to new communities encounter many different circumstances. For example, it makes a difference whether you've been there (say, as an assistant city manager) or whether you are just arriving. Is the organization falling apart or just in need of fine-tuning? Is there consensus among elected officials on matters of vision and philosophy?

What are the expectations of the governing body with respect to the manager? What is the level of involvement of the community in the government—and vice versa? All these are issues that have to be assessed before starting a change effort. If you discover a clear vision and consensus in the community, that leads to one strategy. If there is a crisis atmosphere and significant conflict, that leads to another. For a certain amount of time, Bob O'Neill advises: "Just keep your mouth shut and listen. Try to capture what is the dynamic in the community and the organization."

Jan Perkins described this period as one in which she specifically listens for the questions others were asking before making their decisions. If staff members are dealing with capital improvements, do they only involve other staff? Do they also ask whether members of the community might want something different? And if so, how do they go about involving the community? Listening for the right questions can give you the right answers. And, depending on what you learn, you can experiment with different responses. During this period, the "successful manager tries lots of different hats and a lot of different exposures." You can listen and learn but you can also "test the waters" with respect to possible solutions.

The listening/learning period can take a long time (these three managers described this period as taking up to 18 months) and is a difficult one, especially when the manager would like to establish some early successes. Several staff members were surprised by how much time their managers took in assessing the situation, but thought in retrospect that had been a good way to proceed. One of her staff members described Jan Perkins's style during this early period in this way: "You have to go slow to go fast." You have to spend a lot of time doing your homework. You have to find out what employees are thinking, that is, what is the organizational culture. You have to learn the expectations that the governing body has, and how you can work most effectively with them. And you have to get a sense of the community. Who is involved? How are they involved? How can they be more fully involved?

Similarly, one of Bob O'Neill's department heads commented, "It's been a lot slower than I thought. And I think Bob is very smart and savvy in doing that. He's not willing to act precipitously. There's been some criticism for going too slow, but he's certainly not indecisive. He doesn't mandate change. He just gently guides you in the right direction." And Phil Penland was recognized as being "realistic in knowing it doesn't take a day or two." You have to think long term.

Because there is so much to learn and because what you learn during this period is so critical to your later strategies and, hopefully, successes, the early period is very important. But it's also difficult personally, because of the stress and anxiety it produces. For one thing, it just takes a lot of time and energy. In answer to a question about how she gathers information, Jan Perkins commented, "I do it all. I ride in police cars. I go to every work group in the city. I visit all the fire stations. I schedule meetings all over the place—just to listen to what people are saying and hear what they are doing." And that takes an enormous amount of time and energy.

This period is also difficult because the manager is constantly on display. One commented, "When I came here, you had to be on all the time. Every movement you made; every body twitch; everything was being interpreted by everyone. There's a huge anxiety that builds up based on that. Once you've been there a while, the attention drops. Or at least you are not as sensitive to it." It takes a substantial amount of self-confidence, as well as physical stamina, to maintain the rigors of the early months on the job.

Phil Penland was also particularly helpful in emphasizing that what works in one community may not necessarily work in another. A manager needs to adapt his or her style and approach to new conditions. Penland put it this way: "You have to gauge the community and what will work. When I came from Deland, I had to change my style. They didn't like change. If there was a criticism it was that I was too conservative. I really wasn't. I just understood what they would do and wouldn't do. You have to speak their language to move them along."

One popular recommendation recently has been that a new manager should try to capture the "low-hanging fruit," that is, make those changes that are easy and that demonstrate early success. All of the managers we talked with admitted to picking that fruit. (We should point out, however, that the low-hanging fruit is not always policy related. Significantly involving employees in an organization where that has not been the norm may itself be low-hanging fruit.) But in any case, "It's there to be picked. You do it." But there were caveats as well. Most important, as these managers pointed out, you don't want to miss the fact that you have long-term issues that you need to work on. You can't just work on the easy problems. And you have to be sensitive to the fact that gathering low-hanging fruit is often more of a political strategy than an organizational development strategy; that is, while you may earn political points in this way, the long-term impact on the organization is likely going to be minimal.

Plan Strategically, though Pragmatically, for Change

The three local government leaders we studied were consistently recognized for their ability to think strategically and conceptually. They seem to have a sense of where the organization and the community are going and how the various parts have to fit together to make that happen. Indeed, to some employees, this capacity seems quite remarkable. For example, Phil Penland's fire chief felt that Penland "always has the big picture in mind, even though he may not immediately share it with us. He moves at a different level, which sometimes can leave me wondering where he's going. But when I finally start to put the puzzle together, it makes sense. He sees things the rest of us don't see."

Similarly, Bob O'Neill was described as a strategic, conceptual manager, not just a "day to day" manager. Employees in Fairfax County felt that, until O'Neill's arrival, their work was "just getting through the day and doing whatever the board had asked us to do at the last meeting. There was not much discussion of where we are going and where we want to be. A lot of the issues that have now come to the surface were starting to form during that time. The health of the organization was not being watched. The community and how it viewed county government was something that we weren't that concerned with, except providing services on that particular day. All of this was bottled up and Bob said a few key things. It's been uncorked."

Of course, the things O'Neill said had to do with strategically focusing on those things that make a difference. In his case, the admonition to managers and employees was to create a more efficient and creative organization. He tells his top managers quite simply to ask, "What is it you're doing to assure that your organization is better tomorrow than it is today? If you don't do that, then what's the value of senior management, senior leadership?" Similarly, Jan Perkins concentrated on citizens and customers, quality and innovation, while Phil Penland was able to make change a positive force in his community. In each case, the manager's role was to see the big picture, then translate that picture into words and actions that would make a positive difference in the community. The words ultimately chosen were simple but they gave focus to the work of the organization and its employees in a way that made sense to them.

While known for their ability to think strategically, these leaders were careful to point out that you can't think of everything in advance. Rather they followed a strategy referred to in *The Pursuit of Significance* as "pragmatic incrementalism": "Change occurs through a free-flowing process in which the manager pursues a wide variety of often unexpected opportunities to move the organization in the desired direction." Though the manager's vision for the future is clear, the exact steps to get there are not laid out in advance. Rather the manager takes advantage of chance and opportunity to move in the right direction. In this sense the manager is like a surfer who would like to end up safely on the shore, but knows that a great deal of cleverness and spontaneity will be required along the way.

The managers we talked with clearly employed this approach; indeed, they advised against being overly structured in planning change. Jan Perkins put it fairly directly: "Don't overplan. Things are changing so rapidly that any plan that is too detailed today simply won't fit the circumstances tomorrow. Just create the outline, the structure. That's enough." You may have a set of values that you carry with you and you may have a sense of where you want the organization to be and where you want it to go. But your success also depends on the situation, on luck, and on opportunity. She added, "If you are going to be a good leader you have to take all that into account. You may be able to do a little something over here and then you do a little something over there, but all the while moving in the same direction."

Bob O'Neill used a sports analogy to make this point. He points out that in football you call plays in a huddle, then hope that everyone does exactly what they are supposed to do. In local government, he continued, "We're playing soccer. There are no time-outs, no time to plan each individual move. So we have to build a capacity for the players to make a decision on the fly, based on the set of circumstances, consistent with values and constructs that we have put together. In today's world I think we'll be much more successful playing soccer than playing football."

In this process, the manager depends on luck and opportunity, but also on an intuitive sense of how things need to come together. Every manager knows the importance of good timing, but these leaders pointed out that timing is not merely accidental; rather it comes from the manager's having a sense of the big picture and knowing when things need to happen. The big picture is always in the forefront: For example, they are always trying to make something happen that's going to improve what they do. O'Neill explains, "There are certain things that require other players to be participants and so you have to assess opportunities and whether you are likely to be successful. You have to know your stakeholders and where they are. You have to find the level where you can work. So there are times when we focus on the internal and times that we focus on the external and visible. You just get that sense." And, continuing the sports metaphor, O'Neill reminds us that great football running backs like Walter Payton and Barry Sanders cut away from people they can't possibly have seen. They simply felt it. "Intuition makes the great running back." And a great leader.

Build Support for the Change Process Both through Involving Everyone You Can and through Modeling the Change Process in Their Own Behavior

All of the managers we talked with followed a strategy of open communication and significant employee involvement in the change process. While the particular approach chosen differed from place to place—from O'Neill's task forces to Penland's quality improvement teams to Perkins's collaborative problem solving—what was most significant was the manager's commitment to involving people throughout the organization and the community in the change process.

O'Neill's task forces provide a good example. While the task forces dealt with important substantive issues facing the organization, it was clear that O'Neill also wanted to use the task forces to demonstrate a "new way of doing business," one in which there would be high levels of employee involvement and open communications up, down, and across the organization. "How you go about it is two or three times more important than the technical or substantive part of it," he commented. "If we do this substantively well, but don't engage the workforce and don't communicate about what the changes are, it will fall on its face. We can do it less well technically, but communicate it well, and it will be enormously well received. And that's our choice. If I have to make a sacrifice, I'll make it on the technical side. I can fix that."

A part of the manager's role in leading change is to generate or at least identify good ideas that the organization can pursue. Phil Penland spoke of this process as one that is multi-faceted. "A lot of ideas come from this office. Many come through brainstorming with department heads. And the best ideas for operations come from employees. And we spend a lot of money sending people to conferences, hoping they will pick up something they can bring back here." One of Penland's staff members pointed out Penland's own role in encouraging innovation. "Phil gets chagrined when he sees another city doing something we should be doing or should have thought of. So he encourages an attitude we think of as the Altamonte Way. We want to be leaders, not followers. Phil praises innovations and reinforces the idea that change is good."

The manager's own role in generating ideas should not be underestimated. Penland, for example, tries to stay current with the latest management thinking in business as well as the public sector. He then tries to find what is written and shares that material with others, especially his department heads. He commented, "I read a lot about things going on elsewhere, especially in the private sector. I try to turn the ideas, to adjust them so they will work here in government, in Altamonte Springs. I try to find what is written and share that information. We then set aside time at the end of staff meetings. What are we doing already? What might work?" The manager's office can be an incubator for good ideas, but they need to be shared widely through the organization to eventually take root.

One of Bob O'Neill's department heads suggested that O'Neill seems to like to shake things up a little and then let people figure out the right direction. "He doesn't tell you how it's going to come out. He doesn't make it easy to get from this point to this point. But that's good. There's not a grand plan laid out for you. He probably always knows the answer. But I think he wants you to figure it out."

Jan Perkins pointed out that the manager has to act as a coach, but also has to model good ideas and indeed an attitude that encourages the search for new ideas. "You have to provide leadership by walking the talk. It's important that people believe that the world can be different if you want it to be. People have to know that how we have done things is always open to improvement. Sometimes you just have to say 'time-out.' Is this how we want to be solving this problem? You have to resist the temptation to just order the answer." But as a staff member commented, "Jan is very good at recognizing obstacles and removing them so that we can get to where we need to be." Perkins and several staff members felt that early in the change process in Fremont, they had pushed too hard. They wanted to get people involved but it seemed forced at first. Once they eased up a little, then they started seeing the results. "When we stopped pushing it and started modeling, that's when people really got it."

Implement Specific Changes, but in Doing So Encourage a Broader Positive Attitude toward Change and Innovation

All of those we talked with recognized the importance of putting change in context for their employees. As one manager put it, "It's helpful for people to understand that change is not just my weird idea, it's something that's being thrust upon us." Certainly people recognize change in the world of technology, but there are also changes in the workforce, such as family medical leave, telecommuting, and job sharing. And there are new global economic institutions and the pressure on public institutions to do more with the dollars they have. As one department head in Fairfax County put it: "If you are aware at all of those changes that are going on, how could you not expect that those would impact your workplace? You have to let people know the idea of change isn't just something that a new executive is bringing in. You are going to be constantly buffeted by a changing world. So you might as well prepare yourself to embrace change, because change is part of your life." Consequently, a key message in all three communities we visited was the need to continually improve ourselves. We have to do better every day. We have to change how we do business. We have to recognize and embrace change as an opportunity.

Soon people throughout the organization understand how important change is. We asked several front-line employees what the message was that they were getting from the manager. The answers were often similar. "It's not like we go out every day and say what can we do differently. But we look for opportunities. We never go back. We always keep a little bit. We learn something." Another staff member noted a change in the way people approach one another as well as the way they approach their jobs. She said, "I see cultural change here in terms of how people approach problem solving. Everybody has ideas. But you have to create an environment in which there is not deference to authority, hierarchy. To hear someone say 'do what you're told' smacks in the face of change. You have to create a climate in which people feel comfortable saying things that might improve the work."

A part of that climate is setting expectations with respect to risk and opportunity. All three managers want their employees to understand that there is no penalty for trying something, even if you fail. There is no penalty for taking risks as long as they are taken for the right reasons. And that's an idea that is energizing. As Penland put it, "It emboldens people; it emboldens me!" At the same time, the managers we talked with understood that there is a fine line between encouraging risk and discouraging risk adverse behavior. It is the latter they propose. O'Neill pointed out that for the city manager or county executive, a willingness to take risks is part of their "leadership profile." You may have to stick your neck out on occasion, but you have to figure out when it's worth it and when it's not.

O'Neill put it this way: "When you say take a risk, I think what you have to say is that what we're talking about is a calculation of risk." One of Penland's department heads described Penland as a risk taker, but not a gambler. But in any case, the primary problem these managers see is getting people away from their natural predilection for risk-*averse* behavior. Employees need to understand that "you have to push where you are all the time."

Institutionalize the Change

One question that came up repeatedly in our discussions was to what extent were the changes that had occurred institutionalized, that is, a part of the organization's profile rather than a particular manager's program. Generally, the sentiment seemed to be that after about five years of solid organization development work, the changes would be solidly in place to the point that they would probably stay, even if the manager were to leave. One staff member in Fremont commented, "I think (the changes we've made) would stay in place, though it's hard to know what a new manager or new council would bring. Someone would have to really work to change things. They probably could dismantle what we've done, but it would be difficult." But clearly there will be greater opportunities for the changes to remain in place if the manager remains with the organization. It's not surprising that all three managers we studied are committed to their communities for the long term. Jan Perkins, for example, underlined the importance of "continuity in the manager's position" for changes to have the positive effect in the community that you desire.

What seems most important in institutionalizing the change process is to make changes in the organization's culture as well as in specific policy areas. Once ideas such as involvement and communication, quality and innovation, collaboration and engagement become embedded in the culture of the organization, people will begin to automatically look for ways to extend these values. They will become attuned to new opportunities that they previously wouldn't even have recognized as opportunities. They will begin to ask such questions as "How can we communicate more effectively? How can we come up with better ways of doing things? And how can we more effectively engage the public in the work of government?" Establishing questions like these as the norm rather than the exception seems to be essential to the process of institutionalization.

Leadership and Learning

We can draw many lessons from the three case studies presented here. But it's hard to avoid the conclusion that the single most significant element of leading change in American local government today is the manager's capacity to learn. More than anything else, these three managers and those around them emphasized the importance of the manager's taking time early on to learn everything possible about the community and the organization before making changes. Although some decisions may be thrust upon the manager early in his or her tenure and some unique opportunities such as personnel changes or reorganizations may present themselves, the general lesson seems to be that the manager's initial investment of time and energy in learning the community and the organization will pay off in the long term. That is, to the extent that the manager's learning is successful, later changes will be far better informed and stand a much greater chance of succeeding. There are four areas of learning that seem most critical and that form important lessons for future leaders.

Know Yourself and Your Values

The managers we studied were not merely doing a job; they had each made a personal commitment to their communities and their organization. It was a commitment that expressed deeply held personal values and it was a commitment that meant that other aspects of their lives would often have to compete for attention. Jan Perkins spoke of the values that she carried with her. "I start with fundamental values. Wherever I go I take these with me. They have to do with a deep belief in the democratic way, in democracy in local communities. I really do believe if we're going to have healthy communities, people who live and work in those communities need to be a part of finding solutions. It's really just a core value I have. In government, it means that we can't assume that we know it all. We know some of it, but there's a whole lot of other stuff out there that people know or value or feel that's very valuable data." Each of the managers with whom we spoke expressed similar deeply held values, values about democracy, values about local government, and values about the important role of public service in our society. Their work had indeed become an expression of their selves.

In many cases, their commitment to a core set of values (and their commitment to the kind and amount of work needed to actualize those values) meant that these managers would have to make sacrifices in other areas of their lives. The demands of meetings from early in the morning until late at night, day after day, takes its toll on one's personal and family life, and other managers or students need to be clear about the demands of leading change. Leading change of the type we have described is more than a full-time job and should be recognized as such. It is hard, demanding, and stressful, both physically and psychologically. Again, for the managers we studied, a very strong set of values drove their work. Other managers lacking such a commitment would likely find the demands of leadership too high. But for these managers a set of core value commitments made the sacrifices worthwhile.

Know the Community

As we saw in the case studies, these three managers and many of their staff members spoke of the importance of their being involved in the community and being knowledgeable of nearly everything happening in the community. The purpose of that engagement is not merely to help move particular issues along, although that is not unimportant. One manager, encouraging his employees to become more involved with the community and more active in listening to citizens, put it this way: "Why would you want to go out into the community and tell them what to do? You know it won't work. Why pick a fight and then get forced into doing something you don't want to do anyway? You don't give up any of your professional values by involving the citizens. In fact, in the long run, you are likely to be more successful than you would have been the other way." Though it appears time-consuming, public engagement can in fact be a very effective long-term strategy for achieving organizational goals.

But in addition to the practical benefits of citizen involvement, the managers we talked with held a deep personal commitment to the involvement of the community in the work of government. Phil Penland talked about the importance of those in the community defining the kind of community they would see as ideal, the kind of place they would want to live and to work and to invest. Similarly, Jan Perkins commented, "We see the trees that need to be trimmed. We see the potholes. But the way we go about it may differ from what the community wants. We need to listen. We need to engage the community in everything we do." Not only because it helps, but also because it's the right thing to do.

Know the Organization

As we noted earlier, each of the managers we studied emphasized the importance of getting the best possible people involved in the organization, then encouraging open communications and sincere employee involvement throughout the organization. All three managers took advantage of opportunities early on to bring the right people into the organization. Rarely did that involve firing people. Indeed, Bob O'Neill noted that people often distinguish between a strategy of change through getting rid of people and change through developing the skills of those who are there. O'Neill and others came down firmly on the side of developing existing employees.

But where vacancies do occur, there is the opportunity to consider how the organization might be restructured and how new people might be brought in to meet the current needs of the organization. These managers largely saw reorganizations as symbolic, unless it occurred where the previous organization had been built around the skills and abilities of a particular person who had now left the organization. One staff member in Fremont reported, "Every time someone would leave, Jan would see that as an opportunity to reassess whether the organization was structured at its best."

And once the structure and the people are in place, the manager has to simply get out of the way and let them do the work they can do. Phil Penland noted that it's worth a great deal to attract and retain good people. "We have good department heads. We have people in the 'skill positions' who are head and shoulders above their peers in any other organization around here. We have more skill here than you will find in much bigger organizations. Now we pay a lot more than other cities. But it works." It works for the community and it works for the manager, because as Penland noted, one definition of leadership is that "real leaders are ordinary people who have an extraordinary staff."

Know the Governing Body

The relationship between a manager and the governing body is absolutely critical to bringing about successful change. As one manager put it, you want a board that is either engaged in the change effort or at least neutral toward it. You can't bring about change with a hostile governing body. Jan Perkins's city council is an example of a governing body actively involved in the change process, even from the early days of planning for change. But even so, Perkins talks about the importance of constantly communicating with the board and cultivating their trust. And in part, trust is built by delivering the goods. Both Perkins and Penland, given their somewhat longer tenure in their communities than O'Neill, seem to have established such confidence among members of the governing body that their councils are quite receptive to their bringing specific and well-developed proposals forward (as opposed to a set of alternatives). Perkins told us that the Fremont council has "developed an expectation that we will have worked out all the kinks in a project before we bring it to them." Penland recalls from his early days in Altamonte Springs, "When I first came here I hadn't gotten the feel of the community and I would take alternatives to the commission. One commissioner came to me and said, 'You know, we're looking for leadership from the city manager. I don't want a menu. We're paying you to make a recommendation.' So I began to do that and still do." These managers seem to prefer that style, but they recognize that while the governing body should not be involved in internal management, they reserve the right to "take our heads off if we're wrong!"

In Fairfax County, Bob O'Neill worked to build trust and confidence among the members of his board. The key seems to be that the board come to recognize, as O'Neill put it, "we're trying to accomplish what they are and that 'we add value' to the process." One manager pointed out, however, that "(the political world) is a world of anecdotes, not a world of analysis," so it's important for the manager to work to build a personal relationship with members of the governing body and also to work among various constituencies in the community to create support. "If a board member walks down the hall or goes to a community meeting and asks someone how it's going and they say 'terrible,' then I'm in trouble. So I work with those groups that are likely to be asked. In addition to the board member's own interest, their constituents' interests are important."

The relationship between manager and governing body is an important topic in council-manager governments. Whereas the traditional description of the council-manager relationship posited a fairly strict separation (at least around some issues), O'Neill reports that he enjoys the fact that both "sides" bring important perspectives to the table. "Elected officials bring a very different set of perspectives and values than we bring. The sharper the divide between the policy/political context and administrative, the quicker you get in trouble. I want to muck around in their world and they ought to be able to muck around in mine. The dynamic of that produces a better result. Is the potential for misbehavior there? Absolutely. Is the potential there for all the problems we thought about in graduate school? Yes. But there is an important perspective offered by the board. We get solutions and approaches from the board that are terribly constructive. Do I always agree? No. Do they? No. That's fair. So I want them actively engaged, not a disconnected board of directors. I want them to understand the difficulties of what they are facing. Our staff comes up with textbook answers that are perfectly right, but they don't understand the political dynamic."

In many cases, the political world and the technical/administrative world seem to be separate cultures, and some have recommended that one important aspect of the manager's role is to translate back and forth between the two cultures. Generally, these three managers agreed, but O'Neill pointed out that the work of translating often needs to go well beyond the manager's office. "We need translators between the political and the technical world, that's true, but if it's just me, we're in trouble—especially in a bigger system. The staff needs to be involved with the board, with stakeholders, and with each other. That's where we'll get the best results."

Conclusion

The type of leadership demonstrated by the three managers who were the focus of this study is clearly different from the traditional top-down, internally focused management that has long characterized public management. In the older view, the leader was expected:

- to come up with good ideas about the direction the community and the organization should take.
- to decide on a course of action or a goal to be accomplished.
- to exert his or her influence or control in moving the community and organization in that direction.

These three managers seem to model a somewhat different style, one in which the leader's role is:

- to help the community and the organization understand their needs and potential.
- to integrate and articulate the community's vision and that of the organization.
- to act as a trigger or stimulus for group action.

The new leadership for change in American local governments is a much more open, free-flowing, engaging, collaborative form of leadership than that used in the past. But, based on the experiences and successes of those managers who have been our focus here, it is an approach that reaps tremendous benefits for not only the managers but also for the public they serve.

Certainly other managers might well benefit from the experiences of these three managers, not only in terms of the specific approaches they took in leading change, but in the way they pursued change. As we have shown, there are specific steps that each of these managers took to bring about change. But cutting across these steps is the important relationship between leadership and learning. Other managers wishing to be more effective in bringing about change in their communities would do well to consider what they have learned and what they might learn about themselves and their values, the community, the organization, and the governing body.

In the end, once again, as in *The Pursuit of Significance*, we must also comment on the relationship between leadership and public service. The three local government leaders whose work we studied have demonstrated immense capabilities for bringing about change in their communities and their organizations. But the change is not at all random. Rather the changes these managers are pursuing are the kind that makes a difference in the lives of citizens. The work of these managers is not merely technically competent; rather they are doing something significant, something worthwhile in their communities. In the work of these managers, we see that the grand ideals of public service are alive and well in American local government—and, we suspect, throughout public service at all levels of government.

Appendix: Methodology

The research reported here was based on a series of semi-structured interviews conducted by both authors in the three communities. In each case, we interviewed the city manager/county executive first, asking for an overview of the community and of their efforts to bring about change. We then interviewed eight to 10 other people, all situated to observe the work of the manager in leading change. These people included primarily department heads in city government, but also members of the governing body, members of the manager's immediate staff, representatives of employee unions, and front-line employees.

In these interviews we asked about the manager's approach to leading change—essentially what he or she had done, when did they do it, and what effect was it having in the organization. We asked not only about substantive changes that were underway in the communities and in the local governments, but also about the process by which the different managers tried to bring about change. Following these interviews, we held a final interview with the city manager/county executive in which we asked more generally about his or her approach to change and about what advice they would give to others involved in trying to bring about change in local government. The interviews were transcribed, then used as the basis for developing the material in this report. Though we have sought to maintain the anonymity of all the interviewees, with the exception of the managers themselves, we have used quotation marks to indicate direct quotations, even where we have not identified the person who made the statement.

Endnotes

1. Robert B. Denhardt, *The Pursuit of Significance: Strategies for Management in Public Organizations,* Wadsworth Publishing Company, 1993.

CHAPTER SIX

The Importance of Leadership:
The Role of School Principals

Paul E. Teske
Professor and Director of Graduate Studies
Political Science Department
State University of New York at Stony Brook

Mark Schneider
Professor and Departmental Chairman
Political Science Department
State University of New York at Stony Brook

This report was originally published in September 1999.

Introduction

While educational reform movements have been fairly common throughout this century, the publication of the Department of Education's study "A Nation at Risk" in 1983 propelled education to an even more prominent place on the nation's political agenda. Since that report, myriad reforms designed to provide more American students with a better education have dotted the landscape. Indeed, the level of educational reform activity is now so intense that some analysts argue that we are engaged in too many reforms, without paying enough attention to whether these reforms actually work. In the resulting "policy churn," new reforms are introduced repeatedly without any sustained effort to integrate new approaches into the core practices and learning environment of the school (Hess 1999).

Based on our observations of a set of principals in New York City, we argue that despite these myriad reforms, there is one essential ingredient common to successful schools that is easily overlooked in pursuit of the educational "reform du jour"—and that is focused, consistent leadership by principals over time. We believe that such leadership is essential to high-performing schools, especially in central cities, because a strong principal defines the culture of schools and integrates the concern for high performance into the mission of the school. Moreover, we argue that change in school practices takes time, so that longevity in leadership is essential to the creation and maintenance of successful schools. Such longevity can also act as a corrective to hyperactive reform activity that is often concerned more with the "show" of reform rather than with actual improvement.

We are not alone in linking focused leadership and longevity to success. For example, Lee and Smith (1994: 32-3) argue that schools "should decide on a modest number of reform strategies, should work hard to see that these reforms are engaged profoundly in the school, should continue their commitment to those particular reforms over a sustained period, and should not attempt too many reforms simultaneously." Similarly, Hess argues, "Evidence on the performance of parochial schools and high-performing schools suggests that the best schools are able to develop expertise in specific approaches. School improvement required time, focus, and the commitment of core personnel. To succeed, the leadership must focus on selected reforms and then nurture those efforts in the schools." (Hess 1999: 7)

We also argue that one of the conditions linking leadership to strong schools is autonomy. In this, our position is congruent with the central vision motivating many of today's educational reforms, which share a vision of a system of education built around small, autonomous schools, unburdened by large administrative structures. Stimulated by the work of Coleman and colleagues (1966; 1982; 1987), numerous empirical studies have identified a set of factors that constitute a framework for school effectiveness

(Purkey and Smith 1983; Rowan et al. 1983; Hallinger and Murphy 1986; James and Levin 1987; Hill et al. 1997). The school-level variables that have been most commonly cited as central to the success of schools include: a clear school mission, a cohesive curriculum, high expectations for students, instructional leadership, instructional time that maximizes students' opportunity to learn, administrative autonomy, parent contact and involvement, and widespread student rewards.

These characteristics of effective schools stand in stark contrast to the characteristics of schools operating in the much more common heavily bureaucratized "factory model" of education that came from the pursuit of "one best system" of education (e.g., Darling-Hammond 1997; Hill et al. 1997). The resulting bureaucratization of education insulated schools from external forces while, paradoxically, reducing the discretion of school leaders, especially principals. Hill (1994:40) describes the limitations of this system:

> Rule-bound, it discourages initiative and risk taking in schools and systems facing unprecedented problems. Politically driven, it allows decisions reached from on high that satisfy as many people as possible to substitute for the professional judgement and initiative of competent, caring professionals in the school and classroom. Emphasizing compliance, it defines accountability as adherence to process, when results are the only appropriate standard. Organized to manage institutions and minimize conflict, it ties up resources of permanent staff and the management of routine operations.

We argue that one of the biggest costs of this overly bureaucratic system is the extent to which it restricts principals, prevents creative leadership, and ultimately reduces educational success.

Principals as School Leaders: A Review of the Literature

While the importance of principals to the quality of schools may seem obvious, in fact scholars have only recently begun to examine educational leadership. Studies on the topic suggest that in the past, principals were able to succeed, at least partially, by simply carrying out the directives of central administrators (Perez et al. 1999). But "management" by principals is no longer enough to meet today's educational challenges—instead principals must assume a greater leadership role.

According to Drake (1999) a leader "envisions goals, sets standards, and communicates in such a way that all associated directly or indirectly know where the school is going and what it means to the community."

While managers rely on the authority given to them from above (Buhler 1995), leaders seek to create a cooperative culture in which everyone has a responsibility to lead and to suggest changes when necessary (Drake 1999; Perez et al. 1999). Still, since both managerial and leadership aspects must ultimately be integrated by the principal, it is important to understand the tensions between the two leadership forms.

Burns (1978) argues that there is a distinction between transactional and transformational leadership. Transactional leaders take a more managerial approach; they get things done by clearly defining the task to the followers and providing whatever immediate rewards they can. Transformational leaders, in contrast, work with both external environments and within the organization to map new directions, obtain necessary resources, and respond to present challenges and future threats. The transformational leader recognizes that change is imminent and even strives for its creation.

Applying this to schools, Aviolio and Bass (1988) argue that although transactional and transformational leadership can represent two discrete forms of leadership, effective school principals exhibit characteristics of both by maintaining short-term endeavors through transactional leadership and by inciting change as a transformational leader. A number of studies emphasize the importance of transformative leadership for school principals (Fullan 1996; Hord 1992; Leithwood, Tomlinson & Genge 1996; Wood 1998; Sergiovanni 1992; Conley 1997; Perez et al. 1999; Reed and Roberts 1998).

Other researchers have argued that the most important goal of a leader is to create an effective organizational culture (Schein 1985). By establishing a consistent and shared culture, the principal engages the staff, students, and community in a sense of belonging and a shared sense of commitment to the success of the school (Deal 1987; Deal and Peterson 1990; Sashkin and Walberg 1993; Purkey and Smith 1983). Deal and Peterson (1990: 7) define school culture as "the character of a school as it reflects deep patterns of values, beliefs, and traditions that have been formed over the course of history." They found that successful principals tend to employ several common strategies to shape school culture. These include:

- a clear sense of what is important (history, values, and beliefs)
- selecting compatible faculty
- dealing with conflict
- setting a consistent example
- telling stories that illustrate shared values
- nurturing the traditions that reinforce school culture.

To the extent that the principal is able to include parents, staff, and students in implementing the principal's vision, all these actors are likely to share in the sense of accountability and responsibility for the vision (Perez et al. 1999).

The term "vision" is often used in the current context of leadership studies. According to Perez et al. (1999: 6) "a vision includes strategies for obtaining a desired outcome, provides a picture of what schooling should look like (i.e., its content) and how educators can recreate or process this mental picture in real life." Implementing a vision is not instantaneous; it requires repeated cycles of reflection, evaluation, and response, and only the principal can sustain it (Lashway 1997). A principal's vision must also be related to the existing needs and culture of the school (Keedy 1990), and it must be focused and consistent. Lee and Smith (1994: 158) analyzed performance from 820 secondary schools and found that coherent, sustained, and focused reforms resulted in the best outcomes for students.

Pushing further on this "bottom-line" connection, the issue is whether principals really can affect student achievement. Studies have shown that the establishment of an effective school culture and the academic success of students are positively correlated, thereby establishing principals as contributors to student achievement—the principal helps create the culture that, in turn, enhances student performance.

While case studies show a strong connection between principal leadership and student academic success, only a few reliable statistical studies examine this connection. Eberts and Stone (1988) surveyed 14,000 elementary schools to determine whether or not a principal's leadership does improve student achievement. They conclude that the principal's behavior does affect student performance levels, and that the principal's skills in conflict resolution and instructional leadership are the most important factors. In a follow-up study, Brewer (1993) found a positive correlation between the high academic standards set by the principal and student performance and test scores. Furthermore, Brewer (1993) showed that student achievement levels were higher in schools where the principal had hired like-minded teachers who shared the principal's goals and who were able to implement effectively the principal's vision. Clearly, this research suggests that strong leadership by principals can lead to effective schools with high student achievement.

A recent study of American high schools by *U.S. News & World Report* (1999) reinforces the importance of principals and suggests that parents shopping for schools should talk to principals, asking many of the kinds of questions we asked in our interviews. Specifically, their report suggests that principals should have an academic mission they can summarize easily, they should give teachers a stake in school leadership, and they should know how to seize opportunities to expand their autonomy.

We probe these and related issues further in our study.

The Role of Principals in Creating Effective Schools: The Case of New York City

Our goal is to understand how principals operating within a highly rule-bound public system are able to gain enough autonomy to implement their vision of effective education to create successful schools. In particular we study the aspects of leadership and vision that seem most important in changing school culture and in creating effective schools. To do this, we studied in-depth eight successful schools in New York City. To mirror the distribution of New York City public schools, we divided our set of schools into four elementary schools, two intermediate schools and two high schools. Below, we report the results of our fieldwork for the elementary schools first and then we discuss the results of our study of the junior and senior high schools.

A Brief History of New York City Schools

The New York City public school system is a massive, highly bureaucratic organization that serves more than 1 million children. The New York City school system has experienced many changes over time, most of which led to more bureaucratization. In the early 1800s, local non-profit organizations ran the schools for a small number of children. Over time, society recognized education as a valuable commodity, and as a way to achieve social change. The city government eventually took over control of public education to meet the growing demands of the population.

Philosophical and political battles emerged in this process, which Diane Ravitch (1974) characterizes as the "Great School Wars." The first "war" was over public financing of schools, the second was over shifting power from political machines to a central Board of Education, while the third was fought over the curriculum and length of the school day. The fourth, and most relevant here, was the fight over decentralization, which began in 1969.

Decentralization created 32 community districts that have some latitude to experiment with different forms of school organization. Elementary and intermediate schools are mostly under the jurisdiction of these 32 community districts, while the high schools are mostly controlled by the central Board of Education. The central Board of Education also maintains control over most of the school budgets, although districts have a limited range of flexibility. All of the schools are also governed by the central union contract with the city teachers, as well as union contracts with school principals and custodians.

Since decentralization, some districts have experimented with various forms of school choice for parents and greater autonomy for schools. Elsewhere we have examined the performance of one such district, District 4, encompassing East Harlem, in some detail (see, for example, Schneider, Teske, and Marschall, 2000).

Our goal is to identify the characteristics of principals that are associated with successful schools. Our first task was to identify successful schools and then to identify the role of the principal in creating such success.

Profiles of Successful School Principals

Before summarizing our findings across schools, we first present elements of each principal's leadership and vision, managerial style, approach to the school's diverse constituencies, and various contextual factors.

Elementary Schools

P.S. 161

Public School (P.S.) 161 is a neighborhood school located in Crown Heights, Brooklyn.[1] The school is overcrowded, leading to large class sizes that average 29 students in the kindergarten classes and as many as 35 students in the 5th grade classes. The school is a very high performer in all standardized tests. In a new New York State test, P.S. 161 achieved the second-highest 6th grade reading scores in the entire state, without any adjustment for demographic characteristics. As a result, the school has attracted national attention.

P.S. 161 At a Glance	
School (District)	District 17
Grades	K-8
Enrollment	1,400
% Black/Hispanic	90% / 8%
% Free Lunch Eligible	100%
Principal	Irwin Kurz

A visitor is immediately impressed by how well the school maintains a sense of organization and decorum. Uniforms are mandatory. Classroom walls and hallways are plastered with cheerful posters and examples of students' academic work. The high level of commitment to the students' academic success is apparent from banners displaying the names of various universities throughout the country in the front hall lobby.

Irwin Kurz has been the principal of P.S. 161 for 13 years.[2] Employed by the New York City school system for the past 30 years, Kurz was initially an elementary school teacher, then an assistant principal. A self-proclaimed benevolent dictator, Kurz holds all school participants and employees (teachers, parents, students, and staff) fully accountable for the responsibilities their respective roles require. He has clear goals, sets guidelines, and holds himself and others responsible for producing results. By continuously giving resources to his staff, Kurz aims to remove possible excuses for not achieving good results. Should teachers not be able to respond to his demands, Kurz has no qualms about firing them or suggesting that they relocate to another district or school.

Kurz states that the most critical aspect of his job is selecting staff. Thus, he personally interviews all the teachers, and hires only those he feels will best fit his vision. He believes that, despite his high expectations, his respect and fair treatment of the teachers is a significant factor in the high rate of teacher retention. Kurz only employs staff with extensive teaching experience; few of his teachers have less than six years of teaching experience. He has also implemented a peer observation program, where teachers can learn from observing each other.

The most important aspect of Kurz's vision is his emphasis on student performance. Without hesitation, he will implement whatever reform is necessary for the increased academic success of his students. For example, Kurz has established a standardized math program, mock tests, and paraprofessional tutoring for children who require extra assistance. He also has established a strong and consistent curriculum based on reading. He states that although nothing in this school is on the cutting edge, the school has achieved academic success primarily because everyone in the school shares his belief in the potential of every student.

In implementing his vision, Kurz at first encountered resistance from a community that was hesitant to change the status quo. Opposition came from both the parents and teachers, who were all used to a more laissez faire attitude in a school that had been ranked 13th out of 16 schools in its district. Following a difficult year of resistance, Kurz was able to change the attitude of the school community. The teachers' union representative we interviewed acknowledged that prior to Kurz, the school had a poor reputation. Kurz immediately set a tone of orderliness and strong expectations, which led to some successes, and to many teachers and parents adopting his vision. This parental support was reflected by 96 percent of his students agreeing voluntarily to wear uniforms.

Kurz does not complain about a paucity of resources but is more concerned with how they are allocated. In fact, he would rather have more space than additional money. Although Kurz professes to bending the New York City school system rules at least moderately, he claims that a mastery of the rules of the system is even more essential in gaining greater autonomy.

The representative to the teachers' union believes Kurz leads by example and that students and teachers emulate his devotion and commitment.

Teacher morale is high and while Kurz pushes them hard, he does not look to break any teacher's contracts. Parents are involved in the school community and are kept well-informed, especially through PTA meetings. Several programs work to bring the school and community together.

Community Elementary School (C.E.S.) 42

C.E.S. 42 is a neighborhood school located in the central Bronx. Class sizes are large; according to teachers, they are too large, especially in grades K-2. Limited amounts of classroom seats are reserved for children outside the district. The school displays a definite sense of spirit, with bulletin boards, hallways, and classroom walls plastered with colorful posters and students' work. Uniforms are optional.

Sandra Kase has been principal of C.E.S. 42 for the past 12 years.[3] Prior to becoming principal, she spent 10 years as a teacher of early childhood education and as a resource teacher. Following her 10 years of teaching experience, Kase worked for the district office as a staff coordinator and administrator, where she was able to develop networks and to observe models of schools and principals.

C.E.S. 42 At a Glance	
School (District)	District 9
Grades	Pre K-5
Enrollment	620
% Black/Hispanic	52% / 48%
% Free Lunch Eligible	100%
Principal	Sandra Kase

Kase is a strong and aggressive leader. She has clear expectations of her teachers and requires that the staff support her ideas. When first coming to the school, she explained her vision and expectations to the teachers, and asked that they leave (she would help them find another school to work at) if they did not agree with her ideas. Although she says that the organizational culture of her school is "flat," rather than hierarchical, with everyone involved in the shared decision making, she has clear ideas of what she wants and will do whatever she can to implement her standards.

Kase wants the teachers to feel that accountability is shared. Teachers are hired using a school-based staffing option, in which a committee (which includes Kase as a member) is responsible for hiring new teachers. She feels that staff selection is of utmost importance. New teachers are hired after a formal interview, a classroom demonstration, and a writing sample. Since Kase believes that it is the job of the school to train the teachers, C.E.S. 42 has a strong mentoring system. Teachers of the same grade level share free periods, enabling them to work together and share ideas.

Before Kase became principal, the school employed a "drill and grill" curriculum, teaching only the basics. Kase's first goal was to modify the culture of the school by adding special programs, new clubs, and extracurricular activities.

On the practical side of instituting her vision, Kase made it a priority to renovate the building, an 80-year old structure. She painted walls, bought new desks, and hung up bulletin boards and posters.

Kase believes in community involvement. C.E.S. 42 has a neighborhood watch group, an active PTA, and strong parental support and involvement. Upon becoming principal, Kase approached the ministers in the community, asking for their help.

Kase believes that issues of money and space are only details in the obstacles encountered by a school principal. Her biggest challenge rests with the constantly changing rules set by the city, state, and federal government. But, mainly because of her successes, Kase was able to carve out autonomy for herself. Kase also gains greater autonomy by gathering money from outside grant sources for extra curriculum development in math, writing, science, art, computers, and music.

According to the school's teachers union representative, Kase's strong and effective leadership makes this school unique. Leadership is top-down and teachers have a solid grasp of what is expected of them. There is pressure for the teachers to succeed in terms of test scores, active parental involvement, and the continued progress of students. Kase's vision that every child has special abilities and talents is clear. Sometimes, however, the ideas and goals clash with the actual implementation. Class size is an interfering factor; it is difficult to reach each child when there are 32 children in a class. Furthermore, the ambitious portfolio assessments for each child are demanding on the teachers.

P.S. 29

P.S. 29 is a neighborhood school located in the South Bronx. Although the school aims for a small class size of 18 to 19 students, this year there are 22 to 25 children in each classroom, due in part to an influx of students enrolling from outside the school boundaries.

The principal, Dorothy Carmichael, was the assistant principal prior to 1996, when the long-serving principal left. More than P.S. 161 and C.E.S. 42, the school has a broad-based system of management. Carmichael works very hard to implement a bottom-up decision-making team. This was illustrated by the fact that this was our only interview that included three other staffers in addition to the principal.

Teachers and administrators choose textbooks and make decisions together. The school provides an extensive staff development program for entering teachers, making them feel comfortable both professionally and emotionally.

P.S. 29 is divided into units; each unit works to develop and assist one another. The teachers of the same grade level are all free once a week at the same time so they can collaborate on curriculum issues. Teachers have the leeway to teach the subjects in their own creative manner.

Carmichael expects that all students should be able to fulfill their potential and work to their fullest capabilities. While greater academic success is the primary goal for each student, she believes that children should be able to master other areas as well. Students of different ability levels are grouped heterogeneously; those students needing extra help stay after school for special programming. Other special programs include an integrated literature and science/mathematics curriculum, and a 4th-grade greeting card business.

P.S. 29 At a Glance	
School (District)	District 7
Grades	Pre K-5
Enrollment	830
% Black/Hispanic	36% / 63%
% Free Lunch Eligible	98%
Principal	Dorothy Carmichael

According to Carmichael, the biggest obstacle to further success is the teachers' union contract. In trying to reallocate resources, she has faced some frustrating dead-ends and feels that some staff are often reluctant to go beyond what is prescribed of them.

The school has an active Parents' Association. Parents have been trained to work in classrooms together with teachers and para-professionals. Attempting to make parents feel more comfortable in the school, Carmichael has instituted educational programs and free medical screenings for the parents themselves.

According to both the assistant principal and a teacher within the school, the school's success comes from the fact that teachers feel that they are heard and respected; Carmichael is open-minded and flexible.

The Neighborhood School (P.S. 363)

P.S. 363, The Neighborhood School, is an alternative school of choice, located in Manhattan's East Village. Class sizes are large, but the classes are of mixed age and ability level. A neighborhood group started the school seven years ago (hence the name) in an effort to attract and accommodate the changing neighborhood, a very artistic and politically active area. Both students and staff portray a sense of individuality and informality. Hemphill (1997) describes students in the school with "purple hair" and "sitting on

P.S. 363 At a Glance	
School (District)	District 1
Grades	Pre K-6
Enrollment	235
% Black/Hispanic	15% / 45%
% Free Lunch Eligible	100%
Principal	Judith Foster

the floor," a style we also observed. The school perpetuates an atmosphere of respect and teamwork, providing a nurturing and supportive environment in which students develop a strong academic foundation and are encouraged to also fulfill their creative potential.

Judith Foster, director of the Neighborhood School, was a substitute teacher for a number of years and a teacher in this school for seven years before becoming director. She still identifies with the teachers and includes them, as well as the needs of the parents and students, in her decision making. She hires teachers who share her vision, and if they do not work out she recommends that they go to another school. The teacher's representative supported these concepts and credited Foster for an open communicative environment. The PTA representative noted that Foster solves problems and runs the school but is careful to include everyone in her decisions.

The progressive pedagogy of the school emphasizes group learning as well as individual development and attention. There is also emphasis on the social and emotional development of the students. Foster feels that the curriculum is more in-depth than most other schools at the elementary level. Since the central Board of Education does not always agree with progressive pedagogy, this can create tensions; for example, Foster does not support standardized testing and feels that students can be evaluated in different and better ways.

The challenge in implementing her vision of the school was actually getting the school started. Over time, she has not changed the vision of the school but has tried to make the relationships between students, parents, teachers, and staff more friendly and open. Her biggest constraint is planning time within the school, as considerable time is spent at external meetings.

Next, we turn to the four intermediate and high schools we visited.

Intermediate and High Schools

The New School for Research in the Natural and Social Sciences (J.H.S. 230)

The New School for Research in the Natural and Social Sciences located in central Brooklyn, is part of a community district that has recently converted nine of its middle schools into magnet schools using a grant from the U.S. Department of Education. The district defines the goals of their magnet schools as: 1) implementation of high-quality classroom instruction for students in the curricular areas of the magnet program; 2) achievement of systemic reform, providing all students with the opportunity to

J.H.S. 230 At a Glance	
School (District)	District 15
Grades	6-8
Enrollment	200
% Black/Hispanic	20% / 35%
% Free Lunch Eligible	80%
Principal	Anthony Galitsis

achieve high standards; 3) design and implementation of innovative educational practices and methods; and 4) promotion of diversity balance. Parents from all over New York City can apply to have their children attend these schools, but preference is usually given to those students already in the district. Seats are determined by a lottery basis.

Since the New School for Research in the Natural and Social Sciences opened in September 1998, it cannot yet be legitimized as a "success." Still, the "buzz" about the school is very good, and parents in the district seem to like it.

The principal, Anthony Galitsis, has a Ph.D. in chemistry and has been in the New York City public school system for 35 years. For 12 years, he was Central Board Director of Science Curriculum.

The mission of the schools is "to provide students with the skills, background, and experience to become expert problem solvers." The school runs on the philosophy of Paul Brandwein's "ecology of achievement" where students get considerable hands-on research experience. The school emphasizes group work and uses the students' natural curiosity as a driving force for learning.

Galitsis explicitly employs a shared leadership style. New teachers are chosen by a panel of teachers, parents, staff, and the principal. In creating this school, and as a pre-condition for accepting the job, Galitsis was given considerable autonomy by his district superintendent, who favors choice and school-level autonomy and accountability.

Galitsis works to create an open relationship with teachers, who are given the autonomy to explore teaching methods they feel are important. Given that the school combines math and science teaching together, the biggest obstacle they face is finding qualified teachers, many of whom come from the New School for Social Research in New York.

J.H.S. 99

Junior High School 99 is located in District 4, Manhattan, or East Harlem. District 4 is a national model for public school choice, having initiated choice in 1974. All junior high students in District 4 must choose a school to attend; there is no default neighborhood option. J.H.S 99 is far from the top school in the district, but it has improved substantially in recent years.

J.H.S. 99 is an alternative school that has four mini-schools within it, all directed by Leslie Moore. Moore has been in the New York City public system for 31 years and had been a director in another alternative school in District 4.

J.H.S. 99 At a Glance	
School (District)	District 4
Grades	6-8
Enrollment	1,100
% Black/Hispanic	34% / 58%
% Free Lunch Eligible	80%
Principal	Leslie Moore

The Manhattan East Center for Arts and Academics has over 275 students in the 6th, 7th, and 8th grades working on advanced coursework. The Academy of Environmental Science Secondary School (grades 7-12) focuses primarily on math and science. A visitor sees plenty of computers in the Julia de Burgos Academy of Computer Technology (grades 7 and 8). The fourth school is being converted into a computer-oriented school for bilingual students in kindergarten through 12th grade. Students are chosen for these schools based on district regulations, academic ability, and an interview.

Each of the four schools has a director with the autonomy to hire teachers who fit into the mission of that particular school. Moore views her role as that of "CEO," getting outside grants and bringing in special programs. She stays out of most "nitty-gritty" daily activities, unless she is called upon to solve an important problem.

When Moore took over in 1992, the school building was "a mess." Instead of student work on the walls, it had obscene graffiti. There had also been some controversy about her appointment because Moore is white, and the vast majority of school students are Hispanic or black. The first part of implementing her vision was to make the school a secure, nurturing environment for both children and teachers. She believes she was selected because she was perceived as "tough," which she said is accurate. She renounced any previous "deals or favors" people had made, and she "excessed" eight staff members who were not doing their jobs. Generally, she worked around union and bureaucratic constraints to get the staff members she wanted.

Moore does believe that financial resources could be enhanced. For example, she is budgeted about $35 per student per year for textbooks, which currently buys about one book. Thus, she spends considerable time seeking outside grants.

Moore believes that parent involvement is valuable but not critical to success. In fact, the current state mandate for Team Leadership, which includes 50 percent teachers and 50 percent parents, seems problematic to Moore in a junior high school setting where the students turn over every two to three years. The same parents will not continue on the team, causing low stability, high turnover, and the need for lots of ongoing training and re-training.

To Moore, success is defined by test scores, acceptance into selective, elite high schools, high levels of daily attendance, very low dropout rates, and safety of the building. Also, as a choice school, parents signal their interest by applying in large numbers. Total enrollment has grown from 750 to 1,100 students in recent years. The district has pushed Moore to accept the larger number, which she has done, but she does feel there is both a physical limit and a maximum size that they are now very close to.

A teacher representative agreed that morale was high and that teachers worked very hard for Moore, but enjoyed it. Few leave the school. Moore leads by making teachers feel like part of the team.

The International High School (IHS)

The IHS was founded in 1985 in collaboration with LaGuardia Community College at CUNY. It is an alternative, multicultural high school designed to help recent immigrants with varying degrees of English proficiency. There are 440 students attending the school. The principal is Eric Nadelstern. The mission of IHS is to provide its students with the linguistic, cultural, and cognitive skills needed for success in high school, college and beyond.

International High School At a Glance

Grades	9-12
Enrollment	400
% Black/Hispanic	25% / 38%
% Free Lunch Eligible	85%
Principal	Eric Nadelstern

Specifically, the school believes: 1) students should learn to speak English; 2) learning another language is an advantage; 3) high expectations along with support systems are essential for success; 4) students learn best in heterogeneous groupings; 5) in career-oriented internships; 6) teachers must participate actively in school decisions.

The school emphasizes team teaching and teachers develop the actual curriculum. Teachers are chosen by a panel of staff and are given considerable autonomy. There is generally no need to fire teachers, because of this selection method. Teachers work in groups to improve themselves. Currently, the curriculum is divided into 12 courses. While team teaching is the biggest strength of IHS it is also a challenge to overcome. Sometimes team teaching is more work for the teachers, and loyalty sometimes flows more to the team effort rather than to the school as a whole.

Nadelstern's leadership style is to let teachers have as much control and autonomy as they prove themselves capable. Teachers, instead of only the principal, help to evaluate each other. Decision-making is shared collectively by parents, teachers, and students. Maneuvering around the central Board of Education is crucial in order to develop the school in the ways that Nadelstern sees as necessary.

The Landmark High School

Landmark High School is located on West 58th Street in Manhattan in the upper floors of a larger school building. The school was started in 1993 with the mission of dealing with at-risk students who would otherwise drop out of high school. The school receives financial support from the Annenberg Foundation.

In theory, half of the students are chosen from a list by the school and the other half are chosen by the Board of Education. In reality, though, the rules are not clear and the city system often

Landmark High School At a Glance	
Grades	9-12
Enrollment	330
% Black/Hispanic	25% / 71%
% Free Lunch Eligible	83%
Principal	Sylvia Rabiner

"dumps" children in the school at the last minute, often those with the biggest problems, who end up taking up the most time of teachers and staff.

The principal, Sylvia Rabiner, uses a leadership style that is consultative but top-down. She relies on creativity in dealing with bureaucratic constraints. She "counsels out" teachers who do not fit with the school's mission and helps to find them another job through her school system contacts.

Teachers have some autonomy within the school's framework, but not an unlimited amount.

Her vision largely involves day-to-day coping with the myriad problems of the students. Success is defined by graduation and pursuit of further education by the students. Rabiner finds that she must often utilize creative maneuvering to circumvent the restrictions of the central Board of Education to accomplish the goals of the school.

Rabiner feels that the soft money grant from the Annenberg Foundation is critical to her school's mission. One example is a school yearbook. The Board of Education said she had to use student affairs money to pay for it, but there was only $320 allocated for it. A high school yearbook costs about $6,000, so only through the flexibility of the Annenberg money were they able to have one. In addition, one cannot "roll over" Board of Education budget monies from one year to the next, limiting flexibility.

The school has a five-year waiver from standard testing, and utilizes portfolio assessment, around which the whole curriculum and school organization is structured. Rabiner is concerned that the current push for standardized testing and "one size fits all" will jeopardize her school's approach.

Principals as Leaders of Successful Schools

All of the schools we studied are high value-added and/or high-performing schools—but they vary on many important dimensions. Class sizes ranged from large to small, children of different ability levels were either integrated or separated, management was both collective and top down, teaching styles were either formal or informal in nature, halls were quiet and orderly or loud and lively, parents were intimately involved or not closely involved, and school size varied widely, from 200 to 1,400 students. However, there was one thing shared by all these high-performing schools: strong and consistent leadership by the school principal.

Each principal we studied was integral to defining the culture of the school, whether they had created it or adapted to it. At the elementary school level, Kurz's exceptional professionalism and organizational skills coupled with a quiet but stern demeanor structure the atmosphere of the school: Students walked in orderly lines, teachers dressed in professional business attire, and attention was paid to the cleanliness of the school. Kase's approach employed similar characteristics, but in a more relaxed environment. At the other extreme, Foster's open approach to child development and problem solving is mirrored by her collective office space; students, parents, teachers, and even a rabbit frequent Foster's space, a spatial exemplar of the constant interaction between students, staff, and administration. In between, Carmichael simultaneously fashioned a sense of leadership, respect, and authority for herself, while stressing the importance of teachers' contributions and collaboration. Since they came into dysfunctional schools, Kurz and Kase can be considered the most transformational leaders, while Carmichael was part of a continuing success story, and Foster was part of an effort to explicitly create a new school and culture.

At the higher grade levels, there was also variation on the theme of strong leadership. Like Foster, both Galitsis and Moore were essentially starting up new operations, with different approaches, one from scratch, one by re-orienting existing programs. While both high school principals, Rabiner and Nadelstern, work with a challenging student population, they have developed creative teaching approaches that seem to be working. Galitsis and Nadelstern seem oriented more to sharing responsibility, while conditions lead Moore and Rabiner to asset their own authority more within the school.

Despite these differences, all of these principals were exceptional leaders. They all worked to develop both a clear and consistent school culture and a community that is supportive of the school. As a result of their leadership, all of these high-performing schools possess the criteria set forth by Deal and Paterson (1990) in their definition of an effective school. They share a strong set of values that support a safe environment; high expectations for every student; a belief in the importance of basic skills instruction; clear performance goals and continuous feedback; and strong leadership and a belief in its importance. Each principal had a vision and an articulated mission for their school. The specific mission varied across the schools, but in each school the mission is clear and has been consistent and stable over time. In all cases teachers and parents bought into the vision and culture that the principal created, in part because they were and are involved in that vision.

In short, while the exact nature of that vision and the associated pedagogical approaches do not seem essential, it is important that an articulated vision exists that permeates all aspects of school culture with consistency, clarity, and stability.

School Principals as Entrepreneurs

Schneider and Teske (1995) have studied public entrepreneurs—individuals who have revitalized and transformed local governments. They argue that an effective entrepreneur (or to use other terminology a transformational leader) is:
- alert to opportunity and unfulfilled needs

- able to carry the reputational and emotional risk involved in pursuing a course of action with uncertain consequences, and
- able to assemble and coordinate teams or networks of individuals and organizations that have the talents and resources necessary to undertake change.

The principals we studied have many of the hallmarks of the other public entrepreneurs Schneider and Teske analyzed. In an era where the autonomy of the school principal is being constantly challenged, the success of these schools was created by the principal, as they initially took risks, seized opportunities, and worked to establish a cohesive, like-minded network of parents, teachers, and staff.

All of these principals felt that much of their success came from having some autonomy from the central Board of Education constraints. In practical terms, each principal had considerable experience within the school system. This allowed them to learn, firsthand, what worked, and what rules could be ignored and what rules could not be ignored. This suggests that even these successful principals, individuals who should have "earned" a certain amount of autonomy from central administrators, are still not given enough freedom to run their schools in a manner consistent with their pursuit of quality education. These principals all fought to increase the policy space they had, describing autonomy as something they "took" rather than something that was "given" to them.

Not surprisingly, given the labor intensity of education, in schools at both the elementary and secondary level, the most important issue facing these principals seems to be their relationship to teachers. All of these principals emphasize the need to have teachers who share their vision. These principals have developed various ways to ensure that their teachers are team players. For example, in many of these schools a panel of teachers, parents, staff, and the principal jointly choose new teachers, and by so doing help to ensure that new teachers understand and buy into the mission and style of the school. Since, given the union contract, it is difficult to simply fire a teacher, the most successful principals have evolved strategies to help teachers who don't buy into the vision find alternative schools, "counseling them out" and working with the district to find another school for them (on the issue of the teacher's contract and principal discretion, see Ballou 1999).

This personnel strategy is essential for a variety of reasons. Most obviously, having developed this shared culture among the staff, most of these principals give their teachers a large degree of autonomy, which teachers appreciate and which allows them to develop professionally. As in any team situation, when the players share a vision, the need to monitor individual members declines, and more energy can be devoted to the real tasks of the organization.

Given that principals in the New York City public school system earn only a little more than advanced teachers, who have far fewer headaches, and earn far less (as much as 50 percent less) than principals in nearby suburban schools, it is no wonder more exceptional principals do not emerge. It is also a wonderful surprise that at least these strong and successful principal did emerge and stay in the system.

Conclusion

Leaders Are an Essential Ingredient of Successful Schools

Although our schools were not chosen randomly—and eight is a small sample of the nearly 1,000 public schools in New York City—some patterns are nonetheless evident in our study.

First, it is important to note that many of the inputs into education that are often emphasized by different educational reforms were not critical to the success of the schools we studied. For example, for most of these successful principals money was not a central issue—although they all would like additional resources, the problems they faced were not overwhelmingly resource-based. And, while parental involvement was important to some principals, other principals recognized limits on how much parents could help.

For us, even more interesting was the range in the size of these highly successful schools: Some of these schools were large (1,400 in one elementary school) and others were small (200 students). Similarly, some had relatively small class sizes, while others had large and overflowing classes.

Finally, some of these schools were schools of choice, but most were not. Choice gives school leadership more autonomy, since alternative schools and schools of choice are subject to fewer restrictions than their regular public school counterparts in New York City. But in the high-performing neighborhood schools in our study, the principals had developed strategies to assert autonomy from the central Board and to create effective schools, even without being a designated choice school.

Despite this wide range in school structure and resources, we do not mean to imply that successful schools are idiosyncratic creations. We believe that leadership is an essential ingredient and that there are commonalities across the actions of these successful principals that contributed to their successes:

- *Controlling staff hiring and development practices is critical.* This allows teachers to develop professionally and frees the principal from many of the time-consuming tasks of dealing with staff who do not or cannot work together.

- *Experience matters.* All these principals had considerable time in the system and drew on this knowledge base to identify strategies that gave them the policy space to pursue their goals.
- *A coherent educational mission throughout all grades in the school.* A defined articulated mission helps mobilize the staff and the school community. But it is important to realize that while a coherent mission was common in all these schools, the specific approach to education varied widely across the schools.
- *High expectations for students, not just in rhetoric but in practice.* These beliefs were common to every principal we studied and they all expected everyone in the school community to live up to high standards and to enforce those high expectations.

Based on our observations, we argue that the leadership of the principal is a central factor for effective schools. While many of our findings support previous studies on what makes an effective leader, we believe that the autonomy the principal is given or is able to assert is often neglected in the literature. The principals in our study not only worked with what was already in the school, they also created and nurtured a productive school culture by innovative hiring practices and often bending the rules of the bureaucracy to achieve their critical tasks.

Recommendation

Increasing Autonomy Is Essential for Leadership to Emerge

Based on our observations, we believe that greater autonomy is needed in large bureaucratic school systems to increase the number of successful schools. We selected the principals profiled here specifically for their successes—and virtually all of these successful leaders learned to seize autonomy within a highly rigid, rule-bound bureaucratic structure. Providing such autonomy more routinely would save considerable effort, free successful principals to pursue academic success, and generate more positive results for students.

However, we recognize that not all principals will effectively use greater autonomy. Some may use their increased freedom to pursue ineffective policies and inappropriate goals. Thus there is clearly a risk: If greater school-level autonomy leads to abuses at the school level, some *reasonable* regulations must be maintained to insure accountability to public standards. We believe that the level of bureaucratic control now in place—a system that emerged to deal with past problems and, as Chubb and Moe have argued, grew like "topsy"—is now excessive. We need to increase school autonomy while at the same time preserving accountability.

There are changes that can do both. For example, we believe that under a system of greater parental choice, principals would also be held directly accountable to parents and students who can "vote with their feet." We think that increasing accountability through parental choice requires an increase in the amount of reliable information about the schools that is available (Schneider, 1999) and a better understanding of how parents will use that information (Schneider, Teske, and Marschall, 2000). But, realistically, principals are already the single set of school personnel that are held more accountable for outputs than anyone else in the system (Ballou 1999).

We also believe that the ongoing movement toward national and state standards and the move toward more uniform testing procedures will help produce tools for holding schools accountable while at the same time (and perhaps not obviously) create the conditions for more autonomy at the school level. Society will set the goals and standards, while schools will be given the autonomy to develop the ways of best achieving those ends.

Thus, we also recommend that school systems, especially large urban systems like New York City, act to reward successful principals more, and to reassign or terminate unsuccessful ones more frequently. The rewards can include salary increases, since principal salaries are low compared to the responsibilities of the job and to salary levels in nearby suburban school systems. But rewards must also include greater autonomy to make the job more interesting and rewarding. Autonomy is probably most important in the selection and retention of staff. Successful principals should also be given greater flexibility in the use of their school budget.

We also find that consistency of leadership is important. Here we agree strongly with Hess, who argues that frequent leadership turnover "disrupts administrative support and increases the emphasis on initiating rather than executing reform. The need to design and launch new initiatives reduces the resources available to diagnose problems and implement remedies." (Hess 1999: 160) Indeed, most of these successful principals have been in their positions for a number of years (or as in one case, followed in the steps of a leader who had been principal for a long period). We recommend that the system use some of the rewards noted above to try to maintain consistent leadership in successful schools.

Another common theme in the leadership style of the principals we studied was their respect for the teaching profession. To varying degrees, these principals gave autonomy to the teachers in their classrooms— because they trusted their teachers and had worked hard to make sure that teachers and staff were united in their beliefs and pedagogical approaches. To do this, staff development is clearly important. Teachers were made important members of the school community by their involvement in administrative decisions, and they helped to set the goals in several schools.

While it is important to develop good relationships with the teachers of the school, it may be even more important to choose the teachers that one is working with. These principals made success happen not only by transforming existing school practices but also by recruiting new members who supported the school's mission. Therefore, the principal plays a critical role in developing school culture not only by influencing the teachers and students within the school, but also by showing leadership when choosing the people that will belong to the community. At present, principals are only able to do this by going around standard New York City Board of Education procedures that emphasize hiring based on tenure, not suitability (see Ballou 1999 for details on this process).

There is no secret to the success of the effective school principal, no magic formulas, and no hidden models. Rather, the schools succeeded to a large degree because of the alert, consistent, resourceful, and sustaining energy of the school principal. There is no inherent reason that strong principals should be in such short supply in New York City and in other public school systems. Reforms that help to "deregulate" the schools are likely to create the conditions under which more such principals will emerge. More autonomy is essential and more rewards for success are also critical in encouraging such leaders to emerge.

But structural reforms need to be matched by a psychological change on the part of principals. While reforms that reduce central bureaucratic controls encourage those conditions, ultimately, to create better schools for more of our children, principals must think of themselves as both innovative managers and creative leaders.

Appendix:
Methodology

Selecting Elementary Schools

We chose the particular elementary schools to study by first identifying "high-performing schools" using test score and demographic data. Using two separate studies (one by the Board of Education and one we prepared ourselves), we identified about a dozen schools that were performing at least 15 points higher than demographic characteristics would otherwise "predict."[4] We cross-referenced these schools against those selected in *The Parents' Guide to New York City's Best Elementary Schools* (Hemphill 1997). We then selected a stratified random sample of these high-performing schools in order to include a range of school types in terms of pedagogical approach and demographic makeup.

We contacted the schools we identified as potential participants by mail, followed by telephone inquiries about one week afterward to ensure receipt of the letter and to arrange for a date and time to meet with the principal. We interviewed school principals for at least 45 minutes with a prepared interview question format. The goal of these interviews was to understand the extent to which they changed the culture of their school and to identify the managerial reforms they credit most with improving performance. The principals' interviews provided both factual information with respect to their previous experience in education, beliefs, roles, and personal and school-wide values; the schools' present operations; and also valuable perception-based data based upon the principals' successes and failures in implementing many of the reforms and cultural changes. In most cases, we also interviewed the head of the teachers' associations and/or other parent leaders to gain another perspective on the principal's influence within the school community.

Selecting Intermediate and High Schools

Without a common metric of test scores across all such schools, we chose our two intermediate and two high schools based upon the reputation of the schools and their principals. We received recommendations from three knowledgeable sources: Clair Hemphill, award-winning journalist who covers and writes books about New York City public schools; Sy Fleigel, director of the Center For Educational Innovation; and Diane Ravitch, former U.S. deputy assistant secretary of education and scholar of the New York City system. We chose the specific schools for variation by area of the city and by type of school.

Endnotes

1. The reader may be confused by the various names and terms for these New York City schools that follow. Historically, the NYC Board of Education assigned a number to each school building—for example, elementary schools are called Public Schools (PS) "x" such as P.D. 161. Similarly, Intermediate Schools (I.S.) and Junior High Schools (J.H.S.)—the terms differ mostly for historical reasons, although intermediate schools often have a different configuration of grades than grades 7-9 typical of many J.H.S.s— are also assigned a number. Some schools that formed more recently were started as "Community Schools" to emphasize their ties to neighborhoods. (hence C.E.S. 42). Many schools also have "names" in addition to their official numbers. In addition, some schools have broken up into "mini-schools" within a single building, as in J.H.S 99, described later, In addition, when we refer to "neighborhood schools," we mean those that gather their students form within a defined set of geographic boundaries, while "alternative schools" emphasize particular themes and allow students to choose to enroll in that school even if other schools are physically closer.

2. In August 1999, Irwin Kurz was named one of five superintendents in the New York City school system to oversee failing schools. Mr. Kurz will be responsible for schools in Brooklyn.

3. After our interviews, Sandra Kase accepted a position working with the central Board on schools that were failing and had been placed on the state's special list of failed schools. An interesting future question is whether her ideas have become institutional- ized or whether they require her sustained leadership presence.

4. In more technical terms, we regressed the test scores of each elementary school against a set of student demographic characteristics (including NEP, LEP, turnover, and other demographic indicators). We then calculated the residuals from this regression equation. Schools whose observed performance was at least 15 points higher than that predicated by the regression equation were identified, and the schools we studied were selected from that population of high-performing schools.

Bibliography

Anderson, Shirley. "High School Principals and School Reform: Lessons Learned From a Statewide Study of Project Re:Learning." *Educational Administration Quarterly* 31, 3: 405-423.

Aviolio, B. & B. Bass. 1988. "Transformational Leadership: Charisma and Beyond." In J. Hunt, B. Baliga, H. Dachler, and C. Shriesheim (eds.), *Emerging Leadership Vistas* (pp.29-49). Toronto: Lexington Books.

Ballou, Dale. 1999. "The New York City Teachers' Union Contract: Shackling Principals' Leadership." Civic Report by the Center for Civic Innovation at the Manhattan Institute, New York, New York.

Brewer, D.J. 1993. "Principals and Student Outcomes: Evidence from U.S. High Schools." *Economics of Education Review.* (12) 4:281-292.

Buhler, P. 1995. *Leaders vs. Managers.* Supervision. 56:24.

Burns, J.M. 1978. *Leadership.* New York: Harper & Row.

Chubb, John and Terry Moe. 1990. *Politics, Markets, and America's Schools.* Washington, D.C.: Brookings Institution.

Coleman, James, E.Q. Campell, C.J. Hobson, J. McPartland, A.M. Mood, F.D. Weinfeld, and R. L. York. 1966. *Equality of Educational Opportunity.* Washington, D.C.: Government Printing Press.

Conley, D.T. 1997. *Roadmap to Restructuring: Charting the Course of Change in American Education.* Eugene, OR: ERIC Clearinghouse on Educational Management, University of Oregon.

Deal, T. 1987. The Culture of Schools. In L. Sheive and M. Schoenheit (eds.) Leadership: Examining the Elusive. *The 1987 Yearbook of the Association for Supervision and Curriculum Development* (pp.1-15).

Deal, T.E. and K.D. Peterson. 1990. *The Principal's Role in Shaping School Culture.* Washington, D.C.: Department of Education, Office of Educational Research and Improvement.

Drake, Thelbert L. and William H. Roe. 1999. *The Principalship.* D. Stollenwerk (ed.) Upper Saddle River, NJ: Prentice Hall.

Eberts, R. and J.A. Stone. 1988. "Student Achievement in Public Schools: Do Principals Really Make a Difference?" *Economics of Education Review* (7)3: 291-299.

Fullan, M.G. 1996. Leadership for Change. In K. Leithwood, J. Chapman, D. Corson, P. Hallinger, and A. Hart (eds.) *International Handbook of Educational Leadership and Administration* (pp. 701-722). Dordrecht, The Netherlands: Kluwer Academic Press.

Gardner, Howard. 1995. *Leading Minds: An Anatomy of Leadership.* New York: Basic Books.

Goldman, Elise. "The Significance of Leadership Style." *Educational Leadership.* April 1998. (pp. 20-22).

Hanushek, Eric. 1986. "The Economics of Schooling: Production and Efficiency in Public Schools." *Journal of Economic Literature* 24:1141-1177.

Heck, R. 1992. Principals Instructional Leadership and School Performance: Implications for Policy Development. *Educational Evaluation and Policy Analysis*. 14 1):21-34.

Hemphill C. 1997. *The Parents' Guide to New York City's Best Public Elementary Schools.* NY: Soho Press.

Hess, Frederick. 1999. *Spinning Wheels: The Politics of Urban School Reform.* Washington, D.C.: Brookings Institution.

Hord, S.M. 1992. *Facilitative Leadership: The Imperative for Change.* Office of Educational Research and Improvement. Contract No. RP 91002003. Austin, TX: Southwest Educational Development Laboratory.

Keedy, J.L. 1991. *School Improvement Practices of Successful High School Principals.* West Carrollton, GA: The West Georgia Regional Center for Teacher Education.

Lashway, L. 1997. *Visionary Leadership.* Eric Digest 110) EA 028 072.

Lee, Valerie and Julia Smith. 1994. "Effects of High School Restructuring and Size on Gains in Achievement and Engagement for Early Secondary School Students." Madison, WI: Wisconsin Center for Education Research.

Leithwood, K. 1994. "Leadership for School Restructuring." *Educational Administration Quarterly* (29): 498-518.

Leithwood, K., D. Tomlinson & M. Genge. 1996. Transformative School Leadership. In K. A Leithwood, J. Chapman, D. Corson, P. Hallinger, & A. Hart (Eds.), *International Handbook of Educational Leadership and Administration: Part II* (pp. 785-840). Dordrecht, The Netherlands: Kluwer Academic.

Mitchell, D.E. & S. Tucker. 1992. Leadership as a Way of Thinking. *Educational Leadership.* 49(5), 30-35.

Perez, Anna L., Mike M. Milstein, Carolyn J. Wood, and David Jacquez. 1999. *How to Turn a School Around: What Principals Can Do.* Thousand Oaks, CA: Corwin Press.

Purkey, S.C. and M.S. Smith. 1983. Effective Schools: A Review. *The Elementary School Journal.* 83 (4):427-452.

Ravitch, Diane. *The Great School Wars: New York City 1805-1973: A History of the Public Schools as a Battlefield of Social Change.* New York: Basic Books. 1974.

Ravitch, Diane and Joseph Viteritti (ed.) *New Schools for a New Century: The Redesign of Urban Education.* New Haven: Yale University Press. 1997.

Reed, P. and A. Roberts. 1998. *An Investigation of Leadership in Effective and Noneffective Urban Schoolwide Project Schools.* Paper presented at the Annual Meeting of the American Educational Research Association (San Diego, CA, April 13-17, 1998. ED 419 885.

Sashkin, M. and H.J. Walberg. *Educational Leadership and School Culture.* Berkeley, CA: McCutchan Publishing Corporation.

Schein, E.H. 1985. *Organizational Culture and Leadership.* San Francisco: Jossey-Bass.

Schneider, Mark. 1999. "Information and Choice in Educational Privatization." Paper prepared for the conference on educational privatization. The National Center for the Study of Privatization in Education. Columbia Teacher's College. New York: Columbia University. April 9th-10th, 1999.

Schneider, Mark and Paul Teske. 1995. *Public Entrepreneurs: Agents for Change in American Government.* Princeton, NJ: Princeton University Press.

Schneider, Mark, Paul Teske, and Melissa Marschall. 2000. *Choosing Schools: Consumer Choice and the Quality of American Schools.* Princeton, NJ: Princeton University Press.

Schweigr, D.M. and C.R. Leana. 1986. Participation in decision making. In E. Locke (ed.) Generalizing from the laboratory to field settings: Findings from research in industrial organizational psychology, organizational behavior, and human resource management. Lexington, MA: Lexington Books.

Sergiovanni, T.J. 1992. Moral Leadership: Getting to the Heart of School Improvement. San Francisco: Jossey-Bass.

U.S. News & World Report. 1999. "Special Report: Outstanding American High Schools." January 18 issue. Multiple Authors.

Wood, C.J. 1998. Human Dimensions of Supervision. In G.R. Firth & E. F. Pajak (eds.) *Handbook of Research on School Supervision* (pp. 1085-1103). New York: Macmillan.

CHAPTER SEVEN

Profiles in Excellence:
Conversations with the Best of
America's Career Executive Service

Mark W. Huddleston
Dean
College of Arts and Science
University of Delaware

This report was originally published in November 1999.

Introduction

At the top of the executive branch, just below the President, cabinet secretaries, undersecretaries, deputy undersecretaries, and various other transient political figures, are 6,000 or so senior career executives who constitute the heart of our permanent government. These are the men and women who, year after year, day in and day out, manage major federal programs. They maintain our national security, guarantee the purity of our food, protect our natural resources, reinforce the rule of law, facilitate our commerce and otherwise ensure that life in the United States remains safe, bountiful, and civilized. Who these individuals are—their talents, character, commitment to the public good—and how they are selected, developed, and managed are thus questions of considerable interest for those who care about the quality of American government. Excellent public service requires excellent public servants.

This report is intended to assess the health of the personnel system—the Senior Executive Service (SES)—responsible for managing these senior public servants, and hence for underpinning this crucial stratum of American government. The report is based on a series of conversations held in the summer of 1999 with some of the best of the best: 21 of the men and women whose achievements in the SES were so outstanding that they were recognized with Presidential Distinguished Rank Awards, an honor bestowed on only 1 percent of all career federal executives. Among this group are Thomas Billy, whose leadership in redesigning food safety and inspection procedures has markedly reduced food-borne illness in the United States; Franklin Miller, a career Pentagon official who was the key author of the START II treaty and a principal drafter of NATO's post-Cold War policy; James], the government's lead anti-terrorism attorney, a man responsible, among other things, for coordinating responses to the bombings of the World Trade Center and the Murrah Federal Building in Oklahoma City; and Eleanor Spector, who in her role as Director of Procurement for the Department of Defense, has played a pivotal role in streamlining the weapons acquisition process, saving billions of dollars a year in taxpayers' money.

How did these executives approach their work? What characteristics made them such outstanding leaders? What, more generally, facilitates or impedes excellent performance in government today? What does the future hold for the senior executive personnel system? Can Americans rest easy that government management is secure for the next generation, or is there cause for concern?

The SES and Presidential Rank Awards

This is a propitious time to address these questions. In 1999 we celebrated the 20th anniversary of the launch of the SES. Established pursuant to the Civil Service Reform Act of 1978, the SES was the first serious attempt in American history to forge a distinct personnel system for senior career executives. Modeled roughly on the military and foreign services, its members were conceived as the general officers on the civilian side of government—mobile, high-performing managers who could be sent by political leaders from one tough assignment to the next. They, unlike members of the lower rungs of the civil service, would carry their rank with them wherever they went. SES members would even be eligible for positions traditionally considered "political." Moreover, high risk would entail high reward: Basic pay rates would rise, performance bonuses would be generous, and a select few SES members would be eligible to receive presidential ranks, with large cash awards.

As one who has monitored the SES closely over its two decades of life—as an academic analyst, rapporteur for a Twentieth Century Fund study, participant in workshops, and consultant to government agencies—I, like most other observers, have found that few of these expectations have been fully met. Mobility has been minimal. Few SESers have risen to appointee positions. And pay has remained capped, compressed, and generally troublesome. Yet I have also found a continuing appreciation in almost all quarters of the challenges that gave rise to the SES 20 years ago, an abiding belief that the system, however flawed, needs to be fixed rather than abandoned; it is to this end that this project has been mainly devoted.

One part of the system that has functioned very well indeed, however, is the presidential rank award program, and as it is also central to this report I shall describe it in some detail. Intended to recognize particularly outstanding performance among career members of the SES, the presidential rank award program provides for two levels or ranks, "Meritorious" and "Distinguished." The rank of "Meritorious Executive," which may be given to no more than 5 percent of the government-wide career service in any one year, is reserved for members who have made "sustained accomplishments." SESers so recognized receive a one-time, lump-sum payment of 20 percent of base pay. The rank of "Distinguished Executive" is bestowed for "extraordinary sustained accomplishments." Recipients of the Distinguished Executive rank, whose numbers may not exceed 1 percent of the career SES, are granted a lump-sum award of 35 percent of base pay.[1]

In addition to the broad requirements established in law that recipients show "sustained" "or extraordinary sustained" accomplishments, each year OPM publishes a set of specific criteria against which rank award nominees

are to be judged. For the 1997 round of awards, there were seven such criteria. Nominees were to show:

1. career achievements that are recognized throughout the agency and/or
   acknowledged on a national or international level;
2. specific achievements of cost reduction or cost avoidance;
3. successful use of human resources as evident through improved workforce productivity and effective development and recognition of subordinates;
4. personal initiative and innovation in meeting the administration's goals
   and policies;
5. substantial improvement in quality, efficiency, and customer service;
6. unusual levels of cooperative effort with other federal agencies, government jurisdictions, or the private sector;
7. especially successful efforts in encouraging and maintaining a diverse
   workforce.

Following their own procedures, agencies are permitted to nominate up
to 9 percent of their career SES members for rank awards, providing that no
more than one member is nominated for the Distinguished rank for each
five members nominated for the Meritorious rank; agencies are also pro-
hibited from nominating a member for a rank award that he or she has won
within the past four years. Once the nominations are submitted to OPM,
typically by late January, and checked for compliance with basic eligibility
requirements, executive review boards are convened. There is one review
board (the "D Board") for Distinguished Executive nominees, which meets
in Washington, D.C., usually in March. Four review boards ("M Boards"),
which meet in four locations around the country, are empanelled for Meritorious Executive nominees; the four M Boards usually meet in the late
spring, which allows them to review the Meritorious award nominees who
did not make the cut for the Distinguished rank. Each of the D and M
Boards is composed of three individuals from the private sector selected by
the Director of OPM and the White House.

After each board member rates each nominee, scores are summed, and
a ranked list forwarded to OPM. OPM's Office of Executive Resources
establishes "cut scores" that reflect allowable numbers of recipients under
the law in each category and weighs the distribution of awards by agency
and "other relevant factors." The director of OPM then reviews the list of
potential winners and forwards the information to the agency heads for final
certification. After this "eyes only" process is completed, the director trans-
mits the list to the President for his approval. Final announcement of awards
is usually made by the White House in September or October, with an
awards ceremony held early the following spring.

The Design of the Study

This study is based on the 1997 class of SES Distinguished Executives, a cohort chosen because it was the one that had been most recently announced at the time the research was launched. Comprised of 54 men and nine women, the 1997 class came from 21 separate nominating agencies. Approximately two-thirds of the winners were located in agency headquarters or regional centers in the greater Washington metropolitan area. It was this geographic subset, drawn for ease of interviewing, that comprised the frame for the sample in this study.

My initial research plan called for me to conduct in-depth interviews with eight or 10 selected executives. Expecting it to be difficult to find willing participants, I wrote letters of inquiry to all 41 award recipients living in and around Washington, introducing myself and explaining the purposes of the project. I then followed each of these letters with a telephone call requesting an appointment for an interview. To my surprise, the acceptance rate was very high—nearly 70 percent if we exclude from the base people who were wholly unavailable owing to relocation, retirement, or travel. As I decided it would be ill-advised (and certainly ungracious) to stop making follow-up phone calls after I had met my initial target of eight or 10 executives, I wound up making appointments with all 21 of those who were available.

Because this set of 21 executives over-represents headquarters staff and women, and because it does not include, owing to the vagaries of responses from potential interviewees, winners from two relatively large agencies—National Aeronautics and Space Administration (NASA) and the Department of Veterans Affairs—it cannot be considered a rigorous representative sample. It does contain considerable variety, however. The 15 men and six women in the final set of respondents come from 16 different agencies. Their ages range from mid 40's to mid 60's. Although most are general "managers," with backgrounds in finance and administration, a few are scientists or engineers, and a handful are attorneys.

At the time of the interviews, their average length of service (mean and median) in the SES was nearly 13 years. One respondent was a charter member of the SES; the newest had been appointed in 1993. Sixteen of the 21 executives had previously won rank awards, three at the Distinguished level, 13 at the Meritorious level; one, indeed, had received three previous awards, including a Distinguished rank in 1990. Two of the respondents had left federal service between the time of their award and the interview, one to retire, the other to take a job in the private sector. Although many of the executives, over the course of their careers, had experience in more than one agency, as executives they had moved little: Only three of the 21 had held SES jobs in agencies other than those in which they had won the

1997 Distinguished rank award; this is a pattern that holds for the SES as a whole.

Nineteen of the executives were interviewed in person, in their offices; owing to scheduling problems two interviews were conducted by telephone. Each interview lasted approximately one hour, and was semi-structured and open-ended, taking the form more of what I have described as a conversation. Although I had a list of broad topics to cover—what makes a successful executive, career history, the current state of the SES, and so forth—each interview had its own unique character, reflecting the interests and perspectives of the particular executive.

The Conversations

From these interviews emerged six broad themes. The first deals with the qualities that produce excellence in administrative leadership. The final five themes bear on the state of the senior executive personnel system today and its likely fate as we move into the next century.

The Art of Excellence: Qualities of an Outstanding Senior Executive

One of the main aims of this project was to try to understand what qualities or characteristics made these award winners what they are. How does one become "distinguished" from a group, the broader SES, that is already quite distinguished? Exactly what constitutes excellence in public service?

These are questions, as I knew going in, with elusive answers, not the least because I had a small sample and no control group. Still, there is value in asking people who are acknowledged to be excellent to reflect on exactly how it is that they do what they do. So as not to run into an immediate brick wall of modesty, I approached this subject indirectly. What, I asked each of the executives, do you tell young people on the verge of joining the SES, the GS-14s and GS-15s in candidate development programs? What qualities make really successful senior executives?

The recipe, according to these distinguished executives, is deceptively simple. It has only four key ingredients: have a clear strategic vision for your agency, animate other people, work hard, and have integrity.

Four Qualities of an Excellent Executive

- Strategic vision
- Ability to animate others
- Ethic of hard work
- Integrity

Thomas J. Billy[2]
Department of Agriculture
Administrator, Food Safety and Inspection Service

- Reduced food-borne illness in the U.S., significantly improving public confidence in food safety
- Developed a multi-year regulatory strategy to reform the federal meat and poultry inspection system

To have a clear strategic vision means knowing exactly where you want your agency to go. You have to have "that funny feeling in the pit of your stomach," as Thomas Billy, administrator of Food Safety for the U.S. Department of Agriculture (USDA), put it, that you're headed in the right direction. Moreover, Billy added, "You need to set impossibly high goals." His strategic vision for the next five years is that "the food Americans eat will pose *no* risk." At first glance, he said, that sounds crazy. "But it starts you thinking. We may not have *all* the answers, but we can start now to plan the laws, design the regulations, and develop the technologies we need to get there." Michael Delpercio, director of ship operations for the Maritime Administration, used a similar example: "My goal was that every ship in the fleet get activated on time. Period."

Although all of the executives talked about the importance of articulating a vision, setting goals, and having a performance orientation, they did so in common sense terms. Across the board they rejected canned techniques and modish nostrums. "I tell young people to ignore management speak and the buzzwords of the week," said Lawrence Wachs, USDA's associate budget director. Deputy Inspector General for the Department of Health and Human Services (HHS) George Grob agreed: "Management theories and fads, which always come with new administrations, are things to live through, not to use."

The greater challenge for a leader, of course, is learning to **animate other people**. I use the word "animate" here rather than the more traditional "motivate" to convey the sense of enthusiasm, even exhilaration that these executives seek to inspire. It is essential, noted Kathleen Peroff, deputy associate director of the Office of Management and Budget (OMB), "to keep the people who work for you energized and excited." Carol Okin, associate director of the Office of Merit Systems Oversight and Effectiveness for the Office of Personnel Management, agreed, "My subordinates do the real work. They make me look good."

HHS's Grob maintained that team-building was the key here. Group work multiplies competence, breeds enthusiasm, and stimulates creativity.

Bradley A. Buckles
Department of the Treasury
Deputy Director, Bureau of Alcohol, Tobacco and Firearms

• Drafted Distilled Spirits Tax Revision Act, which simpli-
  fied tax collection
• Guided ATF's evaluation of adding taggants to explosives

Most important, Grob said, it makes work *fun:* "If you don't hear laughter, you're doing something wrong." It also helps, according to Grob, to develop incentives that fit what your subordinates really want, which for most federal employees is "to make a difference." To that end, he has developed a ritual for his staff, akin to a Presidential signing ceremony: Once legislation passes that his office had worked on, the staff gets together and identifies the sections on which they had a particular impact. Then, between popping flashbulbs and mouthfuls of cake and ice cream, they sign their names next to the relevant paragraphs.

Much of their success these executives attribute to nothing more than **hard work**. "Everyone has shortcomings," observed William Campbell, director of finance and procurement for the Coast Guard. "Successful executives just work around them. They're like three-legged dogs—they don't know they have only three legs. They just work extra hard." In fact, all of these executives described work schedules that most people would consider crushing, 65 or 70 hours a week on average. And the word "schedule" is probably inapt. As James Reynolds, chief of the Violent Crime and Terrorism Section at the Department of Justice (DOJ), emphasized, "If you want to be successful, you've got to be available. You've got to forget about sacrosanct nights, weekends, and vacations."

"You can't be a successful executive," said Paul Chistolini, associate director of the General Services Administration's Public Buildings Service, "as an '85 percenter.' You have to invest whatever it takes to finish a project." The Coast Guard's Campbell raised the ante even higher: "You have to remember that this is a service business. You give 99 percent, you get an 'F.' If you want an 'A,' you give 100 percent. Excellence is more than doing a job. It is doing it, wanting to do it, in a way that the people you are serving are *delighted.*"

Finally, mentioned more than any characteristic was another enduring virtue, **integrity**. Outstanding executives are not loose with the truth or inclined to try for quick wins by cutting bureaucratic corners. "What makes an excellent executive?" USDA's Wachs asked rhetorically. "In addition to innate ability and intellectual curiosity, it takes integrity and a desire to do the right thing." "Never forget that your role is to be an honest broker," said

William H. Campbell, Jr.
Department of Transportation
Director of Finance and Procurement

- Fostered improvement and customer service in the Coast Guard's finance and procurement program
- Promoted competition through innovative management of the Competition Advocacy Program, saving the Coast Guard $60 million annually

Steve Colgate, assistant attorney general for administration in the Department of Justice. "Honesty and integrity are everything." Eleanor Spector, director of procurement for the Department of Defense (DoD) agreed, "Integrity and honesty are the standard traits of leadership."

A Changing Sense of Vocation: Today's Senior Executives Commit to Government Service; Tomorrow's Will Commit to a Profession

One of the first questions that I asked in every interview was, "What led you into the federal service?" With all but a few of the executives, I got answers that started with words like "calling" or "vocation." These are men and women who are products of the 1960s—the *early* 1960s—a time before Americans became deeply and routinely cynical about government and what it could accomplish. Even some of those whose chronological age would have put them in middle school in 1962 and 1963 talked about how inspired they were by John F. Kennedy's impassioned call to serve our country; more than one, in fact, had a bust of JFK in his or her office. But—and this is a sad commentary on our own time—this was not always an easy topic for them to talk about. Phrases like "the nobility of public service" were spoken with a sort of guarded embarrassment. The unspoken question, "Will I be thought silly or old-fashioned?" seemed to hang in the air. For instance, after he talked about the continuing importance of attracting young people to government to work for "the public good," one executive asked, "Does that sound corny?"

To some young people, it may well sound corny. And that may create new challenges for the higher civil service and American government down the road. Although most executives expressed high levels of satisfaction with the quality and character of new recruits to their agencies, there was a pervasive sense that a sea change is underway with respect to motivation and commitment. As HHS's George Grob put it, "There isn't such a public

Paul E. Chistolini
General Services Administration
Deputy Commissioner, Public Buildings Service

- Created a Pentagon-wide recycling program that saved
  $50,000 per year
- Started an employee tutoring program at GSA for sixth
  and seventh graders to receive basic computer training
  and be exposed to a wide range of job skills in a work
  environment

service vocation among [the younger] cohort today. They are more narrowly focused. I said, 'I want to be a government employee'. These young people are more profession-focused." The widespread expectation is that most people entering government service today will be around for a few years and then move on, perhaps to the private sector or the nonprofit sector, perhaps to state and local government, perhaps even to return eventually to the federal government. They will commit to interests rather than institutions.

This sort of "in-and-outing" has some distinct advantages for the government, of course, as many of the executives observed. Certainly it will provide a regular infusion of fresh ideas and maybe greater adaptability. In an era that will undoubtedly see even faster change and a greater need to incorporate innovative technologies, there is much to be said for such qualities. At the same time, it is hard to imagine how the federal government will function without considerably more continuity, especially in the senior ranks, than such career patterns will afford. Institutional memory is scarcely less important than institutional adaptability. As Larry Massanari, regional commissioner of the Social Security Administration, put it, "the culture of responsibility" that now undergirds the public service cannot be maintained without a high level of commitment to the organization by employees.

Part of the answer may lie in an observation made by Dennis Williams, deputy assistant secretary for budget at the Department of Health and Human Services: "There is," he said, "a place for continuity and a place for change. We don't need both at all levels of government." Put into other words, this means that we need to design personnel systems that ensure that, however limited the tenure of employees in most lower and mid-level jobs, there is considerable continuity for those marked for promotion to senior ranks. This is a theme to which we shall return.

Although "Gen Xers" are presumably still some years away from most SES slots, there is, according to several executives, another generational

Stephen R. Colgate
Department of Justice
Assistant Attorney General for Administration, Justice
Management Division

- After the Oklahoma City bombing, led the Marshals
  Service blueprint for protecting vital federal interests
  against terrorist attack

problem on the horizon that we may need to worry about rather sooner. The downsizing and hiring freezes of the 1980s and early 1990s so decimated the middle management ranks of some agencies that the talent pool of up and coming SESers isn't nearly as deep as it ought to be. Social Security's Massanari pointed out that a "retirement wave" is moving through his agency now. When it crests in 2004-2005, "there will be a mass exodus, and we don't have the cohort ready to step in." Lawrence Wachs of USDA expressed a similar concern: A whole class of agency heads is about to retire and "there isn't the talent base to replace them." For Wachs, though, the problem had less to do with earlier bouts of downsizing than with a young SES cohort that was inexperienced and inadequately trained.

It is tempting to dismiss these concerns as the curmudgeonly grumblings of the soon-to-retire. Which of us, after all, has not looked over our shoulders at the next generation, shaken our heads sadly and sagely, and announced that these young people simply don't measure up? In this case, this is a temptation to be resisted, for at least three reasons. First, there is a lot of data around to support the conclusions of these executives. It is a fact that workforce mobility and attachments are changing; and it is a fact that in the 1980s, the federal government experienced, at least in certain agencies, what a Brookings Institution conference called a "quiet crisis," hiring and retaining fewer of "the best and brightest."

Second, even when their conclusions differed, the empirical observations of the distinguished executives about the skill set of the rising cohort were remarkably similar. Almost everyone I spoke to praised the technical competence of would-be SESers but questioned their leadership skills and political acumen, a point we shall explore in more detail later.

Third, the fact that exceptions to this pattern were noted consistently by executives in certain types of agencies may well prove the rule. Respondents from the Bureau of Alcohol, Tobacco and Firearms (ATF), the Bureau of Prisons, Secret Service, and the Violent Crimes and Terrorism Section of the Justice Department, in particular, stressed that there was no dearth of talent in their pipelines. As Bradley Buckles, deputy director of ATF, put it,

Michael Delpercio, Jr.
Department of Transportation
Director, Office of Ship Operations

- Enhanced readiness, responsiveness, and capacity of the Maritime Administration's sealift assets of the Ready Reserve Force (RRF)
- Directed management initiatives that improved the RRF and saved over $9 million in one year

"We are not just an agency, not just a job. Law enforcement attracts people with a life-long commitment." Similarly, Lewis Merletti, former director of the Secret Service, stressed that while the "24/7 demands" of the job take their toll in terms of turnover, his agency tends to draw people with fierce loyalty and dedication to the organization and its mission, people who "would rather die than fail." Besides, as Justice's James Reynolds noted, if you are interested in doing this kind of work, "you have to do it by working for the government."

All of these comments underscore the unique strengths of military-like agencies when it comes to certain matters of personnel management and, by contrast and implication, the particular weaknesses of civilian agencies. With this in mind, we shall turn from the broad theme of generational mobility and commitment to particular problems in recruitment and career development that emerged in these conversations with America's distinguished federal executives.

Excellence is Serendipitous: Far More Attention Needs to Be Paid to Executive Development

That Americans are, thanks in large part to the men and women of the Senior Executive Service, the beneficiaries of truly excellent government is beyond dispute. Reading the nomination forms for these presidential rank award winners is an inspiring, humbling, and gratitude-evoking experience. Leafing through these files leads one to think how very lucky a society so enamored of bureaucrat bashing is to have such remarkable public servants.

And luck—or "serendipity," as Carol Okin from the OPM put it—is precisely the focus of the third theme that emerged from my conversations with these career executives. The United States government has for years churned up senior managers from the depths of federal agencies with the regularity of boulders rising in the fields of New England. Nineteen ninety-

George F. Grob
Department of Heath & Human Services
Deputy Inspector General for Evaluation and Inspections

- Reduced excessive Medicare and Medicaid payments by $1.6 billion in 1996
- Pioneered the use of customer satisfaction surveys for Medicare

seven, the year that my respondents received their rank awards, was no fluke. This has gone on for decades. And, more to the point, it has gone on without apparent exertion or design by federal personnel managers; indeed, some would say that it has gone on *despite* the exertions and designs of federal personnel managers.

Like farmers harvesting bumper crops without ever seeding, watering, weeding, or fertilizing, Americans and their elected officials have consistently received the fruits of outstanding administrative leadership without investing any time or effort. We have taken what might be called, to pursue the agricultural metaphor, a "Field of Dreams" approach to senior executive development: "If we need them, they will be there." That this complacency has seemingly been rewarded for decades should not lead to further complacency. Listening to some defenders of our senior executive personnel system, one is reminded of the old joke about the man falling from the top of the skyscraper. "How is it going?" shouted a startled onlooker as the fellow zipped past the 20th floor. "So far, so good!" was the cheery response.

In fact, defenders of the senior executive personnel system were in short supply among the 1997 distinguished executives. Even those who believed their own agencies were well stocked with future administrative leaders were critical of career development efforts. "Haphazard" and "slipshod" were words I heard more than once. K. Darwin Murrell, director of the Beltsville Area Agricultural Research Service (ARS), suggested that training and development has actually deteriorated in recent years. A once reasonably vigorous program in his agency built on superiors identifying potential leaders early and ensuring that they were given appropriate "developmental assignments" has been replaced by an undirected, applicant-driven system. Official candidate development programs have become so clogged with self-selected, often unqualified people, most of whom are destined to fail, that no one takes the new program very seriously.

Perhaps the most common complaint was that the current executive development "system," a word to be used advisedly, tends to produce officials who are technically competent but managerially lost and politically

Larry G. Massanari
Social Security Administration
Regional Commissioner, Philadelphia

- Leader in improvements to telephone service to the public. SSA's 800 number received a Hammer Award
- Short-term Disability Project reduced pending initial disability claims by 119,000

clueless. Most SES candidates, observed ATF's Buckles, are "naïve about the political process." To succeed at the highest level, said USDA's Wachs, you have to understand the system, especially the budgetary, legislative, and regulatory processes. "I am continually amazed that SESers don't know this stuff. But they often don't." Like Murrell, he noted that his agency had had a better development program in the past, which he in fact had run for three years; but it, too, died, a victim of turf battles. What will happen, Wachs wondered, when the next generation of senior executives, unprepared as it is, is forced to testify on the Hill or is confronted by Dan Rather? Wachs made it clear that it was not a thought he relished.

Franklin Miller, principal deputy assistant secretary of Defense for international security policy, was especially critical of career development programs in the Department of Defense (DoD). In fact, until recently, there simply *were* no career development programs for civilians in DoD, at least not in the Office of the Undersecretary of Defense for Policy (OUSD). One could, he noted, "be the German desk officer for 20 years without being disturbed or developed. Consequently, people become so narrow that they are rightly not looked upon as material for higher positions in the SES, much less than for deputy or assistant secretary slots." Although Miller has made an enormous personal commitment to building a career development system in OUSD/P—with systems of rotation, promotion tied to training, opportunities for advancement to job slots normally held by political appointees, and so forth—he is not especially sanguine that his reforms will take root. Although there were a few very significant exceptions among the political appointees he worked with, people who had provided critical support for his initiatives, Miller observed that those in a position to make a difference simply don't have any incentives to care about career development.

In the absence of overall systems of career development, many of the award winners have become personally dedicated to mentoring younger executives or encouraging internship programs. For instance, Janet Menig, the deputy chief of staff for installation management in the Defense Department, was cited in her nomination form as "the consummate mentor, tutor, trainer

Janet C. Menig
Department of Defense
Deputy Assistant Chief of Staff for Installation Management
(Army)

- Improved the efficiency and reduced the cycle time to
  produce products that saved $3 million in the first year
- Led the effort for parametric modeling to reduce amount
  of planning and design costs for military construction

and developer of professional staff personnel and talent." Gary Thurber, associate director of the Defense Logistics Agency, was praised for his establishment of an "Entry-Level Intern Program to recruit college graduates in multiple academic disciplines." William Campbell of the Coast Guard was cited for his "avid mentoring of his people [including] providing career strategies for increasing their experience through high-visibility assignments, education, and training opportunities." Were he not to do this, Campbell explained, his subordinates would get stuck, presumably like Miller's German desk officer, in one spot, and would become, in Campbell's words, "caricatures of themselves. They will have done one thing and been successful, and then will use this as a default setting. What makes you successful coming up will not make you a successful senior executive."

But personal mentoring and internship programs alone—even the Presidential Management Internship program, which was consistently cited as a real bright spot in the federal personnel system—obviously cannot fill the career development vacuum. What is needed is a more fully articulated structure that directs career development from recruitment to retirement, a structure in which the needs of the government for executive talent are treated as a question of design, not a matter of chance. The changing character of the workforce makes this even more essential.

Again, it is the military-style organizations such as ATF that provide the most instructive examples. Bradley Buckles described an expansive executive development program within his agency, organized under the auspices of a central executive development board. This is a serious, high-profile enterprise, which Buckles himself, as ATF's chief operating officer, chairs. Leadership candidates are regularly moved across ATF's various directorates in an effort both to combat "stove-piping" and to expose officials to all segments of the agency. This effort supports and is supported by a strategic team orientation that pervades ATF. ATF's assistant directors, each head of a directorate, constitute a board of directors, which has corporate responsibility for the whole agency. Each assistant director is forced

Lewis C. Merletti
Department of the Treasury
Special Agent in Charge, U.S. Secret Service

• Innovated protection techniques to assure the security
  of the President
• Increased female agents by 29 percent and minority
  special agents by 48 percent in Presidential Protection
  Division

to think of ATF as a whole when important decisions are confronted. More-over, all projects are organized on a team basis, with members drawn from all germane directorates. Dr. Kathleen Hawk Sawyer, director of the fed-eral Bureau of Prisons, oversees a similar executive development program, which initiates and oversees training opportunities for upper-management staff in the Bureau.

Interestingly, despite the military's well-deserved reputation for training and officer development, this culture does *not* rub off on civilian structures embedded in defense agencies. Indeed, DoD's Miller emphatically rejected my suggestion that it might have helped him to initiate a career development program because his shop was surrounded by good military examples. Phys-ical proximity to the military seems to be much less important than cultural proximity, a fact that obviously increases the challenge government-wide.

Who will pick up this challenge? Can the structure of the SES itself accommodate the needs of career development? What leadership can the Office of Personnel Management provide?

The SES as a System: OPM Needs to Take the Lead in Helping the SES to Reach Its Full Potential

As it was originally framed, the SES was to be far more than a classifi-cation and pay scheme for the "supergrades" (GS 16 to GS 18) it mainly replaced. Instead, it was to constitute a government-wide corps of senior executives, high-performing generalist managers who would be flexible, responsive, and mobile. Because rank would inhere in the person and not in the position, in principle a cabinet secretary or other high-level appointee with a particular management problem would be able to reach into this rich reserve of talent and pluck from Agency A an SESer with just the right sort of abilities to solve a problem in Agency B. When that problem was sorted out, then off he or she would go to put out the next administrative fire.

Franklin Carroll Miller
Department of Defense
Principal Deputy Assistant Secretary of Defense (International
Security Policy)

• Recognized nationally and internationally as a key policy-
maker in nuclear deterrence, arms control, and counter-
proliferation
• Played a major role in NATO and was instrumental in
building ties between DoD and the Ministries of
Defense of the Newly Independent States

This is not how the system has worked. Consider these comments,
bearing in mind that they come from the *crème de la crème* of SESers.
Eleanor Spector, procurement chief at the Pentagon, said that while she supposed "the SES has some prestige, it actually has no content. It really isn't
any different from the supergrades." After averring that he was probably the
worst person to ask because he doesn't "pay any attention to the SES," the
Department of Justice's James Reynolds said that the "SES is relevant only
as a pay grade. I don't see any real difference between the SES and the old
supergrades." Buckles of ATF was similarly dismissive: "The SES is irrele-
vant. The status is meaningless. I have no connection to other SESers, no
kinship. It is just like if everyone who is a GS-14 got together."

Virtually identical words came from almost every other interviewee,
usually accompanied by a puzzled look, as in "SES? Why are you asking
about that?" Although hanging prominently on the wall in almost every
winner's office was the framed Distinguished Rank certificate—which is
itself dominated by the stylized shield that is the emblem of the SES—no
one had any sense of identification with the SES as a system. It is simply a
pay grade or a vehicle for receiving a well-deserved cash bonus.

The SES may yet emerge from the shadows and provide the basis for
government-wide career development. Certainly some key officials in the
Office of Personnel Management think that it can, at least with some tweak-
ing. In the spring of 1998, OPM released what it labeled a "Framework for
Improving the Senior Executive Service," better known simply as the
"Framework Document." Among other things, this document set forth proposals to replace the SES with a Senior Civil Service (comprised of a man-
agement-oriented Senior Executive Corps and a specialist-based Senior
Professional Corps), foster career development and "continual learning,"
strengthen accountability, increase rewards, and enhance flexibility at the
agency level.

K. Darwin Murrell
Department of Agriculture
Deputy Administrator, National Program Staff, Agricultural
Research Service

- Created a research program to find ways to conserve
  and reuse agricultural water
- Used existing resources to tackle emerging and crosscutting food and agricultural issues, including assem-
  bling multidisciplinary research team

By OPM's own account, though, support for these proposals was less
than overwhelming, a judgment that the distinguished executives generally
share. In their conversations with me they were particularly disturbed by
what they saw as OPM's continued push for interagency mobility. "OPM
doesn't get it," Lawrence Wachs said. "SES jobs are not interchangeable
pieces." Similarly, William Campbell insisted that "OPM is fixated on
mobility. Some jobs, including a lot of SES jobs, need stability." In fact,
Campbell noted that for years the Coast Guard had filled his own position
with flag officers, who had to rotate every two years. They finally decided
that this wasn't working and redesignated the position for a civilian, who
would not be subject to rotation.

This is not to say that the executives dismissed mobility out of hand.
Some of them, in fact, were models of mobility, having served in a wide range
of agencies and positions. Stephen Colgate, Department of Justice, suggested
that more selective rotation programs be developed within specific areas such
as finance and budgeting. Based on his earlier career as a uniformed officer
in the Navy, Michael Delpercio expressed a view with even more nuance,
commenting that many people misconstrue mobility as it takes place in the
military and then misapply it in civilian settings. Officers are not rotated willy-
nilly through vastly different assignments, he said. Instead, "careful skill sets
are built. One takes the same experience from ship to ship."

Career-Political Relations: Frictions Remain, and Too Often Elected
Officials and Political Appointees Unfairly Target Career Executives

Relations with political appointees and the broader structures of government constituted another major theme in my conversations with these
distinguished executives. Based on many published reports over the last 20
years, I had expected to hear a lot of complaints about political interference

Carol Okin
Office of Personnel Management

Associate Director, Office of Merit Systems Oversight and Effectiveness

- Transformed a financially troubled national/international training function into a real business that became a privatization candidate
- Revitalized OPM's merit systems oversight program, turning it into an effective force for good government

---

in the SES by unqualified political appointees. In fact, I heard almost none of this. On the contrary, I often heard praise for the quality of the appointees with whom these executives had worked.

What I did hear was a persistent undertone of frustration with the amount of effort it takes to make the career-political relationship work. And the effort, according to these career executives, is very one-sided. "You have to educate them," noted Eleanor Spector. "Sometimes they just assume that you would have gotten a job outside if you were any good. Yet when they give a speech as they are leaving, they always say, 'My biggest surprise is how good the career people are.'"

Part of the problem is that careerists are initially misperceived as incompetent. A larger part is that they are misperceived as partisan. Almost without exception, appointees arrive deeply suspicious of the political leanings of careerists. As one executive put it, "I was viewed by Clinton appointees when they first came in as a right-wing troglodyte. If the Republicans win, I'll be viewed by their appointees as a left-wing liberal." This sort of misperception is a problem that starts at the top, suggested DoD's Miller. "The accepted logic is: Be responsive to the President. Fill the halls with appointees. Otherwise, bureaucrats will wait out the administration and do what they want." This is, he said, "deeply wrong," a view that every other executive shared.

While some could cite exceptions, the widespread view was that, as Stephen Colgate of the Department of Justice put it, "if you're going to succeed in this business, you have to be totally apolitical. Your job is to implement, not formulate policy. You have no agenda." Education's Steven Winnick told me, with a sort of wry pride, how he, as a senior career lawyer in the department during the Reagan administration, had played a key role in drafting the legislation that was meant to abolish his own job and the rest of the agency. Indeed, a recurrent motif as we discussed this point was the extent to which these executives try to reach out to understand and embrace

Kathleen Peroff
Office of Management and Budget
Deputy Associate Director, Energy and Science Division

- Led contracting reforms at Energy to save $10.5 billion over five years via increased competition, fixed price, performance-based contracting, and private-sector risk-sharing
- Led development of a science initiative for improvements to Energy's large science facilities to increase operational effectiveness

each administration's priorities. "If you are going to be successful, you have to mesh what you are doing with the political agenda," noted Carol Okin.

Although most of the career executives seem resigned to the inevitable frictions of the appointee system—one colorfully described his role as a "shock absorber" between the political structure and line employees—they expressed greater unease about the increasingly corrosive atmosphere of American politics in general. Some traced this to the 1994 Republican takeover of Congress, which led, in their view, to a breakdown of the bipartisan consensus that had reigned on a broad array of budget and policy issues. Others, like the Bureau of Prison's Kathleen Hawk Sawyer, see a rise in "incivility in the culture generally."

Whatever the cause, the consequences have been ominous for some senior executives. Several cited vicious personal attacks by members of Congress—Republicans and Democrats, by the way—during the course of congressional testimony. One even pulled out of a desk drawer a copy of an op-ed piece, in which a prominent member of the House of Representatives not only excoriated this particular executive, by name, for articulating what was in fact a settled department position, but even insinuated that the executive had been unethically influenced by a government contractor. "Not only has the environment become hostile," observed Justice's Colgate. "The shield has eroded. The career service used to be out of bounds in the wars between legislative and executive branches. Not any more."

The Rewards of Public Service: Not Only Is The Pay System Broken, but More Attention Needs to Be Paid to Non-Monetary Compensation

Gary Thurber is the ranking civilian in the Defense Logistics Agency, an organization of 51,000 men and women whose mission is to keep the mil-

James S. Reynolds
Department of Justice
Chief, Terrorism & Violent Crimes Section, Criminal Division

- Enhanced the Department's ability to address and resolve critical issues relating to terrorism and violent crime
- Implemented a plan to capture and prosecute terrorists responsible for the World Trade Center bombing

itary supplied with everything it needs—"except bullets"—to do its job. "If they wear it, eat it, or use it, we supply it," Thurber noted. Last year, Thurber spent over $5 billion on fuel for the Pentagon—and returned a profit of $1.3 billion to American taxpayers. He is, in fact, the largest buyer of petroleum products in the world.

What would Thurber have earned last year in a job of this scale and responsibility in the private sector? While it is impossible to know for sure, there are some rough benchmarks. For instance, according to a survey in *Virginia Business,* it took a compensation package in excess of $1 million just to make the list of the top 100 best-paid executives in Virginia. Gary Thurber was paid $125,900 by the U.S. government in 1998, as were many other senior career executives in the Washington area. Even more perverse is the fact that there is no distinction among the top three pay grades within the SES. Thanks to the pay cap, ES-4s, ES-5s, and ES-6s all earned precisely the same amount—$125,900 in 1999.

Fortunately for the average U.S. taxpayer, who may well consider $125,900 a handsome salary indeed, Gary Thurber feels no resentment about his salary. "It is my choice. And I can live well enough on it." And, equally fortunately for the taxpayer, many other executives echoed his sentiment. "I make enough," said USDA's Wachs. "Money is not an issue for me personally," agreed Paul Chistolini, associate commissioner of the Public Buildings Service at the General Services Administration.

Still, frustrations remain, not so much about the absolute level of the pay as the pettiness that surrounds the issue and the negative signals that are sent by Congress and the White House. As a group, these executives perfectly illustrated the old management maxim: Pay is never a satisfier in the workplace, but it may well be a dissatisfier. "No one is in this for the money, but the compensation system is broken and pay compression is a serious problem," said DoD's Miller. Even Gary Thurber chafed at the "nickel and diming" on salary by politicians. William Campbell of the Coast

Kathleen Hawk Sawyer
Department of Justice
Director, Bureau of Prisons

- Streamlined major Bureau of Prisons divisions; enhanced technological capabilities to improve services and reduce costs
- Planned and directed an extensive prison construction and expansion program to match increasing inmate population

Guard described himself as "not bitter, but disappointed about pay. The people who set pay make it clear that they don't value the contributions of senior executives."

So what keeps these distinguished executives going? In every case, the answer I got was the same: the work itself. "No matter how much my counterparts in the private sector get paid, I don't know any one of them in the private sector who says his work is challenging," said Lawrence Wachs. "When I leave work in the evening, I can think about the food stamp program and say to myself, 'I did something good today. I fed a bunch of kids.'" Similarly, Thomas Billy, head of food safety for the USDA, mused, "Yes, I am underpaid and I've thought about the private sector. But I like what I'm doing and I'm making an important contribution." OMB's Kathy Peroff agreed: "The pay isn't fantastic. The hours are long. You are often not appreciated. But the opportunities I've had to participate in policy-making are extraordinary. I have seen things and met people that have enriched my life enormously."

Then why fix the pay system, when career executives are so enamored of their jobs that they will never leave anyway? But to think of it in these terms would be a very serious error. It is exactly this attitude—or at least the perception of this attitude—that most dismays senior executives. They feel, in a word, unappreciated. "You always hear from political appointees, after they leave in a year or two, about how burned out or overworked they are," noted Franklin Miller. "But somehow this is not recognized or appreciated as a phenomenon in civil servants." In George Grob's words, "politicians do not honor good management." Although he thinks that politicians "have punched themselves out on bureaucrat bashing, there is still a fundamental lack of appreciation for the work of public servants."

Ironically, one of the examples several executives cited as proof of the lack of appreciation they receive was the SES presidential rank award ceremony itself. In years past, said another, "winners were invited to the Oval

Eleanor R. Spector
Department of Defense
Director of Procurement, Office of the Undersecretary of
Defense (Acquisition and Technology)

- Streamlined the procurement process and created automated standard contracting software
- Facilitated integration of the defense and commercial industrial bases

Office. That really meant something. It was a big psychic reward. It doesn't happen any more." Several recalled with pride that in 1989 George Bush made much of the fact that his first public meeting was with his "management team," the assembled members of the Senior Executive Service. "President Bush was proud of his public service," observed George Grob. "He said to us, 'Of all the candidates who ran for President, I had the best SF-171' (the standard government employment form). That meant something."

When Kathleen Hawk Sawyer says, "I really don't want a lot—just a little recognition," she is right on target: It really isn't a lot to ask. It costs politicians and the public nothing. But it is a lot to receive. In fact, the symbolism of Oval Office visits and presidential handshakes means more than a lot to members of the SES. It is a source of vitality. It buttresses their sense of professional responsibility and nourishes their deepest motivation for public service.

Beyond basic appreciation, the one incentive that several executives believed was absent from the current system was opportunity, specifically the opportunity to rise to the assistant secretary level in the federal government. Although such opportunities are officially countenanced by the Civil Service Reform Act, they are almost never made available. The main reason is the widespread but unfounded belief that only political appointees can be entrusted with the administration's policy agenda. "Our government has never really known what to do with civil servants," Franklin Miller pointed out. This is especially true, he said, in comparison with England and the other NATO countries with which he deals regularly. "They have real career systems. People *do* rise on a merit basis to top positions. In the British Ministry of Defense there are four or five political appointees. In the U.S. Department of Defense, there are hundreds." Under the circumstances, there is little room at the top for career federal executives in America.

Gary S. Thurber
Department of Defense
Associate Director, Acquisition, Defense Logistics Agency

* Investigated and resolved major acquisitions problems
* Pursued and implemented key reform activities

Recommendations

Americans have made it clear in the waning years of the 20th century that while they may no longer want *big* government, they do want *good* government—government that is honest, capable, and effective. Americans want government that can protect the nation's environment and public health, government that keeps streets and schools safe. They want government that provides wise leadership in international affairs and facilitates continued economic growth at home. This is not now and never has been an ideological question. It is not about the scope of government. It is about the quality of government, whatever its scope.

Yet the overriding message that I heard in my conversations with distinguished federal executives is that good government in America is in jeopardy. As a nation we have come to take it for granted and have stopped nourishing it at its roots. We act as if there is no connection between the public service we expect and the public servants who provide it. We have been drawing down capital invested by earlier generations, living on the efforts of men and women whose sense of public duty led them to the "noble calling" of government. Who will pick up the torch when they lay it down?

This is a profoundly serious question. Every corporation in America knows that to survive, much less to prosper, it must put the development of executive talent at the very top of its agenda. This is a lesson that we can and must put to work in the federal government. Here, distilled from the conversations reported here and from years of research, are some concrete proposals to do just that, aimed at five important constituencies—the White House, Congress, the Office of Personnel Management, federal agencies, and members of the SES itself:

The White House

* *Re-engage the career service.* The President and his appointees should see career executives for what they are: a tremendous resource that can

Lawrence Wachs
Department of Agriculture
Associate Director of Budget and Program Analysis

- Reorganized USDA to improve customer service and saved taxpayers over $4 billion
- Designed and implemented an automated budgeting computer model that became the prototype system for the federal government

be mobilized to implement the administration's program. Approach them as members of the team, and they will respond in kind.

- *Consider career executives for PAS appointments.* The White House Personnel Office should take advantage of SES provisions that allow careerists to accept political appointments. There is a wealth of under-utilized talent here. A few such appointments will also send very positive signals to the rest of the career service.
- *Participate in awards ceremonies.* A little appreciation from the President goes a long way for career executives. Though it should neither begin nor end there, having the President spend an hour a year at a presidential rank awards ceremony would be a good place to start.
- *Talk about public service in positive terms.* The President can set the right tone by talking about why public service is honorable and important. Failing that, the Eleanor Spectors and George Grobs and William Campbells of tomorrow won't even think about coming to the federal government, and the pickings for the roster of distinguished executives in 2030 will be very thin indeed.
- *Improve orientation and training for non-career appointees.* Several times in recent decades, attempts have been made as part of transition planning to orient political appointees to the special character of federal management, usually in collaboration with a university. Such training should become a routine part of the appointment process. The more quickly appointees learn how things work, the more quickly productive relationships will form and useful work will get done in agencies.

Congress

- *Fix the pay problem.* At a minimum, executive and congressional pay should be decoupled. Current law prevents SES compensation (basic pay plus locality pay) from exceeding level III executive pay (Congressional

Dennis P. Williams
Department of Health & Human Services
Deputy Assistant Secretary, Budget

- Convinced Appropriations Committee to allow the secretary to transfer 1 percent of funds between accounts
- Eliminated one complete organizational level affecting 1,000 employees without separating anyone

pay is set at executive level II). Removing this cap is a matter of both common sense and simple justice: The cap has already erased compensation distinctions—and thus whatever effect graduated material incentives have—among the top three SES pay levels (over 60 percent of the service). Pay compression problems aside, the entire system needs a fresh look, with a greater effort made to ease the comparability gap between public and private sector pay. Failing such efforts, the federal government will be wholly unable to compete with the private sector for top talent in the years to come. The implications for service quality follow naturally.

- *Re-establish a "shield" for career executives.* Continue in hearings and in oversight functions to hold civil servants appropriately accountable, but do so in ways that are commensurate with their positions. Political executives, not career executives, should be the point men and point women for criticism that is essentially political.

- *Join with the President in talking positively about public service.* Members of Congress were all drawn to lives of public service, too. Remembering that—and reminding one's constituents—that the "bureaucracy" is filled with men and women who have been called to serve their country will pay dividends for everyone.

Office of Personnel Management

- *Continue the work started in the "Framework Document."* Although some features of this initiative—especially the mobility provisions—attracted considerable criticism, the spirit of the document was on target. There is a great need to assess the state of the service at a fundamental level and to see how the vision of 1978 can be more fully realized.

- *Support executive development programs.* Some agencies are doing a better job than others in developing executive talent. OPM can play a useful role by highlighting and sharing "best practices" in executive development.

Steven Y. Winnick
Department of Education
Deputy General Counsel

- Established an independent Ethics Counsel Division in the Office of the General Counsel, which is used as a model by the Office of Government Ethics
- Instrumental in recovering a $300 million default payment from a financial institution that participated in the student financial assistance program

- *Invigorate the SES as a corps.* Too few SESers have any sense of attachment to the service, an attitude that ultimately inhibits executive development programs and frustrates other goals set forth in the Civil Service Reform Act (CSRA). More initiatives by OPM's Office of Executive Resources to build *esprit*—workshops, exchanges, lunches, newsletters, and so forth—would be useful (if initially viewed with a jaundiced eye by some SESers).

Agencies

- *Develop career ladders.* Agency leaders need to be more proactive about developing executive talent. The complacent, "they'll-be-there-when-we-need-them" attitude that has prevailed for years in many quarters is getting prohibitively expensive. Talent needs to be identified early and nurtured deliberately. Identifiable career paths need to be laid out, with training embraced as a serious commitment and careful programs of rotation—not blunt, across-the-board mobility schemes—created.
- *Embrace the PMI program.* The Presidential Management Internship program is universally lauded for its ability to attract bright and committed young people to federal service. Investments in this program pay off handsomely for individual agencies and for the government as a whole.
- *Recognize high-performing executives.* Although the Presidential Rank Award program is nominally run by OPM, it is paid for in agency budgets. Agency managers need to recognize the importance of this program—and of similar agency-level programs—and to support them fully.

SESers

- *Imagine a service.* Lay aside cynicism about "one size fits all managers" and anxieties about enforced mobility and think constructively about ways in which a genuine government-wide career executive service could co-exist comfortably with an agency-based administrative culture. Other countries do it. Many of the goals that you embrace and at least some of the rewards that you seek may well depend on the creation of such a service.
- *Continue to mentor the next generation.* Although members of the SES can do little to affect fundamental social norms that appear to be changing a generation's attitudes toward work and public service, they can operate at the margins and help shape the outlooks of at least some of those who will replace them. The 1997 class of distinguished executives was filled with outstanding mentors. All SESers would do well to follow this example.

These proposals are hardly revolutionary. Most of them echo recommendations made for years by a myriad of government task forces and independent commissions. What is different now is that we are that much closer to the day when we need to take them to heart. The Dickensian ghost of civil service yet to come has paid its visit. It is time to heed the warning.

Appendix:
1997 Presidential Distinguished
Rank Award Recipients by Agency

Department of Agriculture
  Thomas J. Billy*
  K. Darwin Murrell*
  Lawrence Wachs*
Department of Commerce
  Alexander E. MacDonald
Department of Defense
  Air Force
    Anthony J. Perfilio
    Gerald L. Yanker
  Army
    Michael F. Bauman
    Janet C. Menig*
    James M. Skurka
  Navy
    Daniel E. Porter
    John E. Sirmalis
    Roger N. Whiteway
  Office of the Secretary of Defense
    Gary W. Amlin
    Michael L. Ioffredo
    Franklin Carroll Miller*
    Eleanor R. Spector*
  Defense Agencies
    Diann L. McCoy
    Gary S. Thurber*
Department of Education
  Steven Y. Winnick*
Department of Energy
  Spain Woodrow Hall
Federal Trade Commission
  Eileen Harrington

General Services Administration
  Paul E. Chistolini*
Department of Health & Human Services
  George Grob*
  Arthur C. Jackson
  Kenneth Olden
  Dennis P. Williams*
Department of the Interior
  Robert J. Ewing
Department of Justice
  Stephen R. Colgate*
  Ronald W. Collison
  William J. Esposito
  Nancy B. Firestone
  Dennis F. Hoffman
  Neil H. Koslowe
  Carolyn G. Morris
  James S. Reynolds*
  Kathleen Hawk Sawyer*
  Gary R. Spratling
National Aeronautics and Space Administration
  Larry A. Diehl
  Roy S. Estess
  Tommy W. Holloway
  Daniel R. Mulville
  Leonard S. Nicholson
  Joseph H. Rothenberg
  Robert E. Whitehead
  Richard J. Wisniewski
Office of Management & Budget
  Philip A. DuSault
  Kathleen Peroff*

* Interviewed for this report

Office of Personnel Management
  Carol J. Okin*
Social Security Administration
  Martin E. Baer
  John R. Dyer
  Larry G. Massanari*
Department of Transportation
  William H. Campbell*
  Michael Delpercio*
Department of the Treasury
  Walter B. Biondi
  Bradley A. Buckles*
  Andrew Cosgarea
  Robert T. Johnson
  Lewis C. Merletti*
Department of Veterans Affairs
  D. Mark Catlett
  Kenneth J. Clark
  Larry R. Deal
  James A. Goff
  Kenneth B. Mizrach

Endnotes

1. Prior to FY1999, the awards were flat payments of $10,000 and $20,000, respectively.

2. Source: Executive Resources Management, U.S. Office of Personnel Management. These are the bulleted points used in the slides accompanying the awards ceremony.

Bibliography

Abramson, Mark A., Steven A. Clyburn and Elizabeth Mercier. *Results of the Government Leadership Survey: A 1999 Survey of Federal Executives.* Arlington, VA: The PricewaterhouseCoopers Endowment for The Business of Government, 1999.

Clinton, John B. and Arthur S. Newburg. *The Senior Executive Service: A Five-Year Retrospective of Its Operating and Conceptual Problems.* Washington, D.C.: Senior Executives Association, 1984.

Huddleston, Mark W. and William W. Boyer. *The Higher Civil Service in the United States: Quest for Reform.* Pittsburgh & London: University of Pittsburgh Press, 1996.

Ingraham, Patricia W. "Building Bridges or Burning Them? The President, the Appointees, and Bureaucracy." *Public Administration Review* 47 (September-October 1987): 425-35.

National Academy of Public Administration. *The Senior Executive Service: An Interim Report of the Panel of the National Academy of Public Administration on the Public Service.* Washington, D.C: National Academy of Public Administration, 1981.

National Commission on the Public Service. *Leadership for America: Rebuilding the Public Service.* Washington, D.C.: National Commission on the Public Service, 1989.

President's Private Sector Survey on Cost Control. *Report of the Task Force on Personnel Management.* Washington, D.C.: Government Printing Office, 1983.

Senior Executive Service Symposium. *The Future of the Senior Executive Service.* Charlottesville, VA: Federal Executive Institute, 1995.

Twentieth Century Fund Task Force on the Senior Executive Service. *The Government's Managers.* New York: The Twentieth Century Fund, 1987.

U.S. General Accounting Office. *Evaluation of Proposals to Alter the Structure of the Senior Executive Service.* (GAO/GGD-86-14, 1985).

_____. *Senior Executive Service: Executives' Perspectives on Their Federal Service.* (GAO/GGD-88-109FS, 1988).

About the Contributors

Mark A. Abramson is Executive Director of The PricewaterhouseCoopers Endowment for The Business of Government, a position he has held since July 1998. Prior to the Endowment, he was chairman of Leadership Inc. From 1983 to 1994, Mr. Abramson served as the first president of the Council for Excellence in Government. Previously, Mr. Abramson served as a senior program evaluator in the Office of the Assistant Secretary for Planning and Evaluation, U.S. Department of Health and Human Services.

He is a Fellow of the National Academy of Public Administration. In 1995, he served as president of the National Capital Area Chapter of the American Society for Public Administration. Mr. Abramson has taught at George Mason University and the Federal Executive Institute in Charlottesville, Virginia.

Mr. Abramson is the co-editor of *Transforming Organizations, Managing for Results 2002, E-Government 2001, Innovation,* and *Human Capital 2002.* He also recently edited *Memos to the President: Management Advice from the Nation's Top Public Administrators* and *Toward a 21st Century Public Service: Reports from Four Forums.* He is also the co-editor (with Joseph S. Wholey and Christopher Bellavita) of *Performance and Credibility: Developing Excellence in Public and Nonprofit Organizations,* and the author of *The Federal Funding of Social Knowledge Production and Application.*

He received his Bachelor of Arts degree from Florida State University. He received a Master of Arts degree in history from New York University and a Master of Arts degree in political science from the Maxwell School of Citizenship and Public Affairs, Syracuse University.

Kevin M. Bacon is a partner, PwC Consulting. He currently leads a major portion of the firm's U.S. public sector practice. In his 21 years with the firm, he has consulted to a wide range of public sector clients in the areas of strategy, process improvement, performance measurement, organizational design, and change management. His clients have included agencies in the U.S. federal government, 15 state governments, many large U.S. local government agencies, and government organizations in Australia and Russia. He has published numerous articles and monographs on public finance, reengineering and change management in the public sector, and performance measurement. He has lectured at the National Defense University, the California Leadership Institute, and the Industrial College of the Armed Forces. He has contributed to two books on change management and leadership (*Better Change: Best Practices for Transforming Your Organization* and *Straight from the CEO*).

In 1972, he received an undergraduate degree in political science from the University of California, Davis. He also studied at the London School of Economics, where he received a masters degree in economics in 1978.

Janet Vinzant Denhardt is Professor in the School of Public Affairs at Arizona State University. Her teaching and research interests lie primarily in organization theory and organizational behavior. Her book (with Lane Crothers), *Street-Level Leadership: Discretion and Legitimacy in Front-Line Public Service*, was published by the Georgetown University Press. In addition, Dr. Denhardt has published numerous articles in journals such as *Administration and Society, the American Review of Public Administration, Public Productivity and Management Review,* and *Public Administration Theory and Praxis*. Prior to joining the faculty at Arizona State, Dr. Denhardt taught at Eastern Washington University and has served in a variety of administrative and consulting positions. Her doctorate is from the University of Southern California.

Robert B. Denhardt is Professor in the School of Public Affairs at Arizona State University and Visiting Scholar at the University of Delaware. Dr. Denhardt is a past president of the American Society for Public Administration, and the founder and first chair of ASPA's National Campaign for Public Service, an effort to assert the dignity and worth of public service across the nation. He is a member of the National Academy of Public Administration and a fellow of the Canadian Centre for Management Development. Dr. Denhardt has published 14 books, including, *Theories of Public Organization, Public Administration: An Action Orientation, In the Shadow of Organization, The Pursuit of Significance, Executive Leadership in the Public Service, The Revitalization of the Public Service,* and *Pollution and Public Policy*. He has published over 50 articles in professional journals, primarily in the areas of leadership, management, and organizational change. His doctorate is from the University of Kentucky.

Mark W. Huddleston is Dean of the College of Arts and Science at the University of Delaware, where he has taught since 1980.

He is a graduate of the State University of New York at Buffalo (B.A., 1972) and the University of Wisconsin Madison (M.A., 1973; Ph.D., 1978).

Dr. Huddleston is the author of *Comparative Public Administration: An Annotated Bibliography* (1984), *The Government's Managers* (1987), and *The Public Administration Workbook (4th ed.)*(2000), and the co-author of *The Higher Civil Service in the United States: Quest for Reform* (1996). He has also written many articles, book chapters, and papers on public administration, particularly the Senior Executive Service. On several occasions in the 1980s he served as a consultant on SES issues to the U.S. General Accounting Office.

In addition to teaching courses in public administration at the University of Delaware, in recent years Professor Huddleston has conducted training and served as a consultant in several overseas settings, including Bosnia, Slovenia, Kazakstan, Mexico, Botswana, Zimbabwe, and South Africa. Dr. Huddleston described his work in Bosnia in detail in a recent article entitled "Innocents Abroad" published in *Public Administration Review* (59, 2 March/April 1999).

W. Henry Lambright is Professor of Political Science and Public Administration and Director of the Center for Environmental Policy and Administration at the Maxwell School of Citizenship and Public Affairs at Syracuse University. He teaches courses at the Maxwell School on Technology and Politics; Energy, Environment, and Resources Policy; and Bureaucracy and Politics.

Dr. Lambright has served as a guest scholar at The Brookings Institution, and as the director of the Science and Technology Policy Center at the Syracuse Research Corporation. He served as an adjunct professor in the Graduate Program of Environmental Science in the College of Environmental Science and Forestry at the State University of New York. He has testified before Congress on many topics, including the environment, science and technology, and government management.

A long-standing student of large-scale technical projects, he has worked for NASA as a special assistant in its Office of University Affairs and has been a member of its History Advisory Committee. Dr. Lambright has performed research for NASA, the Department of Energy, the Department of Defense, and the State Department. Recently, he chaired a symposium on "NASA in the 21st Century." A book will be published from this symposium by the Johns Hopkins University Press. He is also the author of the PricewaterhouseCoopers Endowment grant report "Transforming Government: Dan Goldin and the Remaking of NASA."

Dr. Lambright is the author or editor of six additional books, including *Powering Apollo: James E. Webb of NASA; Technology and U.S.*

Competitiveness: An Institutional Focus; and *Presidential Management of Science and Technology: The Johnson Presidency*. In addition, he has written more than 250 articles, papers, and reports.

His doctorate is from Columbia University, where he also received a master's degree. Dr. Lambright received his undergraduate degree from Johns Hopkins University.

Beryl A. Radin is Professor of Government and Public Administration, School of Public Affairs, University of Baltimore. She served as a Special Advisor to the Assistant Secretary for Management and Budget of the U.S. Department of Health and Human Services for the academic years 1996-98. She was Professor of Public Administration and Policy at Rockefeller College at the State University of New York at Albany from 1994 to 2001. She was also Professor of Public Administration at the Washington Public Affairs Center of the University of Southern California's School of Public Administration from 1978 to 1994.

Her publications have focused on management and policy issues within the U.S. federal government. Her books include *Beyond Machiavelli: Policy Analysis Comes of Age; The Accountable Juggler: The Art of Leadership in a Federal Agency; New Governance for Rural America: Creating Intergovernmental Partnerships*, with Robert Agranoff, Ann Bowman, C. Gregory Buntz, Steven Ott, Barbara Romzek, and Robert Wilson; *The Politics of Federal Reorganization: Creating the U.S. Department of Education*, with Willis D. Hawley; and *Implementation, Change, and the Federal Bureaucracy: School Desegregation Policy in HEW* (1964-68).

Dr. Radin is currently the managing editor of the *Journal of Public Administration Research and Theory* and a Fellow in the National Academy of Public Administration. She is a past President of the Association for Public Policy Analysis and Management, the national public policy organization. Her professional activities also include the American Political Science Association, the National Association of Schools of Public Affairs and Administration, and the American Society of Public Administration.

Dr. Radin received her Ph.D. in Social Policies Planning from the Department of City and Regional Planning at the University of California at Berkeley.

Norma M. Riccucci is Professor of Public Administration and Policy at the Rockefeller College of the University at Albany, State University of New York. She currently directs the Ph.D. Program in Public Administration and Policy.

Her research and teaching interests lie in the broad area of public management. Her work has focused on public personnel management, employment discrimination law, cultural diversity, and labor-management relations in the public sector. Currently, she is engaged in a research project examining the capacity of state and local governments to implement welfare to work laws at the front lines of service delivery.

She is the author of numerous journal articles and books, including *Unsung Heroes: Federal Execucrats Making a Difference* (Georgetown University Press, 1995) and *Managing Diversity in Public Sector Workforces* (Westview Press, forthcoming), and co-editor of *Public Personnel Management* (Longman Press, 2001).

Dr. Riccucci received her M.P.A. degree (1981) from the University of Southern California, Los Angeles, and the Ph.D. degree in public administration (1984) from the Maxwell School of Citizenship and Public Affairs at Syracuse University.

Mark Schneider is Professor and Chair of the Political Science Department at SUNY Stony Brook, where he has taught for 22 years. He has published numerous articles and several books on urban politics, public entrepreneurs, and school choice. Dr. Schneider is currently working on a large project studying the Internet as a means of delivering school-based information to help parents choose the schools their children attend. He earned his B.A. from Brooklyn College and his Ph.D. from University of North Carolina-Chapel Hill.

Paul E. Teske is Professor and Director of Graduate Studies in the Political Science Department at SUNY Stony Brook, where he has taught for 12 years. He has written widely about public policy, regulation, and school choice. With Mark Schneider and Melissa Marschall, he is co-author *Choosing Schools*. Dr. Teske earned his B.A. from University of North Carolina-Chapel Hill and his M.P.A. and Ph.D. degrees from Princeton University's Woodrow Wilson School of Public and International Affairs.

About The PricewaterhouseCoopers Endowment for The Business of Government

Through grants for research, The PricewaterhouseCoopers Endowment for The Business of Government stimulates research and facilitates discussion of new approaches to improving the effectiveness of government at the federal, state, local, and international levels.

Research grants of $15,000 are awarded competitively to outstanding scholars in academic and nonprofit institutions across the United States. Each grantee is expected to produce a 30- to 40-page research report in one of the areas presented on pages 240-242. Grant reports will be published and disseminated by The Endowment. All the chapters presented in this book were originally prepared as grant reports to The Endowment.

Founded in 1998 by PricewaterhouseCoopers, The Endowment is one of the ways that PricewaterhouseCoopers seeks to advance knowledge on how to improve public sector effectiveness. The PricewaterhouseCoopers Endowment focuses on the future of the operations and management of the public sector.

Who Is Eligible?
   Individuals working in:
* Universities
* Nonprofit organizations
* Journalism

Description of Grant

Individuals receiving grants will be responsible for producing a 30- to 40-page research report in one of the areas presented on pages 240-242. The research paper should be completed within a six-month period from the start of the project. Grantees select the start and end dates of the research project.

Size of Grant

$15,000 for each research paper

Who Receives the Grant

Individuals will receive the grant, not the institution in which they are located.

Application Process

Interested individuals should submit:
- A three-page description of the proposed research
- A résumé, including list of publications

Application Deadlines

There are three funding cycles annually, with deadlines of:
- The last day of February
- The last day of June
- The last day of October

Applications must be postmarked or received online by the above dates.

Submitting Applications

Hard copy:

Mark A. Abramson
Executive Director
The PricewaterhouseCoopers Endowment for The Business of Government
1616 North Fort Myer Drive
Arlington, VA 22209

Online:

endowment.pwcglobal.com/apply

Program Areas

E-Government

The Endowment is seeking proposals that examine the implementation of e-government in the following areas: (1) Government to Business (G2B); (2) Government to Citizen (G2C); (3) Government to Employee (G2E); and (4) Government to Government (G2G). The Endowment is especially interested in innovative approaches to providing information so citizens can make their own choices, complete service transactions electronically, hold government more accountable for results, and offer feedback.

Examples of previous grants in this area:
- The Auction Model: How the Public Sector Can Leverage the Power of E-Commerce Through Dynamic Pricing *by David Wyld*
- Commerce Comes to Government on the Desktop: E-Commerce Applications in the Public Sector *by Genie N. L. Stowers*
- The Use of the Internet in Government Service Delivery *by Steven Cohen and William B. Eimicke*

Financial Management

The Endowment is seeking proposals that examine specific financial management issues, such as cost accounting and management, financial and resource analysis, financial risk management and modeling, internal controls, operational and systems risk management, financial auditing, contract management, reconciliation, and overpayment recovery. The Endowment is especially interested in full costs and budgeting approaches for support services and capital assets, retirement, and other employee benefits, and other nondirect costs associated with delivering program services.

Examples of previous grants in this area:
- Audited Financial Statements: Getting and Sustaining "Clean" Opinions *by Douglas A. Brook*
- Credit Scoring and Loan Scoring: Tools for Improved Management of Federal Credit Programs *by Thomas H. Stanton*
- Using Activity-Based Costing to Manage More Effectively *by Michael H. Granof, David E. Platt, and Igor Vaysman*

Human Capital

The Endowment is seeking proposals that examine human capital issues related to public service. Human capital consists of the knowledge, skills, abilities, attitudes, and experience required to accomplish an organization's mission. It also includes an organization's ability to recruit and retain employees, as well as to undertake workforce planning and analysis.

Examples of previous grants in this area:
- Leaders Growing Leaders: Preparing the Next Generation of Public Service Executives *by Ray Blunt*
- Reflections on Mobility: Case Studies of Six Federal Executives *by Michael D. Serlin*
- Winning the Best and Brightest: Increasing the Attraction of Public Service *by Carol Chetkovich*

Managing for Results

The Endowment is seeking proposals that examine how organizations align their processes—such as budgeting, workforce, and business processes—around their strategic goals. This area also focuses on how organizations use performance and results information to make policy, management, and resource allocation decisions. The Endowment is especially interested in how different organizations work collaboratively to achieve common outcomes. The Endowment is also interested in case studies of the use of balanced scorecards, including the measurement of customer service.

Examples of previous grants in this area:
- The Challenge of Developing Cross-Agency Measures: A Case Study of the Office of National Drug Control Policy *by Patrick Murphy and John Carnevale*
- Using Performance Data for Accountability: The New York City Police Department's CompStat Model of Police Management *by Paul O'Connell*
- Using Evaluation to Support Performance Management: A Guide for Federal Executives *by Kathryn E. Newcomer and Mary Ann Scheirer*

New Ways to Manage

The Endowment is seeking proposals that examine specific instances of new ways of delivering programs and services to the public, including contracting out, competition, outsourcing, privatization, and public-private partnerships. The Endowment is also interested in innovations in the way public organizations are managed.

Examples of previous grants in this area:
* Entrepreneurial Government: Bureaucrats as Businesspeople *by Anne Laurent*
* San Diego County's Innovation Program: Using Competition and a Whole Lot More to Improve Public Services *by William B. Eimicke*
* The Challenge of Innovating in Government *by Sandford Borins*

Transforming Organizations

The Endowment is seeking proposals that examine how specific public sector organizations have been transformed with new values, changed cultures, and enhanced performance. This area also includes studies of outstanding public sector leaders.

Examples of previous grants in this area:
* Transforming Government: The Renewal and Revitalization of the Federal Emergency Management Agency *by R. Steven Daniels and Carolyn L. Clark-Daniels*
* Transforming Government: The Revitalization of the Veterans Health Administration *by Gary J. Young*
* Transforming Government: Dan Goldin and the Remaking of NASA *by W. Henry Lambright*

For more information about The Endowment

Visit our website at: endowment.pwcglobal.com
Send an e-mail to: endowment@us.pwcglobal.com
Call: (703) 741-1077

About PricewaterhouseCoopers

The Management Consulting Services practice of PricewaterhouseCoopers helps clients maximize their business performance by integrating strategic change, performance improvement, and technology solutions. Through a worldwide network of skills and resources, consultants manage complex projects with global capabilities and local knowledge, from strategy through implementation. PricewaterhouseCoopers (www.pwcglobal.com) is the world's largest professional services organization. Drawing on the knowledge and skills of more than 150,000 people in 150 countries, the practice helps clients solve complex business problems and measurably enhance their ability to build value, manage risk, and improve performance in an Internet-enabled world. PricewaterhouseCoopers refers to the member firms of the worldwide PricewaterhouseCoopers organization.